CRITICAL WAR STUDIES SERIES

Series Editors

Tarak Barkawi (Department of Politics, New School for Social Research) and Shane Brighton (Department of International Relations, University of Sussex)

War transforms the social and political orders in which we live, just as it obliterates our precious certainties. Nowhere is this more obvious than in the fate of truths offered about war itself. War regularly undermines expectations, strategies and theories, and along with them the credibility of those in public life and the academy presumed to speak with authority about it. A fundamental reason for this is the frequently narrow and impoverished intellectual resources that dominate the study of war.

Critical War Studies begins with the recognition that the unsettling character of war is a profound opportunity for scholarship. Accordingly, the series welcomes submissions from across the academy as well as from reflective practitioners. It provides an open forum for critical scholarship concerned with war and armed forces and seeks to foster and develop the nascent encounter between war and contemporary approaches to society, history, politics and philosophy. It is a vehicle to reconceive the field of war studies, expand the sites where war is studied, and open the field to new voices.

FREDERIK ROSÉN

Collateral Damage

A Candid History of a Peculiar Form of Death

HURST & COMPANY, LONDON

First published in the United Kingdom in 2016 by
C. Hurst & Co. (Publishers) Ltd.,
41 Great Russell Street, London, WC1B 3PL
© Frederik Rosén, 2016
All rights reserved.
Printed in India

Distributed in the United States, Canada and Latin America by
Oxford University Press, 198 Madison Avenue, New York, NY 10016,
United States of America.

A Cataloguing-in-Publication data record for this book
is available from the British Library.

ISBN: 9781849044073 *hardback*

This book is printed using paper from registered sustainable
and managed sources.

www.hurstpublishers.com

For Anne

CONTENTS

'Collateral Damage is the unintentional or incidental injury or damage to persons or objects that would not be lawful military targets in the circumstances ruling at the time. Such damage is not unlawful as long as it is not excessive in light of the overall military advantage anticipated from the attack.'

Department of Defense Dictionary of Military and Associated Terms,
US Department of Defense, 2001

PREFACE

All too often, we simplify our accounts of what it means to kill civilians as collateral damage in war. The suffering of the victims and the bereaved and our responsibility towards them do not reduce to the crude equations we routinely apply to explain their fate. In the process of writing this book, I searched for a naturally given right to inflict even minimal collateral damage. I found no such right. What I did find was an age-old moral problem and libraries full of failed efforts to resolve it. We cannot close our eyes to this lack of clarity.

It is our moral duty to be painstakingly clear about what it means to assume the right to take the lives of others as collateral damage. It's a daunting question, that one short book cannot answer alone. While the intellectual challenge of legitimizing what we call collateral damage can be found in all cultures, I focus on the Western perspectives, but hope my observations and conclusions bring this long debate forward.

Frederik Rosén
Copenhagen, 4 November 2015

INTRODUCTION

Never before in history have military powers expressed so much concern for the fate of civilians in war. Developments in humanitarian thought coupled with new strategic and political problems with civilian casualties have pulled collateral damage into the limelight. In contemporary conflicts, where civilian hearts and minds form the currency of power, collateral damage effectively breeds enemy mobilisation. The recurrent humanitarian dilemma of harming and killing some of those we set out to protect casts an ambivalent light on peacekeeping missions, executed as they are under UN Security Council mandates with increasing emphasis on protecting civilians. The moral and strategic dilemmas of collateral damage have swollen to a size where they shape core normative and material aspects of Western military conduct. Yet, at the same time we learn very little about the collateral damage victims. The faces and human destinies behind the numbers of dead and bereaved receive limited attention, as we concentrate on the rights and plights of the violators.

One of the most popular American TV series ever, Homeland (2011–14), illustrates this well. On the one hand, the problem of collateral damage establishes the central plot of the entire series. The main character, American soldier Nicholas Brody, returns home from Iraq traumatised by a brutal imprisonment, but also carrying a savage, scathing anger in his heart. His anger flows from a drone strike, ordered by US Vice-president Walden, which destroyed a school and killed eighty-two children. These included the son of terrorist leader Abu Nazir, Issa, with whom Brody developed a fatherly relationship during his captivity at Nazir's house. Nazir and Brody's mutual loss and anger over US negligence towards the victims fuse their spirits into a shared rage against Walden, who without lifting an eyebrow justifies the strike by stating 'the potential collateral damage falls within current matrix parameters'. And so the scene is set for a drama about causes, loyalties and the question of permissible collateral damage.

On the other hand, we learn very little about the killed children and their families. Brody may to some degree represent the perspective of the bereaved, but he is still too much a Western soldier, and his dilemmas and concerns evidently belong to the military camp. In any case, while the entire plot of Homeland springs from the abstract problem of collateral damage, it pays no particular attention to the collateral damage victims themselves. Could we imagine four seasons of a prime-time TV series following the everyday life of bereaved Iraqi or Afghan families? Not really. Homeland reflects the way the problem of collateral damage has become defining theme in the politics of Western warfare while the victims themselves remain relatively invisible.

We care for the problem, but not for its victims. This is the paradox that created the reason for this book. To unlock the deeper philosophical levels of this paradox I will ask why it apparently remains so exceptionally difficult for us to think about a formal responsibility for killing, say, children as collateral damage. And I will seek out the place and role of the collateral damage rule in our liberal world order: What kind of claim is the claim to lawful collateral damage? Who may claim collateral damage? These are questions with implications. Any answer to them reaches far beyond politics. In fact, as we will see by closer inspection, the problem of collateral damage opens up a gateway that leads to the very heart of theology and political theory; to define, explain and justify collateral damage is to answer the question of who could and should rule the world. Not in terms of actual kings, emperors, presidents, or priests, but in terms of the very form legitimate rule may take and how we may legitimately take military action to realise our hopes for a better world. Again, Homeland nicely draws the lines between formal state authority, embodied in the figure of Vice-president Walden, and alternative forms of authority, embodied in the figure of the terrorist Abu Nazir, as well as Brody, who gets torn apart not by the struggle between state authority and other claims to authority, but by the abyss that opens between them, where ultimate loyalty reveals itself as a free and existential choice, leaving the individual solitary and all at sea.

Until now only two entities have succeeded in making and sustaining a claim to causing death and severe suffering to innocent persons as legitimate collateral damage in the course of realising visions of a better world: the spokespersons of God and of the modern state. Congruently, historical discussions about the category of death and suffering we today label 'collateral damage' point to ultimate authority in governance as a defining focus. As I set out to show, the intellectual debates about authority in governance must thereby be tightly bound to the moral–political–legal status of the corpse of every nameless child whose life is snuffed out by an inaccurate, drone-launched missile somewhere in the tribal areas between Afghanistan and Pakistan. If this is the case, the real protagonist of the TV series Homeland is not Brody, but the dead body of Issa.

We should have serious moral concerns about the killing of civilians in war as collateral damage, not least because history shows that war is expensive and painful compared with other ways of accomplishing our objectives. But that is another discussion. This book seeks not to revisit the many formidable arguments for and against war and collateral damage. Rather it springs from the observation that no study has yet dealt with collateral damage as a puzzle in and of itself. This will be my task. I am after an understanding of what the manifestation of collateral damage victims puts at stake and also of what they stand for in terms of intellectual cargo. We lack such an assessment of how collateral damage, as a separate category of death and suffering in war, fits into our broader notions of authority, state and governance. I see this as a necessary precondition for any further moral engagement with the killing of civilians as 'collateral damage'.

What is collateral damage?

I decided to employ the term 'collateral damage' in this book because of its use in common language and in the military doctrines of major military powers. But while the US military may have pioneered the concept as a military doctrine, in my view they adopted the term to label a category of killings that the laws of war already provided for. 'Collateral damage' was just a name for an already existing rule of international law. The rule is often tweaked and misapplied, but that is also a different discussion than what I aim for. I am interested in the collateral damage rule as an 'ideal type' and the legal codification of a norm that resolves the age-old problem of responsibility for unavoidable and sometimes bad side effects arising from even the most pure-hearted, good-willed actions.

This concept of collateral damage, mediating between a deep-seated true-life problem and a time-honoured social norm, challenges popular accounts of the concept. For instance, we hear how collateral damage should be understood as another of the many military euphemisms, a concept designed and invoked to obscure the human cost of war. Or that collateral damage stands for a 'one must break eggs to make an omelette' type of utilitarian calculation. Or that it represents a sacrifice of civilians or, simply, a category of accidents. Although these explanations may hold some truth, they only skim the surface of the issue and are also too shallow to offer any inroads for our enquiry. The euphemism critique fails to recognise how the problem of collateral damage has always played a most critical role in the intellectual realm of war. Therefore it cannot simply be a euphemism. And utilitarianism is a fairly recent idea, while the problem of collateral damage stretches back to our most ancient debates about war and governance. Similarly, the view that collateral damage is merely an 'accident' fails to capture the moral complexity of the fallout of war and acts of governance more broadly. Furthermore, the rather specific role of sacrifice in more or less all cultures at all times in history makes it, as I will substantiate, difficult to regard collateral damage killings as the sacrifice of civilians in war.

Lastly, and most importantly: collateral damage, as I will speak about it in this book, is per definition not a crime, for then it would not be collateral damage. It is the very lawfulness and absence of formal responsibility that form the contours of the category of death and suffering in war that we call collateral damage. As I devote a chapter to explaining, this lawfulness derives from international law, including the laws of war, and exists independently of whatever we choose to call such incidents or victims. Whether we speak about one or fifty thousand collateral damage victims, whether we speak about civilians killed by a single, small-arms crossfire incident, or huge numbers killed by a nuclear weapon, the category of collateral damage under the laws of war remains fundamentally unchanged. The disagreements concern the scope and application of the rule to those factual circumstances.

Of course, this substantial lawfulness does not free collateral damage from moral critique, although I will contend that the lawfulness of collateral damage expresses a deep-seated moral ethos shared by the international community. Few voices call for zero tolerance of the killing of civilians in war. Yet the scope of lawful collateral damage incidents remains highly disputed. Moral philosophers are mostly preoccupied with scrutinising the principles of proportionality and necessity in order to map out under which circumstances collateral damage may be considered morally permissible; they are not so concerned about the moral acceptability of having such a rule available in the first place. Hence, the rule of international law regulating the killing of civilians as collateral damage sits nicely with most moral systems.

For that reason, while I recognise the desired differentiation between the domain of law and that of morality, as elaborated with greater or lesser success by legal philosophers, the formulae for such differentiation bear no implications for my analysis. Rather, as I see it, law and moral philosophy offer analogous and to some extent intertwined responses to the sort of questions about permissible deaths and suffering that arise from the claim to collateral damage. However, only the legal domain offers a coagulated structure of norms in the form of a rule of international law that is applied to facts on a continual basis. When we speak about collateral damage victims in war today, we speak first and foremost about law. We speak about the application of the collateral damage rule to facts in more or less consistent manners. We speak about an operation of law that singles out the collateral damage victims, who can be physically touched and counted, as part of the supposed necessary and proportionate side effects of acts of war.

Let me emphasise that whether we see explicitly calculated, somewhat foreseen or truly unexpected collateral damage, the laws of war do not view these as separate categories. Regardless of how military organisations may catalogue what they consider different forms of collateral damage, such incidents must all pass the same legal tests of necessity and proportionality. From the perspective of the laws of war, the collateral damage victims sit together, not separated by any 'internal' legal differentiations. The collateral damage rule ultimately presents us with one and only one category of victims. From a legal perspective, we thus see three overall categories of harm and dying from acts of war: We have soldiers harming or killing soldiers as lawful acts stemming from the proportionate use of military force during combat: 'death on the field of honour'. We have soldiers harming and killing soldiers and civilians in ways or for reasons that are not lawful under the laws of war: here we see war crimes. Then we have our third category, which consists of civilians and soldiers whose death and suffering are counted as collateral damage. Unexceptional deaths such as non-combat related accidents, suicide, murder, and illness fall outside these categories.

What is the problem of collateral damage?

To fully comprehend the depth of the collateral damage problem and its contemporary solution in the form of the collateral damage rule, we need to take a big step back from it. Let us start with Adam and Eve. A fundamental constituent of our theme of collateral damage is the gap between perfection and imperfection in human agency. Collateral damage is our recent name for some essentially undesired and regrettable yet unfortunately inevitable side effects

5

of warfare. In the divine harmony of the Garden of Eden, according to the biblical tales, this fissure between perfection and imperfection in human agency did not exist. God and man's actions were one. Perfection ruled but with one crucial exception: a human appetite to taste forbidden fruit. While disagreeing on the source of Adam and Eve's disrespect for God's commandment, and on why the devil tempted them to taste the apple, theologians do agree that the Fall depicts a rupture that hurled man into depravity and sinfulness. The expulsion from Eden laid bare and magnified the gap between God's perfection and man's imperfection. As the story goes, man became failure-prone, condemned to live in a state of permanent fiasco. In the words of Church Father Augustine, the expulsion from Eden changed the human condition from one of *non posse peccare* (unable to sin) to one of *non posse non peccare* (unable not to sin), Augustine is viewed as the key originator of this long-lasting idea of an 'original sin'[1] as the humans' endogenous inability to act without deleterious side effects—an idea, which basically leads to the damnation of children.[2] Historically, the idea of original sin has been viewed as a burden or a weight.[3] But sin is not an abstraction. It is an idea that arose as a response to frustrations about concrete action and the concrete problem of explaining the gap between the ideal and the accomplishable.

What is more, Judeo–Christian concepts of a perfect God have also encountered problems. Humans have not always entirely understood why their omnipresent, omniscient, omnipotent, and omnibenevolent God could or would not remove the tormenting experience of pain and suffering from their world. The story of Job's endless but outwardly meaningless suffering makes a good case. Such doubt called for a defence of God, and hence the theodicy problem. Again, the issue at stake was a gap between promise and performance: a frustration about what God was hoped to be and the experience of the assumed worldly manifestations of his divine powers. Those who argue that human pain and suffering should be viewed as part of God's will still do so in response to a puzzled 'why?' Why suffering? Why pain? In the end, both the idea of sin and the theodicy problem, two crucial institutions in Judeo–Christian theology, seek solutions to the same kind of problem: what do we do when virtuous agency spurs agonising outcomes? What do we do with pain and suffering brought to innocent persons by good-hearted agency? How do we fit such experiences into our worldview and our various ideas of blame and responsibility?

These questions are enduring puzzles and drivers of intellectual history, and they also frame the problem of collateral damage in war. After all, the collateral damage rule suggests a response to the moral problem of killing innocent persons by righteous actions in righteous wars—what I will simply call the collateral damage problem. The idea and concept of collateral damage grows out of an experience of ambiguity created by imperfection and failure-proneness. It points at the rift between the picture-perfect military operations and their agonising side effects. But let's remember that we are speaking about an answer to a question: if no one had asked why such harm should be permissible, the idea of collateral damage would be extraneous, and the collateral damage rule unneeded.

It's a fallen man who fights wars. A creature that cannot not sin. The collateral damage rule of the laws of war embodies this necessity and gives it a legal form: international law firmly establishes the lawfulness of 'proportionate', combat-related, incidental and non-intentional injury and damage. It responds to the question 'why innocent death and suffering?' with an entitlement to blamelessness, legitimised by the idea of necessary failure-proneness. Law thereby accommodates legal space for imperfect judgements, imperfect skills, and imperfect weapons systems. The view that strict adherence to norms and laws jeopardises military missions follows the scheme of failure-proneness. Action needs room for failure, we say.

Flipping the perspective

We often invoke the biblical narrative of the Fall as a caption to the traumatic feelings of regret, shame, guilt and sin that soldiers and nations struggle with in the aftermath of war; a feeling of paradise lost. I suggest we turn this scheme on its head by viewing, in a very secular manner, the story of the Fall as a response to a certain human experience of failure-proneness and the question of responsibility. The narrative of the Fall and its broad appeal did not appear out of the blue. Indeed, most of the Old and New Testament narratives pick their examples, allegories and illustrations from everyday issues to do with family, friendship, food, sex, worship, work, community and war, offering a rich account of many timeless issues relating to man as a social animal. My perspective on our recent conceptions of the collateral damage rule and norm springs from the observation that they may be viewed as a response to the same kind of intellectual puzzle that gave rise to the idea of sin and the theodicy problem. From this angle, the collateral damage rule and norm will be approached as a moral and legal response to the same puzzling gap between the perfect and the imperfect, and to the same questions of 'why?' and 'whose responsibility?' stirred up by imperfect agency. If there is any transcendence in our social world, I suggest we will not find its order in the grand explanations hypothesised by theology or philosophy, but rather in the core puzzles and dilemmas that led to the initial need to formulate these ideas.

I believe the collateral damage victim embodies such a crosscutting puzzle. At its heart, the collateral damage rule implies a bond between the kinds of violence we label collateral damage and the deeper and seemingly insolvable moral, theological and existential questions that have nourished the historical progress of the idea of collateral damage. Just as in the biblical narrative of the Fall, our idea of collateral damage implies a bond between authority and questions of perfection, imperfection, guilt and responsibility. This bond places the problem of collateral damage at the centre of the existential riddles of the individual and collective lives of human beings.

Unfortunately, the current uses of the term 'collateral damage'—and, indeed, our legal, political and moral approaches to address the killing of civilians as lawful 'unintended but perhaps foreseen' side effects of acts of war—fail to consider this bond. It is as though we have forgotten the deep puzzles to which our notion and rule of collateral damage is a response. This perhaps becomes clearest in the increasing labelling of civilian casualties as 'accidental killings'—a somewhat industrial term which differs qualitatively from the notion of collateral damage, vested as this is with grand moral visions of good and righteous governance. In spite of the proliferating debates, the killing of civilians as collateral damage still usually gets treated as a relatively unproblematic incident, legitimised and legalised by the collateral damage rule. It is mostly addressed as a matter of striking the right balance between military necessity and proportionality, thus determining the threshold of unlawful, 'excessive', losses. That may be sufficient from a technical legal perspective. Yet it does not capture the fact that the collateral damage victim stands for one of the most prominent intellectual problems related to human agency and governance.

Obscured by romantic violence

If this is true, then why do the 'inhabitants' of the collateral damage rule, the collateral damage victims, receive so little attention? Despite the roaring buzz of global media, images of atrocities seldom find their way to the broader public. War reporting from the First World War to Afghanistan has given the collateral damage victims little attention. They remain the 'forgotten victims'.[4]

At the same time, it seems that we cannot get enough of war movies and news reports about 'our boys' (and girls) out on the front line. We are, for many good reasons, curious to know how our boys behave out there, at the end of the world, in deep stress and exhaustion, momentarily stripped of ordinary judiciousness and conventions of morality. War coverage and Hollywood feed us, like hungry nestlings, with tales of nationhood, heroic sacrifice, and comradeship. This brings us glimpses of what it means to be a soldier out there, where civilisation ends, where all comfort ends: how does he walk, talk, think, fear, shiver, dream, shoot and survive? What kind of moral animal is he? What kind of moral animal is the human being? The romantic image of war and its violence as a truth-producing event stands tremendously powerful and alluring. We consume with great pleasure and plenty of popcorn.

I do not intend to criticise the soldiers or the military organisations. I just notice how the deaths of others in war seem to interest us only inasmuch as they contribute to shaping images of our own war deeds, sacrifices and failures. It is a cultural phenomenon. When the media, Hollywood, war documentaries and the news deal with collateral damage victims, they typically function as a mirror for reflecting our soldiers' moral conduct and dilemmas or the performance of military technology. The psychological trauma of the soldier who shot dead a little girl makes a more attention-grabbing story than the silenced girl and her bereaved family. We hardly ever look further than the heads of our own troops. There really is very little interest for human life beyond the collateral damage numbers. The story of suffering minor shrapnel wounds without access to morphine or antibiotics or clean water and soap, and the slow, painful death this may cause, is more or less absent from the war narratives in popular culture. Collateral damage victims simply lack a gripping dramaturgy. We build memorials to honour our dead soldiers, but we have no noteworthy memorials for the millions of civilians who suffered or still suffer the horrors of Korea, Vietnam, Cambodia, Laos, Iraq, Afghanistan, or Gaza. We hide away these horrors of war to make war appear sane. But with the absence of the victims, our view over the gap between perfection and imperfection, which collateral damage stands for, also vanishes. That aspect, the lack of representation of the many collateral damage victims, and thus the disappearance of the puzzle of imperfection, makes us incapable of clearly seeing what war today is all about. It makes it very difficult to judge the moral righteousness of fighting wars. Hence scrutinising and exposing the puzzle of collateral damage and its role in our prototypical models of governance is not only about retuning a tangled theoretical chord, but also about invoking the human relation, the ethical bond with the collateral damage victim, which this chord after all embodies.

The present absents

Customary international law and treaties accommodate the lawfulness and civility of the collateral damage rule, yet it still troubles us. In particular, the rising number of civilian casualties in current warfare has turned collateral damage into a contentious moral and strategic problem. The international forces in Afghanistan wrestled with themselves, each other, local authorities, national authorities, world opinion and, not least, the Taliban, about questions of responsibility for civilian casualties. They struggled with an emerging opinion, among the general public and even within the military ranks, that killing civilians as collateral damage should perhaps not be entirely exempted from formal responsibility, regardless of how unintentional and accidental it may be. Military forces increasingly compensate victims and their relatives. Although they emphasise strongly that such compensation functions solely as a strategic 'money as weapon' programme to win (back) hearts and minds, and should not in any way be seen as recognising fault or responsibility, I see some sense of moral obligation looming in the wings.

On the other side of the military officer's desk, bereaved mothers bewail the lack of appropriate recognition, acceptance of formal responsibility and compensation. They cannot understand why foreign soldiers should get away with what they consider to be murder or recklessness. Their loss and sorrow swell too deep and painful to be relinquished in response to the soldiers' promises of a world safe from terrorism. They crave responsibility and representation. They raise the 'why' that keeps producing the answer: 'collateral damage!' The dilemma and the negotiations of the claim to collateral damage stand central to current discussions of war. But the collateral damage victims themselves, the inhabitants of the category of death and suffering we call collateral damage, remain relatively absent.

Outline of the book

To structure my enquiry, I will employ four interwoven concepts of collateral damage: 1) collateral damage as a problem, or 'the collateral damage problem', which denotes how collateral damage stands for an unresolved existential problem of mankind; 2) the collateral damage norm, which denotes the historical formation of responses to this problem, and which distinguishes what we today call collateral damage as a certain category of death and suffering; 3) the collateral damage rule, which is the codification in the laws of war of the collateral damage norm, and 4) the claim to collateral damage, which is the claim to morally permissible and, in recent years, lawful collateral damage stemming from acts of war.

In that way I view collateral damage as both a solution to an unresolvable moral–philosophical problem and a claim: it is a theological–philosophical puzzle-resolver and a political–theological claim to legitimate violence. To unpack this twin topography of collateral damage as puzzle-resolver and claim of authority, I will engage a cross-disciplinary perspective drawing upon law, political science, economic theory, theology, philosophy, ethics and anthropology. The enquiry begins by examining collateral damage in war but then moves beyond that focus to present collateral damage in its broader context as an essential concept or tool of state power. War-related collateral damage merely presents us with our puzzle's most dramatic expression. As we will see, the problem of collateral damage and its proposed solutions denote a wide-ranging philosophical problematic of our theories of governance.

I open the book with an examination of the place and role of collateral damage in the context of current Western warfare. After that follows a juridical examination of the collateral damage rule in general international law. I ask whether we should expect to see incidents of collateral damage being covered by formal responsibility principles in the future. To answer this question I discuss prospects and options within international human rights law, civil law, international customary law, and the possibility of thinking obligations without a "crime". I also demonstrate how drone technology and the new capability of seeing and knowing in war changes key parameters for applying the collateral damage rule. The conclusion is, however, that the collateral damage rule will endure. Then the idea of collateral damage will be examined in the context of just war theory, the doctrine of double effect, theodicy, and utilitarianism. We will see how the problem of collateral damage makes up the formative riddle behind these theories. Having looked into the moral and legal characteristics of the collateral damage rule, I then shift the focus to explore its relation to accidents and sacrifice. First, I explain why and how collateral damage differs from accidents due to its connection to visions of authority. Then I inspect dominant accounts of the role of sacrifice in society in order to make clear why it is wrong to view collateral damage as a sacrifice of civilians.

11

The final chapters of the book discuss collateral damage and its relation to authority. My main question is: if collateral damage so far has belonged exclusively to God or the state, then what becomes of collateral damage in a privatised and fragmented world order, where neither God nor the state hold the position of the principal carrier of authority? I will suggest that any notion of 'decentralised authority', a highly popular diagnosis (and prescription) in current analysis of globalisation and governance, must consider the private claim to collateral damage as a possible tipping point between centralised and decentralised forms of authority in governance.

Altogether, and in a most peculiar way, collateral damage as a problem, norm, rule and claim not only provides us with an avenue for inquiring into the meaning of death on the fields of war but also offers a surprising entry point for inspecting more general notions of governance, legitimate authority, political community, faith, and images of self and society. For that reason I suspect that the collateral damage victim, our forgotten victim of war, may present us with something as challenging as a first philosophy of war and governance.

1

THE THIRD CATEGORY OF DEATH

Some two-thirds of the more than 60 million killed during the Second World War were civilians. Strategic carpet-bombings of civilians and civilian infrastructure were common practice, culminating in the nuclear bombings of Hiroshima and Nagasaki. Seventy years later, the accidental killing by the military of children in a remote rural mountain village in Afghanistan potentially draws news headlines across the world. Militaries increasingly engage collateral damage estimation tools and extensive precautionary measures as standard operational procedure for even minor operations. Certainly, our attitudes towards civilian casualties in war have undergone drastic changes in a continuation of a long-standing process of fortification and nuancing of an old tradition for separating combatants from non-combatants. These changes and the related developments in norms and laws reified and solidified juridically the 'third category' of killings in war that we today refer to as collateral damage. This chapter offers an account of this development and how it formed the recent role of the collateral damage rule in Western warfare. To do so, the chapter first outlines the historical trajectory of this development; it then moves on to observe how collateral damage, as a problem and a rule, unfolds in our present era of urbanised network-centric warfare as a most critical part of civil–military relations in conflict zones.

Calling off wild war: the twentieth-century codification of the battle space

The concept of civilians as a non-targetable category was not established before the emergence of 'just war' theory. However, it has always been an intuitive idea in warfare that not everybody can be the enemy. If we go back in time to the earliest treatments of legitimate targets in war, the question would not be so much about participation in acts of war, but rather a matter of separating guilt and innocence. For instance, Augustine, a father of the Christian church and of just war theory, took a brutally indifferent stand on the question. He refused to condemn the killing of non-combatants with the argument that it might be punishment for their misdeeds elsewhere in life.[1] In the worldview of Augustine, it would be an idolatrous act to make judgements on matters that ultimately lay in the hands of God. It was not that Augustine did not draw a distinction between guilt and innocence, targetable and non-targetable; rather, he rationalised that the question of who belongs where is for God alone to decide. Preceding this we find the separation of legitimate and non-legitimate targets and the constraint of violence as themes in Thucydides' account of the Peloponnesian wars,[2] and the Old Testament frequently raises the issue of God's will and ostensibly undeserved human death and suffering.

The question of curbing (or not) violent force along lines of separation between legitimate and illegitimate targets, or 'guilty and innocent', is at least as old as our first written sources about war. The modern principle of non-combat immunity has its roots in these early debates and, in particular, the distinction that Augustine detailed in his discussion of 'just killing' in war.[3] Later, philosophers of war, such as Thomas Aquinas, Hugo Grotius and Emer de Vattel, all placed the question of indiscriminate killings as central to the war problem, but it was Jean-Jacques Rousseau who brought the question into the modern age by creating a clear category of 'civilians'. He famously stated:

> War then is a relation, not between man and man, but between State and State, and individuals are enemies only accidentally, not as men, nor even as citizens, but as soldiers; not as members of their country, but as its defenders. Finally, each State can have for enemies only other States, and not men; for between things disparate in nature there can be no real relation.[4]

Rousseau wrote in 1762, and soon after his contribution the modern state project took off with great speed. Over the next century organisational capabilities and weapon technologies developed fast, in tandem with the industrial revolution. The Western state projects progressively institutionalised the military as a distinct state branch with constitutionally bound powers, duties and checks and balances. A defining aspect of the modern state project was an increased political–legal categorisation and mapping of all aspects of societal life. This included drawing up the boundaries of warfare according to the Rousseauian dictum, emphasising that civilians are illegitimate military targets.

The first US code of land warfare, the 1863 Lieber Code,[5] which was also the world's first humanitarian instrument, stated that the targeting of civilians and civilian infrastructure should be avoided, but that military necessity was a legitimate reason for overriding this principle. The Lieber Code was introduced through a manual later adopted by Germany, France and Britain. The humanitarian scheme thereby started to take form. In the last decades of the nineteenth century public international law finally gained the status of being a distinct branch of law and an academic field in its own right.[6] The heightened awareness of the legal distinction between civilians and soldiers, in combination with this expansion of international law, led to the birth of international humanitarian law in the form of the Hague Conventions of 1899 and 1907. The Hague Conventions were to a large degree developed as tools of colonial rule, as were most other international legal instruments regulating military intervention and armed conflict at that time in history.[7] Concurrently with the preparatory work for the conventions, in places remote from The Hague, colonial wars in German South-West Africa (Namibia), the Congo Free State/Belgian Congo, the Philippines, South Africa and Sudan ferociously wiped out whole civilian populations. The colonial legacy does cast a shadow over the purported objectives that commenced the era of humanitarian law, but we should not, however, let this eclipse the sincere hope the conventions also expressed for a more humane form of armed state rivalry, with fewer civilian atrocities and an eye open to the danger to civilians. Then came the World Wars.

With the exception of light aircraft and the German 'Paris Guns', which could shell the centre of Paris from a distance of seventy-five miles, the military technologies of the First World War did not really allow for speedy penetration into enemy territory. The bombing of cities by small planes, Zeppelins or long-range cannons created more fear than casualties. The sluggishness of trench warfare, with its reliance on horse-drawn artillery on muddy dirt roads, created a natural separation of soldiers and civilians, and the relatively equal balance of the military powers prevented military forces from moving far into civilian areas. Wherever the front moved forward the civilians, for the most part, had time to flee. So while civilian suffering and deaths during the First World War were very high, they were mainly caused by famine, disease and displacement.

The interwar period saw a number of international conferences on the issue of refugees and civilians in war, thanks to the Red Cross movement.[8] The concerns included displacement of civilians and harm to civilian infrastructure. Changes mooted included the banning of indiscriminate bombing of civilians, the outlawing of chemical, bacterial and incendiary weapons, and the possibility of legally established safety zones for civilians.[9] The call for the protection of civilians during war thus found its way into international politics. In the early years of the Second World War, the United Kingdom's Royal Air Force and the US Army Air Corps both openly committed themselves to applying the principle of civilian immunity when carrying out aerial bombings.[10] Any general impact of these calls and commitments collapsed utterly with the 'terror bombings' of the second Sino–Japanese War (1937–45) and the Second World War (1939–45).[11] The Japanese bombings of Chinese cities such as Nanjing, Canton, Shanghai, Wuhan and Chongqing, which experienced showers of bombs filled with hungry, plague-contaminated fleas that caused epidemics;[12] the London Blitz; the bombing unleashed on Warsaw, Berlin, Dresden and Rotterdam; and the US bombing of Japanese cities, all fall into this category of 'terror bombing'. When night fell on 9 March 1945, three hundred US bombers began a merciless firebombing of Tokyo in Operation Meetinghouse. That night some 100,000 civilians burned to death.

Why strategic bombing of civilians is not collateral damage

The strategic aerial bombings of civilians during the Second World War were far from 'unintentional' killing. The bombings were aimed directly at the civilian population but were not based on the assumption that any person belonging to the enemy nation was an enemy and consequently a legitimate military target. The rationale for targeting civilians during the Second World War, and throughout the nuclear age, was to convey the message that their regime could not protect them and that it was therefore better to surrender.[13] The aim was to weaken the war spirit of the enemy nation by exhausting its civilian base. The strategic bombings were 'attacks on morale', an expression that, according to US laws of war specialist W. Hays Parks 'became a shibboleth, a mantra, exhorted as a matter of blind faith by air power advocates on behalf of aviation service survival and development in post-World War II budget battles with land and naval forces'.[14] The 'attacks on morale' culminated with the nuclear attacks on Japan.

The official policy was that strategic bombing was a last recourse to put pressure on enemy regimes; and as 'neither the British nor the American government was prepared to publicly justify their strategies of deliberate bombing civilians',[15] they maintained that the 'casualties were the unintended consequence of attacks on military and industrial targets'.[16] After the war President Truman, confronted with criticism for massacring civilians, defended the Hiroshima bombing as targeting a military base[17] and thus tried to ascribe the many civilian deaths to the category of combat deaths that would later be dubbed 'collateral damage'. Yet, even if the immediate American response was that Nagasaki and Hiroshima hosted military hubs, it was soon agreed that the nuclear attacks targeted, above all, the civilians, of the Japanese empire. Polls in the aftermath of the war proved that most Americans knew about the devastating collateral effects of nuclear weapons on civilians but that they still approved them as a legitimate weapon.[18]

The deliberate and systematic targeting of civilians during the Second World War was, however, fundamentally different to what we today label collateral damage.[19] Strategic bombing founds its logic on ideas of persuasion and coercion: we shoot to hit civilians. We target civilians, but as a means to put pressure on politicians and generals, as opposed to an end in itself. In contrast, collateral damage as a rule and as a claim founds its logic on inevitable side effects: we shoot so as to avoid hitting civilians. The defining features of being an unintentional side effect and the prohibition of deliberate or indiscriminate attack on civilians and civilian objects (which was later codified in the Additional Protocols to the Geneva Conventions, 1977) clearly separate collateral damage from strategic bombing. It could be argued that the suffering of civilians was an undesired but necessary side effect of terror bombings, but their whole point was to strike terror into the hearts of civilians. Civilian suffering stood as the primary and desired goal, even as a means to other ends. In contrast, collateral damage in itself produces no 'positive' effects whatsoever; it is not a means to anything, but just a problem. To view collateral damage killings, as we talk about collateral damage in this book, as belonging to the same category of civilian casualties as strategic bombing is therefore wrong. Even if the victims might not agree, politically, morally and legally these are two entirely different forms of death and suffering.

Still, the parties engaged in the First and Second World Wars clearly distinguished between death and suffering caused to those who took direct part in hostilities and to those who did not.[20] This made it possible to hold entire civilian populations hostage, or to view the military–industrial complex as turning civil workers into military targets. And the lived-through dilemma of balancing military utility against civilian immunity intensified and deepened the debate about the scope of permissible killings of civilians in war.

COLLATERAL DAMAGE

Response to atrocities and the development of international norms

The humanitarian law response to the atrocities of the Second World War was among other things to strengthen the conceptual separation of civilians and combatants, known in international law as the 'principle of distinction'. The Fourth Geneva Convention of 1949 codified in legal terms the protection of any civilian during war and prolonged military occupation 'who is not a member of his or her country's armed forces or other militia or militant organization'. The practice of targeting civilians to put pressure on their political leaders was outlawed under an international law regime finding increasing political footing in international politics.

The development of international norms left the world with only two ways of killing civilians in war: as war crimes or as unintended side effects of military necessity; that is, as collateral damage. The distinction between war crime and collateral damage moved the question of intention to the foreground of war ethics. Did they intend to harm the civilians? Did they intend to take all the required precautions to avoid hitting civilians? Was it an act of negligence, or did they perhaps even deliberately aim their weapons at them? What was really on the mind of the soldier who directed the laser guided missile at the wedding?

Paradoxically, the twentieth century swell of political–legal codification of all aspects of warfare was accompanied by a change in the character of war that rendered the new legal instruments difficult to apply. The Cold War power lock did not leave room for any major wars between nations. Except for a few larger wars of intervention—Egypt (1956), Korea (1950–3), Vietnam (1957–75), and Afghanistan (1979–89)—most of the armed conflicts of the Cold War years were military coups or involved armed resistance movements, from African wars to South and Central American guerrilla wars; from the PLO in Lebanon to the IRA in Ireland. Many of the armed conflicts were proxy wars between the superpowers, but nevertheless they were also internal struggles. The wars of intervention in Vietnam and Afghanistan escalated into counter-insurgency warfare where formal militaries confronted combatants who strategically and assiduously oscillated between militia and civilian life. It soon proved difficult to apply the international legal code of belligerent and non-belligerent in a meaningful manner to persons who shifted quickly between appearing as civilians and as combatants; or to those who took up arms without complying with international law's prescription for proper combatant identification by wearing a uniform or carrying visible weapons, and thus disqualified themselves from the protection of the laws of war: 'illegal combatants' were for many years exempted from international legal protection. They did not qualify as prisoners of war under humanitarian law and could, in principle, be treated outside any proscriptions of international law. Added to this difficulty is the question of how to perceive civilian support of armed fractions, since insurgencies often benefit from the sympathy, protection and support of civil society. The difficulty grew as adversaries started to utilise humanitarian law as a strategic tool in what became known as concealment warfare, where belligerents blend with civilians to obstruct discovery and targeting. Or deliberately attempt to drag the enemy into situations where they are likely to, or perhaps even forced to, kill civilians and thus deal a blow to their own legitimacy. Without internationally acclaimed humanitarian norms, such strategies would have little effect. It is the norms that put the price on the civilian heads. This price stands central to the political battle regarding who is to blame for civilian casualties caused by conflicts with militias who decide to fight from civilian neighbourhoods.

Ending illegal combatants

The legal grey zone of illegal combatants turned into a major issue during the Vietnam War where 'suspected illegal Vietcong' became subject to sweeping targeting. As images of the carnage reached the international media it sparked a political outcry, which lead to a reconsideration of the international laws protecting civilians and regulation relating to the status of combatants. The result was the Additional Protocols to the Geneva Conventions of 1977, which stretched the legal notion of combatant further. A person now only needed to grab a weapon in the immediate conflict situation to move from non-combatant to combatant status.[21] Picking up a weapon entitled, in principle, civilians to the protection as combatants under humanitarian law, including prisoner-of-war status. The Protocol also granted civilians non-combat immunity until the moment they pick up a weapon. The 1977 Protocol thereby closed down the legal vacuum of 'unlawful combatants'. It removed the 'void of rights' zone that certain political administrations tried to reinvent in their global war on terror after the 2001 attacks in New York City and Washington DC. The Protocols also expressed a concern for the growing proximity of civilians and combatants and the 'blurring' of battlefield identities. It contained the first clear international legal recognition of the norm that even attacks on military targets must not lead to excessive collateral damage to civilians.[22] While late in history, this may be viewed as the introduction of the human rights era to the battlefield. By emphasising the significance of the problem of combatant identity, i.e. the difficulty of applying the principle of distinction, states simultaneously further extrapolated the distinction between legitimate and illegitimate military targets.

A collective consciousness

Gradually, the distinction between legitimate and illegitimate military targets was inscribed in a detailed and growing body of international legal norms, including human rights law. Today, international law offers a nearly all-embracing legal codification of all aspects of armed conflict; every act of war fits into some nook of international law. Everything that happens on today's battlefield has a corresponding legal code. War is an activity governed by law, observed by law, and communicated to the world through the language of law. Lawyers and legal experts now crowd the military institutions at home and abroad. Legal thinking has spurred a collective legal consciousness about war and warfare that is stimulated by the steady stream of media coverage of war, documentaries, TV series and Hollywood productions.

When it comes to the right to wage war, the 1990s and 2000s presented us with a number of cases where moral and political arguments claimed superiority over international law as codified in the United Nations Charter. Commentators describe this as the return of just war theory to the foreground of politics and the failure of international law to accommodate humanitarianism or to curb aggression. While this may sometimes be true, we increasingly discuss and assess the day-to-day conduct of warfare in legal terms. We talk about what is legal and what is illegal, rather than what is morally good and bad. The tricky question of moral responsibility is exchanged for the liberal institutional language of legal accountability. Today, law occupies the war discourse as a neutral language that offers an exit from the potential deadlock of moral disagreements. And, as David Kennedy, an American professor of law, rightly said, the large infusion of lawyers and legal language into the war apparatus sometimes gives the impression that everything has been taken into account and balanced by skilled professionals.[23] Unfortunately, legal codes are dotted lines rather than brick walls. The post-Second World War strengthening of the distinction between lawful killings and war crimes did not prevent the great military powers from killing or massacring civilians on a large scale.[24] This is well described in the literature yet omitted from the public narrative to the degree that schoolchildren in the West may not have heard about Korea or Vietnam.[25]

Even if not throwing up walls, the legal codes provide us with a language to categorise and order all aspects of death and suffering in warfare. They provide the classifications and language by which collateral damage becomes comprehensible. In this sense, the collateral damage rule defines and ascribes meaning to a particular category of death and suffering related to military operations. It ascribes a place to a certain category of violence within the wider system of states, international law and armed conflict. It orders this third category of death in war politically, legally and morally. Today's notion of collateral damage in war would be, if not obsolete then at least very weakly applicable, if it wasn't for this 'juridification' of warfare, because when we speak about collateral damage in war, we speak about the application of a legal rule.

Military doctrine

In international law, the principle of proportionality in attack originally functioned to curb violence in order to avert retaliation and escalation of conflict;[26] it did not have the moral dimension of caring for civilian lives. However, as twentieth-century developments in international law increasingly restricted the scope of force that might be applied even to enemy combatants, the application of the principle of proportionality gravitated towards the question of harming civilians and civilian infrastructure. Today we talk about proportionality and collateral damage to civilians as two sides of the same coin, as codified in the First Additional Protocol to the Geneva Conventions of 1977. Article 51 para. 5(b) prohibits '[a]n attack which may be expected to cause incidental loss of civilian life, injury to civilians, damage to civilian objects, or a combination thereof, which would be excessive in relation to the concrete and direct military advantage anticipated'. If such harm is not excessive in relation to concrete and direct military advantage, but proportionate, we see lawful collateral damage.

As the problem of harm to civilians developed into a key strategic and moral problem, this rule gained a prominent role. It was adopted in the military doctrines of all modern armies and is now used in nearly all operational steps in Western-led military operations. For example, the US military's formal definition of collateral damage is: 'Unintentional or incidental injury or damage to persons or objects that would not be lawful military targets in the circumstances ruling at the time. Such damage is not unlawful as long as it is not excessive in light of the overall military advantage anticipated from the attack.'[27] The US Air Force's 'targeting guide' describes it as 'unintentional damage or incidental damage affecting facilities, equipment or personnel occurring as a result of military actions directed against targeted enemy forces or facilities. Such damage can occur to friendly, neutral, and even enemy forces.'[28] While the definition here is extended to include friendly fire and enemy forces, the concept is mostly used to regulate the legal status of civilian casualties. The doctrine establishes that the killing of innocent civilians in the course of military missions is permissible and legal insofar as it happens as an unintended side effect, and as long as it is not out of proportion with the overall tactical advantage of the concrete situation. Under such circumstances, killing civilians is not deemed illegal, unprincipled, immoral, or unethical. It informs the soldier who kills the child as collateral damage that, formally, nothing is wrong with his actions.

In that way, the collateral damage rule of the laws of war acts not only as a restrainer, but also as an 'allower'. It has become the legal and moral ground for standard pre-operational calculation of expected civilian deaths. The doctrinal language of the US military calls the pre-operational assessment of the acceptable number of killed civilians in a given attack 'collateral damage estimation', abbreviated in military lingo to CDE.[29] CDE tools are increasingly supported by computer modelling and simulation.[30] At the same time we have seen profound developments in military hardware driven by calls for precision-guided munitions, 'collateral damage minimising munition', and drone-based surveillance technology, partly to save soldiers' lives and explore tactical advantages but also to decrease collateral damage.[31] 'It is almost as if the huge resources invested in precision-guided weapons were done solely to reduce the loss of non-combatant life',[32] as one academic writes; and the same may sometimes be said about military doctrinal developments. Collateral damage minimisation has turned into a science and technology in its own right. Still, the care for civilians may not be the main driver of change here. As Professor of political science, Neta Crawford, points out, public legitimacy issues and fear of 'losing hearts and minds' appear to have been more decisive.[33] The proportionality principle's original function in international law to curb violence so as to avert conflict escalation, rather than protect civilians, seems to endure.

Whatever blends of strategy and moral reasoning generated the change, a noteworthy effect of this new sensitivity is that collateral damage has mutated from a being primarily category of law and military doctrine into a crucial sociological component of urban warfare, here understood as low-intensity armed conflicts playing out in densely populated areas. The recent armed conflict in Afghanistan provides the model. In such theatres, CDE emerges as a gauge for more or less any military choice, which in a subtle manner dominates interaction with the local populations: it has become a sociological component of civil–military relations. By sociological component I mean a norm that profoundly shapes social interaction on an everyday level between troops and locals. To understand how the collateral damage rule grew into a sociology of civil–military relations, we need to consider the nexus between the rise of population-centric warfare, risk, and the decentralisation of decision-making power in network-centric military operations.

Population-centric operations and risk

The doctrine of population-centric warfare deprioritises the focus on eliminating the enemy by all necessary force to give room for a form of military engagement that views populations as 'the prize in war',[34] and hence places care for civilians as the foremost priority. While the agenda dovetails with the development of the international Protection of Civilians regime, from a military perspective, the idea of population-centric warfare emerged primarily as a response to the realisation that losing the political and moral support of the population in conflict zones entails, odds-on, a larger strategic setback than failing to take out the enemy. It was a response to the way war and peace increasingly blend together as fighting plays out in populous areas where civilians struggle to carry on their daily doings; where discontent with one group of fighters pushes non-combatant loyalty towards the other, but often in an erratic manner; and where friendliness tipping into unfriendliness does not necessarily depend on any deeper political convictions. It was a response to the challenge of protecting civilians in conflict theatres where people oscillate between civilian and enemy identity in somewhat unpredictable manners.

At the core of such urban warfare theatres stands unpredictability, uncertainty, ambiguity, and thereby a conflict environment defined by risk. Fire may arrive from everywhere and anywhere, everyone and anyone. A civilian car could carry explosives. A dreary-looking person could be wired by cell phone to a hidden bomb. Enemies place improvised explosive devices (IEDs) and wait patiently for their target to arrive, or ambush, habitually encroaching upon their target disguised as civilians, or infiltrate behind enemy lines for 'insider attacks'. The unknown is inscribed in every person, every road, every house, every car, truck, tree, and stone. As the soldiers find their way through fields, bush, villages, and inner-city areas, they must be cautious and aware that friendly looking persons and items may mask hostile power. It is an uncanny experience of friendliness turning against you. Being a squaddie in population-centric urbanised warfare feels like being in a computer game where seemingly innocuous characters and surroundings instantaneously turn into fire demons. In population-centric operations—where the civilians may stand for the princess who the soldiers attempt to seduce through hearts and minds campaigns—the soldier may not live long enough to reflect upon the transformation. Warning time has become extinct, if not negative: the soldier may not know before the attack that it is imminent, or may never even know that there was an attack at all. When warning time dwindles to nothing, planning becomes really difficult.[35]

The keyword here is not military threat but risk. We could speak of masked intentions and masked threats, but the effect is risk. In contrast, threat is about the known, the unambiguous and measurable, and involves perceptions of intentions and capabilities.[36] The threat of an army equals its hardware, intelligence, military culture and the cleverness of its commanders, and outcomes may be forecast by assessing these parameters. Yet if the (possible) enemy appears ambiguous, unpredictable, without a clear form and substance, devoid of clear capabilities and points of engagement, perhaps even void of clear motivations and ambitions, we are no longer talking about threat, but about risk. When picking up indicators of hostile intent, there is a risk that what is contained in the 'black box' is malicious; there is also a chance that it is benign.

In such an inherently unpredictable milieu of fluid and polymorphous identities, the checkpoint emerges as a paradigmatic piece of equipment. Squads patrolling the countryside may also be considered a sort of 'mobile checkpoint'. By establishing bottlenecks, checkpoints slow down movements and allow better inspection. They basically function like a sieve, which, ideally, only non-hostile civilians get through. On the other hand, in steadily reshuffling environments, checkpoints make obvious points of engagement for adversaries. Soldiers constantly encounter suicide vehicles and persons suddenly pulling AK-47s from under a burka. Situations demanding instant fire response are everyday experiences for any soldier moving outside the military fortresses.

Risk turns proximity into a key factor. A suicide bomber throwing him or herself upon a vehicle causes much more damage than if detonating a couple of metres away. A suicide car needs to get really close to hit its target. Afghan police trainees, translators or base staff frequently turned on their own colleagues or foreign mentors, sometimes acting out of personal discontent rather than conflict-related matters. While soldiers may be trained in attentiveness, reaction times, and procedures for fast-moving situations, they cannot really plan for apparently harmless people suddenly turning on them. Due to the constant fear of explosives and ambushes, fire typically gets unleashed at the slightest suspicion. However, an approaching person who fails to respond could be well intentioned but simply inattentive rather than loaded with explosives. Perhaps the checkpoint is new or badly marked. Perhaps the person is unfamiliar with checkpoints. Perhaps the person misunderstands waving and shouting. Perhaps the person suffers from impaired vision or hearing, a common problem in countries with poor healthcare. Hence the approaching civilian is subjected to the risk of being misunderstood—and shot. If you as a civilian want to pass the checkpoint, you had better reckon the risk and shape yourself up accordingly.

The 'checkpoint-encounter' epitomises the issue of risk, which defines the fundamental uncertainty of the situation. There is the risk of the soldier being killed, and the risk of the soldier killing the wrong person; but risk does not have a single object, as is the case with threats. In threat situations you can trust what is threatening as a known that can be avoided. In situations defined by risk the only certain thing is risk itself. This calls for a form of precaution where odds are computed and chances taken. Yet calculations cannot eliminate risk. Risk remains, and remains essentially unpredictable.

Risk, hence, can stand alone—an unquantifiable noun taking no definite article. No matrix of demarcated agencies or clear points of engagement. Statistics may be employed but offer no sanctuary. Risk is unbounded, open to interpretation and always in the eyes of the beholder. The truth does not reveal itself until its actualisation, and then it may be too late. And so trust erodes on both sides. Soldiers don't trust civilians. Civilians don't trust that soldiers will see them as civilians and they view checkpoints and encounters with soldiers as always involving some risk. By opening fire on a suspicious-looking person before that person gets too close, the soldier refuses to carry the risk of letting the person get a bit nearer and perhaps show good intentions. As an American soldier in Afghanistan told a journalist, '[t]he procedure is, if you believe there's any danger to yourself or your unit, you have every right to open fire.'[37] The 'better safe than sorry' attitude makes collateral damage an ordinary checkpoint effect, and nervousness at checkpoints continues to be a main cause of collateral damage.[38] In 2010, commenting on the continuing problem of checkpoint killings in Afghanistan, the then NATO commander, General Stanley McChrystal, acknowledged, '[w]e have shot an amazing number of people, but to my knowledge, none has ever proven to be a threat.'[39]

However, losing uniformed personnel may not pose the main problem to the overall mission: today, information travels faster than bullets and reports about collateral damage may be swiftly funnelled through various media into local, national and global hearts and minds. Waiting to shoot may kill you and cause a local tragedy for comrades, friends and relatives. But pulling the trigger on the wrong person may backfire on the whole mission due to loss of hearts and minds and political support, and thus perhaps contribute to global tragedy. Thus, the responsibility to fire or not cannot be reduced to a local ethical question of an isolated soldier's life or an isolated individual's life. As Professor of political science, Martin Shaw, has argued, risk has become a 'currency of Western warfare', where the 'life-risks' of soldiers and civilians are constantly assessed and computed against each other.[40] The balancing of expected or latent collateral damage against force protection constitutes the principal issue of population-centric warfare, and affects the everyday social interaction between soldiers and civilians on multiple levels.

Without exception, states today, as in the past, privilege force protection and insist on their right to do so to the extent that we might view it as a generally accepted—even legal—norm of armed conflict.[41] From an international law perspective we see the seeds of customary international law, which develops from the sum of what states do and what states believe is right to do. If such a rule consolidates it must, however, be considered a rule of the most powerful, and not of the victims, and therefore prone to be haunted by its inner normative tension: it is not at all obvious who should carry the burden of the double-edged quality of risk.[42] Since the risk of the situation was created in the first place by the presence of the soldiers, and not by the civilians who need to be out in the streets and the fields to carry on their daily doings, a strong moral claim can be made that the soldiers should carry the risk burden. Whether or not soldiers actually have 'every *right* to open fire' if they believe there is a danger to themselves or their unit, is thus a serious moral question.[43] The problem of collateral damage resides at the heart of it.

Network-centric warfare and the decentralisation of decision-making power

David Kilcullen writes in his book, *Out of the Mountains. The Coming Age of the Guerrilla*, that 'history suggests that there will be a strong, continued demand into the foreseeable future for military operations against a variety of nonstate actors', predominantly in urbanised and networked environments.[44] Kilcullen sees this face of the new complex urban conflict environment in

Syria today, where 'rebels are fighting from house to house and block to block in several cities'.[45] In this regard, he considers Afghanistan to be the 'defining experience of modern conflict for many of the developed world's armies and air forces—the model, in effect, for twenty-first-century warfare'.[46] I adhere to Kilcullen's analysis, which suggests that population-centric, urbanised warfare, characterised by uncertainty, volatility, complexity and risk, will dictate future Western military operations. This will probably not be as large-scale hearts and mind campaigns, but do-no-harm to civilians will most likely stand as a doctrinal cornerstone. Furthermore, network-centric military operations, which evolved as a response to such risk-saturated conflict environments, particularly in the context of Iraq and Afghanistan, not to mention Gaza, will provide a main organisational set-up for the future use of armed force—including the application of the collateral damage rule.

In brief, network-centric operations rely on 'computer equipment and networked communications technology to provide a shared awareness of the battle space'[47] to improve situational awareness and accelerate the circulation of information so as to increase force agility, and build on four overall assumptions:

1) A robustly networked force improves information sharing;
2) Information sharing and collaboration enhance the quality of information and shared situational awareness;
3) Shared situational awareness enables self-synchronization; and
4) These, in turn, dramatically increase mission effectiveness.[48]

Theoreticians have toyed with chaos theory, complexity theory, and network theory to intellectualise the network-centric approach, yet it is not entirely clear how these occasionally very abstract schemes may increase combat power. Yet the core network-centric warfare concepts still describe very well the military tactics as they evolved, by default and by design, among the international forces in Iraq and Afghanistan. While network-centric communications lines enable commanders to bypass layers of hierarchy and give direct orders to their subordinates, the demand for nimbleness is also realised by giving 'power to the edge':[49] pushing decision-making power out to the sharp end of the structure—ultimately the individual soldier. In practice, such decentralisation typically works by the means of 'intent-based' orders that lay out the overall goal of the operation while leaving plenty of room for the squads to find their own ways. Commanders become responsible for 'creating initial conditions that make success more likely and exercise control by establishing rules of engagement and other control mechanisms that the fighting forces implement themselves'.[50] In that way, the aspiration to respond swiftly and jointly to confrontations encountered by any units in the system drives a flattening or disaggregating of the chain of command, including information access and sharing, to accommodate self-synchronising and adaptable responses by low-ranking personnel in the field. As a result, we see an 'empowerment of individuals at the edge' of the organisation, 'where the organization interacts with its operating environment'.[51] From the perspective of the traditional hierarchical military organisation, the network-centric operations approach fundamentally restructures decision-making power in a way that best can be described as decentralisation.

Logically, with the decentralisation of decision-making power follows also a decentralisation of responsibility—including for acts leading to collateral damage. The collateral damage rule resides, like the rest of the laws of war, in a concept of a hierarchical military structure, implying that lines of command, responsibility and accountability in the military organisations are structured hierarchically. Consequently, a duty-bound soldier who kills civilians as collateral damage in the course of a well conducted deployment of force does in principle not carry personal responsibility. Instead, responsibility flows up the command hierarchy, eventually to the head of the state. Yet, in network-centric warfare, low-ranked individual soldiers play a greater role in executing judgement over individual situations, including the threshold for engaging fire. The individual soldiers thus carry a larger psychological burden when deciding whether to fire or show restraint. They carry the moral burden of not waiting the additional seconds it might have taken for the allegedly hostile person to show their true colours. Responsibility for engaging fire with the risk of creating collateral damage thereby shifts de facto from the central command to the 'decentralised' individual soldier. This again generates some uncertainty about institutional accountability, because, as Eric J. Dahl puts it:

> the law does not always treat junior personnel in the same way it treats senior commanders. While all military personnel throughout the chain of command are expected to observe the same laws and regulations, there nonetheless may be a different standard applied to the decisions of a senior commander, who is expected to have had access to all available intelligence and advice, than to those of junior personnel in the field, who are understood to be making decisions under different and often more challenging circumstances.[52]

Collateral damage as a sociological category

In risk-saturated theatres of conflict, the collateral damage rule becomes more than a rule for legally ordering death and suffering on the battlefield: it becomes a sociological component. Risk entrenches the collateral damage rule as a weighty sociological constituent of civil–military relations that colours any meeting between soldiers and civilians. It becomes central to assessing the conflict zone, which is no longer a landscape but a manscape, a 'human terrain'[53] composed of facial expressions, clothing, body movements, a mobile phone, indicators of nervousness, people suddenly withdrawing from the streets, clean hands on a 'farmer' who one would expect to have dirty hands from work in the fields. How does he make his living? Whose payroll is he on? The conflict manscape is a milieu of indicators, signs and hints of loyalty and belonging; outside exchanges of fire, enemy identity remains hazy. Soldiers need to read any unidentified person they meet on their way as potentially having hostile intentions—and they need to consider 'Trojan horses' among their own fellows when they work as mentors for foreign security forces. However, we might equally turn this description on its head and say that anyone suspected may have no hostile intentions whatsoever. Just as any civilian may hide an enemy combatant, so anyone suspected is potential collateral damage.

Civilians in conflict-ridden areas adopt a similar alertness towards the unpredictability of fire engagement. Among Iraqis and Afghans, the question of responsibility for and lawfulness of civilian casualties emerged as a major issue from the beginning of the international military operations. Civilians acquired knowledge about the collateral damage rule through meetings between the international forces and NGOs and the bereaved and local and national authorities that were held to mediate incidents of collateral damage. As the international forces rolled out compensation programmes for collateral damage, the processes surrounding claims, rejections, approvals and complaints became sites of awareness production too. The painful experiences in Iraq and Afghanistan also generated plenty of attention to the collateral damage rule in the international media. A learning process took place, which educated civil society all over the world about the prerogatives of military force when it comes to the lawfulness of collateral damage.

Now, I am not suggesting that civilians who encounter uniformed personnel in conflict zones necessarily possess any in-depth knowledge of the collateral damage rule. However, in affected areas, civilian awareness of the possibility of being harmed by soldiers who will not be sanctioned provides a perception of the collateral damage rule 'in action'—a perception that in civilian eyes furnishes the international soldiers with an aura of unpredictability and impunity. It is the simple awareness that he will shoot me if he thinks I look suspicious and he may do so without further ado: therefore, raise your head, be alert, answer any requests from soldiers, don't carry items that could give wrong impressions in the eyes of the soldiers. And avoid moving around unless necessary.

I suggest the following formula: For the soldiers, collateral damage defines the tipping point where the risk of causing collateral damage becomes less important than shielding oneself from the risk of being attacked. For the civilians, collateral damage defines the tipping point where the risk of becoming a collateral damage victim becomes less important than ceasing daily comings and goings. In that way the collateral damage rule becomes a constituent of the meeting between humans: and so collateral damage establishes itself as a powerful sociological category.

Here, it makes sense to differentiate conceptually between the political–legal form of collateral damage as a rule, and collateral damage as a sociology of risk warfare. The first is the subject of law while the latter is a subject of sociology. It is about the instilment of the collateral damage rule into the social fabric of the daily encounters between soldiers and civilians. This instilment differs from conventional, pre-action, collateral damage estimations, but, abstractly viewed, only in terms of time and immediacy. While the collateral damage rule remains the same, its function as a cognitive disposition changes in accordance with the perceptions of time and space in risk-saturated warfare, thereby shaping the social reality on the ground.

The ethics of collateral damage

Collateral damage thrives in decentralised, responsive, risk-saturated warfare. As suggested by Major General Charles J. Dunlap Jr:[54] 'Could it be that the nature of today's COIN [counterinsurgency] operations is such that a new paradox is emerging, that is, the more COIN troops you employ on the ground, the greater the possibility of injury to civilians?'[55] Indicators confirm Dunlap's suspicion but we lack hard numbers since collateral damage generally suffers from weak evaluation due to the difficulty of monitoring and investigating acts of war. Enemy contact often occurs in remote areas where the decision to unleash fire at 'suddenly emerging targets' lies in the hands of a cut-off and harassed group of soldiers who have no time to run over their judgement with their superiors. The squad may consist of soldiers with little combat experience and little knowledge of local conditions. Post-action evaluations easily stall in patchy and poorly remembered testimonies from those directly involved. The fog of war was once about the lack of situational awareness and operational transparency for commanders (and in the democratic state, the democratic base). Today it has found a new primary condition as confusion and adrenaline bend the judgement and memory of the individual soldier, who is now more than ever simultaneously combat planner, law interpreter, executor, witness and, not least, his own moral judge. The difference between doing moral good and moral bad may be decided by the seconds it would take approaching people to identify themselves. Risk management is a totally subjective, *in media res* practice that relies on ad hoc individual judgement and decisions. The question of doing bad or doing good is increasingly up to the individual soldier to define. How much risk do I want to carry? Should I have carried more? On the risk-saturated fields of network-centric urban warfare, there are no generals, only general orders.

To sum up, the category of death and suffering in war we call collateral damage has been reified over the last century, and developments in norms and law have detailed the criteria for when civilian deaths may be counted as collateral damage. The threshold for what may be considered collateral damage killings has been lowered significantly and political sensitivity towards collateral damage heightened. It has even been suggested that the lawfulness of collateral damage in war may no longer be as rock-solid as we believe. The question of a possible outlawing of collateral damage killings provides the starting point for the next chapter, where I assess the international legal regime, which provides for the collateral damage rule. It is about how law is tightening its grip around collateral damage, yet failing to capture it completely.

2

COLLATERAL DAMAGE AND THE QUESTION OF LEGAL RESPONSIBILITY

Decisions on making payments in cases of civilian combat-related casualties or damage remain a matter of national discretion. The non-binding guidelines are not intended to alter the legal position and obligations of individual national ISAF forces in Afghanistan, and payments are not an admission of legal liability or fault.[1]

Deputy Secretary General, NATO

As collateral damage turned into a contentious strategic, political and moral problem in current warfare, political and moral concern about these 'lawful' civilian casualties grew among the international community and within military organisations. We see substantial investment in precision-guided weapons, targeting instruments, doctrines and precautionary measures aiming at protecting civilians against the effects of war. We see an extrapolation of procedures for tackling situations where collateral damage occurs as well as education of troops about collateral damage. Lawyers crowd the military organisations.[2] Western states systematically compensate victims and their relatives for acts resulting in collateral damage. Altogether, we have reached a point where the permissibility of collateral damage is gradually being called into question. How far will these concerns take us? Might we even see the emergence of some form of legal responsibility for collateral damage in war? Put in more technical terms: will we see the development of international legal responsibility for 'proportionate' civilian casualties caused by legitimate military operations in situations of armed conflict? This is a critical question to ask for the fate of the collateral damage victims and also for our purpose of capturing the legal complexity of the collateral damage rule. From this book's intellectual perspective on collateral damage, this chapter will function as an exploration and elucidation of the place and role of the collateral damage rule in the context of the laws of armed conflict. Hence, I will push the perspective into general international law to look at how, for instance, the international rules of immunity contribute to the endurance of the collateral damage rule.

To jump to the conclusion of this chapter: nothing indicates that the substantial lawfulness of collateral damage will ever cease. We are dealing with a sturdy legal concept. This finding confirms the thesis of this book: our 'phenomenon', the problem of collateral damage, remains fundamental and lasting. Yet I will in this chapter add some critical nuances. As we will see, for European states bound by the European Convention of Human Rights (ECHR), incidents falling under the traditional international humanitarian law (IHL) category of collateral damage are now sometimes brought within the realm of legal responsibility not by way of substantial unlawfulness but by way of the procedural duty to investigate. This means that collateral damage no longer always remains entirely outside the scope of international legal responsibility. Furthermore, in the European context, civilian courts now have substantial legal authority to decide whether cases of civilian deaths caused by military operations during armed conflict have been properly investigated or not. The effect will most likely be the development of an expanded body of case law on collateral damage incidents and thus an improved knowledge and detailing of this aspect of war. Hence, while the rule endures, procedural laws are gradually invading the collateral damage category.

The collateral damage rule

The question of legal responsibility for collateral damage is no uncontroversial one. While IHL has long sought to protect civilians from the brutalities of war, it is a fundamental principle of IHL that civilian casualties may be lawful as collateral damage. Treaty law in the form of the Geneva Conventions and human rights treaties and customary international law firmly establish that injury or damage caused to persons or objects that are not lawful military targets at the particular moment is legal—as long as the military force applied is proportionate in light of the overall military advantage anticipated from the attack. The basic rules of distinction between combatant and non-combatant and the protection of civilians during armed conflict are cardinal to IHL. They are 'the foundation on which the codification of the laws and customs of war rests: the civilian population and civilian objects must be respected and protected in armed conflict, and for this purpose they must be distinguished from combatants and military objectives'.[3] This protection is not absolute, but depends on the wider body of IHL, including the principle of proportionality, which distinguishes between excessive and non-excessive use of military force and thus, to put it crudely, between the category of war crimes and that of collateral damage.

The principle of proportionality forms part of customary international law. It is codified in the Additional Protocols to the Geneva Conventions, which state the unlawfulness of 'an attack which may be expected to cause incidental loss of civilian life, injury to civilians, damage to civilian objects, or a combination thereof, which would be excessive in relation to the concrete and direct military advantage anticipated'.[4] By applying the term 'excessive' the provision implies that incidental loss of civilian life, injury to civilians, etc., may be deemed non-excessive to the extent it can be considered proportionate compared to the overall military utility, and therefore permissible. Collateral damage is lawful according to IHL as long as it fits the proportionality bill. From the perspective of law, the substantive lawfulness of collateral damage remains the same regardless of the kind of proportionality assessment we apply.[5] To say there may be proportionality is to say there may be collateral damage. We see two sides of the same coin. In this way, the Geneva Conventions may be said to be permissive rather than restrictive. The permissiveness, however, requires that due precautionary measures be taken. As the International Criminal Tribune For The Former Yugoslavia case, *Prosecutor v. Kupreskic*, concluded:

> In the case of attacks on military objectives causing damage to civilians, international law contains a general principle prescribing that reasonable care must be taken in attacking military objectives so that civilians are not needlessly injured through carelessness. This principle [...] has always been applied in conjunction with the principle of proportionality, whereby any incidental (and unintentional) damage to civilians must not be out of proportion to the direct military advantage gained by the military attack.[6]

But while the IHL regime allows for a certain lawful category of necessary proportionate death and injury to civilians, it does not specify or delimit this category any further. Neither treaty law nor customary international law provides any substantial guidelines or definition of collateral damage beyond the principles of proportionality and necessity. As I mentioned in the introduction, whether we speak about one or fifty thousand collateral damage victims, whether we speak about civilians killed by a single small-arms crossfire incident or the deployment of nuclear weapons, the category of collateral damage under international law remains the same. And while the principle of proportionality in IHL has been the subject of intense scrutiny by international lawyers and scholars, seen from an overall perspective, the collateral damage rule stands fundamentally unchanged, whatever standards of necessity and proportionality inform its content.

International human rights law

All of the above is the case under IHL, but today we also have another international regime available, that of international human rights law (IHRL). Could IHRL perhaps overrun the IHL category of collateral damage? Could IHRL potentially amend the legal status of incidents of collateral damage killings by recasting them as human rights questions? Could IHRL 'see' a violation of the right to life (as codified in the International Covenant on Civil and Political Rights (ICCPR) Article 6(1) and ECHR Article 2 in situations where IHL sees lawful killings?

Four legal questions arise when considering a possible human rights approach to the incidents deemed lawful collateral damage under IHL: the applicability of IHRL to situations of armed conflict; the extraterritorial application of human rights; the status of non-derogable human rights norms in times of armed conflict; and, a bit further down the road, the question of state immunity. Let us take these questions one at a time.

The applicability of IHRL in armed conflict

Until recently incidents of civilian casualties in war have been regulated by IHL, a regime which principally governs the conduct of states in armed conflict, including the responsibility for harm caused by state A to citizens of state B. IHRL, on the other hand, is constructed as a regime governing the relation between state A and persons on its territory. The IHRL regime enables individuals to hold states responsible for human rights violations through national courts and, if they decline or are unable to act, international courts. Immediately after the Second World War it was the general conception among international jurists and lawyers that IHRL and IHL were entirely separate legal regimes. IHRL was a national or 'vertical' matter between state and citizen, while IHL primarily regulated the 'horizontal' conduct between states or specific groups engaged in intra-state armed conflict. Yet the post-Second World War evolution of the human rights regime made it clear that such a strict separation was not carved in stone.[7]

The changing view of the individual in international law[8] led to a debate on the applicability of IHRL in armed conflict as a 'diagonal' juridical bond between a state A and the civilians of another state B on a territory outside state A, a debate which stretches back some 40 years.[9] What is new is the intensity of this debate. This may be understood as an outcome of a strengthened international human rights community and a proliferation of human rights case law as well as a reaction to the change of armed conflict in the direction of long-drawn-out, low-intensity, counterinsurgency and peace and stability operations. Such armed conflicts blur the line between war and peace and between international military operations and global law enforcement; they also blur the line between war and crime, since it may no longer be clear whether armed persons or groups belong to an armed resistance group or whether they are taking part in violence for other reasons. In such theatres of conflict, it is no longer clear why IHL should be the only applicable regime.[10]

Crucially, recent years have seen the application of IHRL to situations of armed conflict by both international and national courts. In the international arena, the International Court of Justice (ICJ) has found IHRL to apply in situations of armed conflict in cases before it[11] as well as in relation to Advisory Opinions.[12] Most cited is its 1996 Advisory Opinion on the Legality of the Threat or Use of Nuclear Weapons. In this opinion the Court affirmed that 'the protection of the International Covenant of Civil and Political Rights does not cease in times of war, except by operation of Article 4 of the Covenant whereby certain provisions may be derogated from in a time of national emergency'.[13] The European Court of Human Rights (ECtHR) has been the most proactive court in terms of applying IHRL in armed conflict[14] (see next section), and the Inter-American Court on Human Rights also offers relevant case law.[15]

Recently, the influential United Nations International Law Commission (ILC) concluded that, as a general principle, the existence of an armed conflict does not *ipso facto* terminate or suspend the operation of treaties either between states parties to the conflict or between a state party to the conflict and a state that is not.[16] The ILC emphasises that this includes human rights treaties, although at the same time it points out that derogation from IHRL is possible but should be considered an exception to the rule of applicability.

Of course, the ILC is not a formal source of law and its conclusions merely refer back to the ICJ and the treaty itself. However, its articulation of the norm derogation in IHRL may be said to at least reflect a general way of viewing the applicability of IHRL in armed conflict.

Although this view on the applicability of IHRL has been criticised there is reason to believe that IHRL will find increasing application in situations of armed conflict, either as a *lex specialis*, a complementary regime, or cumulatively together with IHL.[17] This marks an important change in the distribution of rights and plights during armed conflict and, as we will see, the application of IHRL does have implications for the legal interpretation of collateral damage incidents. However, other legal questions arise in terms of the actual application of IHRL to armed conflict, including situations of collateral damage, and to these questions we will now turn.

The extraterritorial application of human rights

It is one thing that treaties are in effect and another thing that they are applicable to a concrete situation. Provided that IHRL is considered 'diagonally' applicable in armed conflict, the question arises whether states may be bound by certain IHRL regimes with regard to their actions in third states.[18] As the applicability of IHRL depends on the international instruments in question, it is not possible to make any assessment of a general state of law *in abstracto*. Each treaty, or even provision, must be assessed individually. However, looking at practice with regard to certain human rights regimes may provide us with a means to reflect on possible future developments. Let us therefore turn to the current state of law with regard to the extraterritorial application of the ECHR by the ECtHR in Strasbourg, an international court considered quite progressive in terms of the development of IHRL.[19]

In its Article 1, the ECHR stipulates that the member states 'shall secure to everyone within their jurisdiction the rights and freedoms defined in [...] this Convention'.[20] The Court has made it clear that the term jurisdiction in Article 1 reflects the 'ordinary and essentially territorial notion of jurisdiction',[21] and that as a general principle the ECHR does not apply outside the European area.[22] Yet the ECtHR has regularly been faced with possible exceptions to this rule. In the case of *Banković v. Belgium* (2001), it had to consider whether the member states of NATO could be held responsible under the ECHR for damage to civilian buildings and several civilian deaths caused by the airstrike on the Serbian radio television headquarters in Belgrade. The Court found that the basis of jurisdiction other than the territorial was 'exceptional and requiring special justification in the particular circumstances of each case'.[23] In this case, it considered that missiles and bombs fired from aircraft were not a sufficient 'jurisdictional link' and consequently the ECHR did not apply.[24]

Yet the most recent practice from the ECtHR reveals some developments in the extraterritorial application of ECHR.[25] In the course of the cases of *Issa and Others v. Turkey* (2004)[26] and *Öcalan v. Turkey* (2005)[27] the Court broadened its interpretation of 'jurisdiction'. The Court's jurisprudence now based itself on 'an expansive but simple rationale for extraterritorial jurisdiction: "control entails responsibility"'.[28] *Issa* concerned an incident in 1995 where Turkish military forces killed civilians during a cross-border attack ('Operation Steel' from 20 March to 4 May 1995) in northern Iraq that 'aimed at pursuing and eliminating terrorists who were seeking shelter' in this area. Due to the extensiveness of the operations conducted—'Operation Steel' included some 35,000 pairs of boots on the ground—the Court:

> did not exclude the possibility that, as a consequence of this military action, the respondent State could be considered to have exercised, temporarily, effective overall control of a particular portion of the territory of northern Iraq. Accordingly, if there is a sufficient factual basis for holding that, at the relevant time, the victims were within that specific area, it would follow logically that they were within the jurisdiction of Turkey.[29]

While clearly indicating that the Convention could be applied, the Court also stated that 'notwithstanding the large number of troops involved [...] it does not appear that Turkey exercised effective overall control of the entire area of northern Iraq'.[30] In that way the Court emphasised that de facto control through local military presence can trigger jurisdiction for the purposes of the Article 1 of the Convention in the 'specific area' under control. In other words, that the ECHR was applicable if the killings had happened in the space under effective control of Turkey's military forces. Scholars generally consider the judgement in *Issa* a significant departure from *Banković* in that it implies that jurisdiction under Article 1 is not only territorial but may instead be bound to the acts of the state.[31] Similarly, in the case of *Öcalan v. Turkey*, the Court found that the ECHR applied to Turkey as Turkish secret agents abducted Abdullah *Öcalan* in Nairobi Airport in Kenya and flew him back to Turkey for prosecution. The Court found that the direct hands-on link *ratione personae* between the Turkish agents and Öcalan sufficed to invoke ECHR obligations extraterritorially, even in spaces (Kenya) remote from the Convention's *espace juridique* (Europe).

The Court seemed to follow a mixture of the 'authority and control over territory' rationale of *Issa* and the 'direct control over individuals' rationale of *Öcalan* when it ruled in *Al-Skeini and Others v. United Kingdom* (2011).[32] The six killings that gave rise to the *Al-Skeini* case happened as British forces engaged in an urban area of the Iraqi city of Basra in 2003. The killings comprised death by a stray bullet, the killing of a man holding a gun at a funeral ceremony (in Iraq it is customary to discharge guns at funerals), the shooting of a person in a house during a night raid, the killing of the driver of a 'suspicious-looking' vehicle who defied the soldier's signals to stop—all typical 'collateral damage' casualties in urban warfare—and two cases of fatal violence of soldiers against detainees.[33]

Relatives of the deceased brought claims before the ECtHR against the UK for failing in its procedural obligations to investigate the killings. The case was thus not about the lawfulness or not of the killings but about the UK military's lack of investigation: it was about procedure. The Court held that the UK exercised authority and control over the territory in question through its military presence, thus establishing a sufficient jurisdictional link to find the Convention applicable. In the words of the Court (the emphasis is mine):

> Following the removal from power of the Ba'ath regime and until the accession of the Interim Government, the UK (together with the United States) assumed in Iraq *the exercise of some of the public powers normally to be exercised by a sovereign government*. In particular, the UK assumed authority and responsibility for the maintenance of security in South East Iraq. In these exceptional circumstances, *the Court considers that the United Kingdom, through its soldiers* engaged in security operations in Basra during the period in question, *exercised authority and control over individuals* killed in the course of such security operations, so as to establish a jurisdictional link between the deceased and the UK for the purposes of Article 1 of the Convention.[34]

The UK had therefore, the Court concluded, breached its procedural obligation under Article 2 of the ECHR to investigate. However, the Court maintained the standpoint expressed in *Banković* that the extraterritorial application of ECHR is exceptional and needs to be justified with reference to general international law.[35]

In clear cases of extraterritoriality, a jurisdictional link between the victim(s) and the responsible state in question needs to be established. The Court seems to have established two categories of cases in which acts of member states outside the territories of the ECHR space are seen to fall under the jurisdiction of the member state: either the member state has 'effective control' over the specific part of the extraterritorial territory, or actual 'authority or control' over persons in this territory. However, it has been suggested that in *Al-Skeini*, which has become the leading case on the extraterritorial application of the ECHR,[36] the Court did not really see these as two separate categories of control but merged them into a new category of 'combination-based jurisdiction'. In this case, the situation does not fulfil the criteria for 'effective control', nor does it fulfil the criteria for 'authority and control over individuals'. Yet the exercise of a certain amount of 'public authority' (which could be viewed as the functional equivalent of sovereignty) combined with the exercise of a certain amount of authority and control over individuals may together give rise to jurisdiction.[37] *Al-Skeini*, however, does not establish the canon for assessing the 'public authority' criteria nor how it should be balanced against the exercise of authority and control over individuals. It is not entirely clear how much concrete military presence and in what form is needed to trigger ECHR jurisdiction. The Court has still to offer a more precise definition of the term 'jurisdiction' in Article 1, and the exact meaning of the term thus remains unsettled. But it is the Court that decides on this, not European military organisations or their states.[38]

The extraterritorial application of human rights obligations remains controversial. This became clear in a quarrel between the ECtHR and the UK about *Al-Skeini* in which the House of Lords, in June 2007, protested:

> the idea that the UK was obliged to secure observance of all the rights and freedoms as interpreted by the European Court in the utterly different society of southern Iraq is manifestly absurd. [...]. If it went further, the Court would run the risk not only of colliding with the jurisdiction of other human rights bodies but of being accused of human rights imperialism.[39]

ECtHR Judge Giovanni Bonello, outraged by this argument, responded,

> I confess to be quite unimpressed by the pleadings of the United Kingdom Government to the effect that exporting the European Convention on Human Rights to Iraq would have amounted to "human rights imperialism". It ill behoves a State that imposed its military imperialism over another sovereign State without the frailest imprimatur from the international community, to resent the charge of having exported human rights imperialism to the vanquished enemy. It is like wearing with conceit your badge of international law banditry, but then recoiling in shock at being suspected of human rights promotion. (...) For my part, I believe that those who export war ought to see to the parallel export of guarantees against the atrocities of war. And then, if necessary, bear with some fortitude the opprobrium of being labelled human rights imperialists.[40]

The heated dispute demonstrates the political stakes at play with regard to questions of extraterritoriality.

It is certain that the *Al-Skeini* case has strong implications for ECHR member states. At the same time the general perception in international law literature seems to be that the extraterritorial application of human rights will become more widespread, also in the context of armed conflict. The strict separation of IHRL and IHL has been broken down and the two regimes will become still more intertwined. Yet the slow and cautious development of the extraterritorial application of the ECHR by the Court, combined with members states' enduring scepticism towards extraterritoriality, indicates the unlikeliness of any comprehensive extraterritorial application of human rights treaty obligations in armed conflict in the near future. Needless to say, the United States steadfastly resists any movement in that direction.[41] However, we need to notice that in the European context it is the civilian courts that decide whether the ECHR applies, and from a legal perspective, this actually places incidents of civilian casualties under the authority of the civilian courts.

IHRL, IHL and due process obligations

If we were some day to see in practice the application of IHRL on a par with IHL in armed conflict, new dilemmas would soon materialise. With regard to the question of responsibility for collateral damage, the substantial legal question of the application of the right to life in armed conflict constitutes the most critical of these: should 'the right to life' under IHRL, as codified in ICCPR Article 6(1) and ECHR Article 2, be applicable during armed conflict to situations otherwise governed by IHL's collateral damage rule? An oft-heard analysis is that IHL and IHRL offer fundamentally different and irreconcilable norms with regard to the question of the right to life. IHL leaves plenty of room for killing non-combatants or combatants *hors de combat* as combat-related collateral damage whereas IHL merely requires that the use of force be not excessive compared with the overall anticipated military advantage. On the other hand, IHRL considers the right to life a peremptory norm. ICCPR and ECHR require that the use of force is proportionate to the aim of protecting life and, furthermore, both instruments place far-reaching investigative obligations on states in order to legitimise any use of force that potentially involves collateral damage.[42]

The apparent norm conflict between IHRL and IHL has often been dealt with by applying the international law principle of *lex specialis*. According to this principle, the provision that offers the most specialised regulation with regard to the specific situation holds precedence. In its Advisory Opinions on the Legality of the Threat or Use of Nuclear Weapons[43] and on the Legal Consequences of the Construction of the Wall in the Occupied Palestinian Territories,[44] the ICJ applied the *lex specialis* principle to conceptualise the relationship between IHL and IHRL.[45] In the first Opinion the Court found that '[t]he test of what is an arbitrary deprivation of life, however, then falls to be determined by the applicable *lex specialis*, namely, the law applicable in armed conflict which is designed to regulate the conduct of hostilities'.[46] In the latter Opinion, the Court found that as regards the relationship between IHRL and IHL, 'the Court will have to take into consideration both these branches of international law, namely human rights law and, as *lex specialis*, international humanitarian law'.[47]

Yet legal scholars are less convinced about such a 'mechanical' *lex specialis* approach to the relationship between IHL and IHRL norms. They mostly agree that 'at the end of the day, the concrete operation of the principles of proportionality seems broadly equivalent in both branches of international law'[48] even if a stricter precautionary norm applies under IHRL. It is argued that Article 15(2) of the ECHR permits derogations from the right to life 'in respect of deaths resulting from lawful military acts of war',[49] and therefore accommodates the proportionality principle of IHL, although as a derogation from the general rule. While the ICCPR does not mention war in the clause concerning derogation from Article 4(1),[50] its drafting history reveals that one of the emergencies considered in Article 4 was, in fact, war, but that the explicit mention of war was withdrawn from the Covenant text as the drafters wished to follow the United Nations Charter in its denial of war as a possibility (except as self-defence).[51] When it comes to the right to life in armed conflict, both the ECHR and ICCPR thus contain provisions on derogation that in fact attune them with the collateral damage rule of IHL.[52]

In this light, the norm conflict between IHL and IHRL seems merely apparent rather than substantial. The norm 'conflict' implies not mutually excluding norms, but rather something like a sliding scale between the application of IHL and IHRL norms. Which norm to apply depends on the facts of the situation. Therefore, in order to establish the relationship between the different norms regarding the right to life during armed conflict, consideration must be given to the concrete situation in hand—with 'soft' law enforcement operations in the context of low-intensity armed conflict at one end of the scale, ranging to full-blown bombing campaigns at the other.

Covering collateral damage with procedural obligations

Both IHL and IHRL obligate states to investigate violations of the right to life, yet IHRL contains much stricter and far more detailed norms and practice than IHL as to both pre- and post-incident assessments.[53] If ECHR applies to a given situation, the investigatory duties could be expected to follow the human rights regime as *lex specialis*, since it here contains the most specialised regulation.

The ECtHR has confirmed its jurisprudence with regard to investigative duties in cases of possible breaches of ECHR Article 2 (the right to life) in a number of cases, most recently in *Al-Skeini*.[54] The Court clearly established that when the ECHR applies extraterritorially, state parties have a positive obligation to conduct independent and effective investigations into possible breaches of ECHR Article 2. Consequently, the Court found that the lack of proper investigation is a breach in itself: it is simply illegal not to investigate. Case law from the ECtHR has clearly established that an effective investigation must be 'capable of leading to a determination of whether the force used in such cases was or was not justified in the circumstances'.[55]

To get a sense of what may be required from European military forces when it comes to investigating civilian casualties, we could look at the ECtHR practice with regard to Article 2 (the right to life). In the case of *McKerr v. UK*, which concerned the duty to investigate of the police, the ECtHR found that:

> the obligation to protect the right to life under Article 2 of the Convention, read in conjunction with the State's general duty under Article 1 to 'secure to everyone within [its] jurisdiction the rights and freedoms defined in [the] Convention', also requires by implication that there should be some form of effective official investigation when individuals have been killed as a result of the use of force.[56]

Furthermore, the Court held that contracting states must take 'whatever reasonable steps they can to secure the evidence concerning the incident, including, inter alia, eyewitness testimony, forensic evidence and, where appropriate, an autopsy which provides a complete and accurate record of injury and an objective analysis of clinical findings, including the cause of death',[57] and also emphasised the need for independence of the investigation. Further, in 1994, the now out phased European Commission of Human Rights (set up under the ECHR) found that:

> [t]here may be cases where the facts surrounding a deprivation of life are clear and undisputed and the subsequent inquisitorial examination may legitimately be reduced to a minimum formality. But equally, there may be other cases where a victim dies in circumstances which are unclear, in which event the lack of any effec-

tive procedure to investigate the cause of the deprivation of life could, by itself, raise an issue under Article 2.[58]

We should of course expect the Court to scale down investigatory duties in impenetrable environments because 'a state's ability to conduct investigations during an ongoing conflict is much less robust than in peace time'.[59] Yet since most of today's military operations take place in low-intensity conflicts, as discussed in previous chapter, this may only be partly true. To be sure, whether states view investigatory obligations as an integral part of military missions or as a separate 'burden' placed on states (by themselves) is a matter of political choice. But the authoritative decision on whether the ECHR applies and if so whether a collateral damage death received proper investigation relies with the Court in Strasbourg, not with the military.

Case law from the ECtHR has thus clearly established that an effective investigation must be 'capable of leading to a determination of whether the force used in such cases was or was not justified in the circumstances'.[60] Applied to situations of armed conflict, the extended duty to investigate under IHRL may thus prove decisive for the choice of norms to be applied to civilian casualties during military operations. In other words, a procedural rule and the facts produced become decisive for the relationship between the two regimes. As the choice of norms 'is a factual one, not a legal one',[61] it seems meaningful to trade in the *lex specialis* approach for an interpretive approach, which emphasises facts and the interpretation of facts as the criteria for the choice of norms. By this I mean that available concrete facts and the assessments of those facts constitute the critical point with regard to determining how to apply the IHL and IHRL norms. This is always the case, one could claim. Any application of law always, of course, comes governed by the facts of the case.

However, this matter of facts before norms becomes particularly noteworthy in our case here. Firstly, because it moves the focus from regimes to facts and their interpretation. Secondly, and importantly, because the interpretive approach emphasises the significance of the quantity and quality of facts for the choice of law—an aspect of critical relevance to situations of armed conflict, where fact-finding may be hindered by volatility and security problems. In this regard, the application of IHRL to the armed conflict introduces new investigatory norms, which may have a critical impact on the choice of applicable norms. The more facts, the more comprehensive the application of law. In that way, the procedural duty to investigate may have a decisive impact on the choice of applicable norms. The next decade of jurisprudence will show us how this new reality may affect the merging of IHL and IHRL.

IHLR and the new duty to investigate collateral damage

Now, what does this mean for the collateral damage rule? In addition to establishing extended investigatory obligations for incidents that may turn out to be considered collateral damage after investigation, the application of IHRL to armed conflict changes the process through which national courts may decide whether a state has lived up to its investigatory obligations under ECHR. Most significant, as *Al-Skeini* established, it is for the ECtHR to decide, first, whether the Convention applies and, second, whether the investigatory duties have been fulfilled. For European states that separate their military justice system from their civilian justice system, this means that military justice may be overruled. The duty to investigate not only authorises civilian courts to act; civilian courts now have a strong say with regard to deciding whether procedural obligations have been fulfilled in the context of armed conflict: again, the final say lies with the Court in Strasbourg, and not with the national military commander.

This implies also that victims' relatives (the victims themselves being dead) acquire a new role in situations of civilian casualties. As the ECtHR found in *Al-Skeini*, where a state fails to fulfil its investigative obligations under ECHR triggered by civilian casualties in military operations, relatives of the victims have the right to have their case heard in national courts. What is more, in the context of the ECHR, if civilian courts are unable or unwilling to act, the case may be taken to the ECtHR.

Hence, the most significant difference between IHRL and IHL is not the extended positive duty put on states to conduct independent investigations, which may simply be viewed as the expansion under IHRL of a conventional IHL norm. The most significant difference is the right of the individuals under IHRL to instigate national or international court proceedings based on alleged legal breaches of the procedural duty to investigate, as we saw in *Al-Skeini*. Let us also bear in mind here that the criteria of jurisdiction depend on control, as discussed above, and not geography or nationality: anyone of any nationality may in principle have their case heard. Compared to conventional IHL, this presents us with an entirely new legal regime for dealing with civilian casualties, including collateral damage, far beyond what IHL has to offer.

ECtHR practice with regard to procedural obligation stemming from alleged breaches of ECHR Article 2 leaves us with the question of the delimitation of access to national courts. After *Al-Skeini*, what constitutes a manifestly unfounded claim under the IHL rule of collateral damage and/or the derogation clauses in the ECHR? To what extent may claimants expect national courts to review decisions based on investigations? Imagine that the UK had actually conducted the investigations that the ECtHR found the UK obliged to under the ECHR in the case of *Al-Skeini*. What if the claimants were to remain dissatisfied with the lack of independence or quality of these investigations? Would the claimants be entitled to have their case heard by a national court? What could block their access to having such cases heard in accordance with the ECHR? What could make such applications inadmissible to the ECtHR? Future cases dealing with the question of the lawfulness of killing civilians in armed conflict will without doubt present us with such legal questions. It remains to be seen how the courts will respond, how they will balance claimants' calls for investigation with the need to protect issues of national security and interest, and what form obstacles to investigation will take in hostile environments.

Individual criminal responsibility

So far we have dealt with state responsibility, since the state remains the primary subject of legal responsibility under IHL and IHRL. Let us examine the prospect of individual criminal responsibility for incidents falling under the current category of collateral damage. International lawyers will probably find this exercise more speculative than valid, if not pointless. I think, however, it is good to clarify this aspect. Compared with current practice with regard to individual criminal responsibility, which so far has only been applied to cases of particularly grave international crimes, the gravity of incidents falling under the legal category of collateral damage is very far from international law conceptions of war crimes. On the other hand, the question of individual criminal responsibility in armed conflicts does appear pertinent in an age where critical decision-making in military operations increasingly gets pushed out to the 'sharp end'. The common legal response to what has been described as 'decentralised authority in global governance' is to attempt to bind decentralised authority with new forms of legal responsibility. The question posed is whether individuals may be able to hold 'decentralised' individual officers legally responsible for acts committed during armed conflict,[62] or whether the 'central' state in such situations will continue to be the primary bearer of legal responsibility. In other words, whether the international responsibility for breaches of ICCPR Article 6(1) and ECHR Article 2 may fall upon individual military officers rather than or in addition to their states. That would indeed require a transformation of the criteria for when individual criminal responsibility becomes legally relevant, including a lowering of the threshold for what kind of breaches constitute an international crime. While not impinging on the legality of collateral damage, such a development could also heighten the legal focus on individual acts in terms of investigating alleged breaches of law.

For the sake of the exercise, let us assume that ICCPR Article 6(1) and ECHR Article 2 will become the primary rules applicable with regard to civilian casualties in armed conflict. Let us also assume that the right to life is peremptory and derogable only as provided for by the derogation clauses of ICCPR and ECHR, thus providing some room for lawful collateral damage. Now, in this connection it has been argued that violations of *jus cogens* rules (including 'the right to life') may penetrate the principle of state immunity and thus radically transform the law of state immunity.[63] If this should happen, it would leave national and international courts with a new legal framework for judging the reach of legal responsibility—including for collateral damage in armed conflict. The question we must answer is thus whether the suggested recent changes in the doctrine of state immunity may further expand access to holding agents acting on behalf of the state, such as soldiers, individually responsible and whether that may prove relevant to the problem of legal responsibility for collateral damage. Finally, zooming in on the somewhat hypothetical question of international criminal responsibility for collateral damage also brings the role of the law of state immunity for the collateral damage rule into view.

The law of state immunity and collateral damage

The international law doctrine of state immunity protects states and their representatives from prosecution in foreign states. This doctrine has traditionally been considered extraneous to the question of collateral damage as IHL provides combatant 'immunity'[64] for lawful acts during armed conflict.[65] However after the Second World War, the Nuremberg and Tokyo processes affirmed the existence of individual criminal responsibility, including command responsibility, for acts unlawful under international law.[66] Today this principle is considered a part of IHL[67] as codified in the Statue of the International Criminal Court (ICC).[68]

Ordinarily, pleas of state immunity arising in a particular legal case before a national court may only be considered after the jurisdiction of the state has been determined, since it is 'only where a state has jurisdiction under international law in relation to a particular matter that there can be any question of immunities in regard to the exercise of that jurisdiction'.[69] It follows that the law of state immunity only becomes relevant for the question of legal responsibility for collateral damage once it has been legally established that a) IHRL applies generally to armed conflicts and b) there is territorial or extraterritorial jurisdiction in relation to the specific alleged IHRL violation. Having settled this in preceding sections, the question to be considered here is whether a plea of state immunity may become relevant in considering acts producing collateral damage as such acts are per definition *jure imperii* (the public acts of the government of a state, often distinguished from *jure gestionis*, the commercial activities of a state).

The law of state immunity

The jurisdiction of a state is limited by the rules on state immunity, which are firmly established in customary international law.[70] Two types of immunity are often distinguished: immunity attaching to acts performed by state officials in the exercise of their functions (immunity *ratione materiae* or 'functional immunity'), and immunity pertaining to representatives of the state (immunity *ratione personae* or 'personal immunity'), the latter encompassing both senior state officials (especially Heads of State, Heads of Government) and diplomats, and the immunity of state officials on special missions abroad.[71] In this way the law of state immunity serves to separate jurisdictions in terms of matters relating to state activities and, further, it functions as an 'intersection of international law and national procedural law'.[72] The law of state immunity is built on the principle of sovereign equality of states. The principle of state immunity may, in fact, be viewed as buttressing the very international system of sovereign states as we know it today: the system would collapse if national courts could sue other states or their statesmen or delegates. The function of the law of state immunity in the international legal order should thus not be underestimated. Immunity makes and shapes state sovereignty.

In 2004 the UN Convention for Jurisdictional Immunities of States and their Property was adopted,[73] some twenty-seven years after the work on it had been initiated. While the convention is yet to enter into force,[74] it is generally seen to reflect customary international law. The Convention reflects the so-called 'restrictive' approach to state immunity, according to which states are only entitled to immunity for acts that are intrinsically governmental (*acta jure imperii*), while acts of an essentially commercial or private nature (*acta jure gestionis*) do not give rise to immunity. Furthermore, according to the restrictive doctrine, individuals may be recognised as third parties in proceedings. This view has gradually superseded the traditional 'absolutist' doctrine of state immunity according to which both acts *jure imperii* and *jure gestionis* may form a basis for claims of immunity.[75]

Paradoxically, however, if or when the Convention enters into force, it will have to operate in a world in which the restrictive conception of state immunity is increasingly being put under pressure by the international human rights movement as well as by the increased delegation of core state functions to private corporations.[76] As Professor Hazel Fox notes: '[i]n one direction, the enhanced status of the individual presses for the lifting of immunity from all claims arising from the conduct of the State; in another direction, the pooling of national powers in non-State entities calls for their protection to enable their proper deployment in public interests.'[77] While the question of whether non-state entities may claim immunity on a par with states is of great relevance to the growing commercialisation of various aspects of armed conflict, it is the question of state immunity for international crimes or human rights violations that has drawn the most attention recently in both theory and practice.[78] In recent years, civil or criminal adjudication in domestic courts has increasingly been viewed as a realistic path to holding states accountable for international crimes and human rights violations.[79]

The law of state immunity and jus cogens

The term *jus cogens* refers to a category of preemptory/nonderogable rules of general international law. Although there is no authoritative definition of this category in international law, Article 53 of the 1969 Vienna Convention on the Law of Treaties defines the legal effect of preemptiveness: 'a peremptory norm of general international law is a norm accepted and recognized by the international community of States as a whole as a norm from which no derogation is permitted and which can be modified only by a subsequent norm of general international law having the same character'.[80] However, exactly which rules are included in this category is not defined by the Convention, or by general international law, and has long been a matter of controversy. Today many scholars argue that rules of *jus cogens* crimes include the prohibition against aggression, crimes against humanity, war crimes, piracy, slavery and slave-related practices, and torture.[81] Some of these rules involve rights of such importance that, as stated by the ICJ (without referring explicitly to *jus cogens*), 'all states can be held to have a legal interest in their protection; they are obligations *erga omnes*'.[82] However, it may be questioned whether the *erga omnes* effect amounts to an actual legal obligation or rather a right to prosecute breaches of such rules.[83] Some international lawyers argue that the *erga omnes* effect implicates a legal obligation and, further, that this obligation includes both a duty to prosecute or extradite if applicable (*aut dedere aut judicare*) and universality of jurisdiction. Further, inherent in the categories of *jus cogens* norms and obligations *erga omnes* is that the rules in question apply both in times of peace and of war.

Therefore, if we dare to imagine that the right to life will someday become considered a rule of *jus cogens* character entailing obligations *erga omnes*, (which it must be stressed is far from legally established), the breach of this norm even in armed conflict would allow all states—or even obligate them— to prosecute the state responsible for any such breaches.

A normative hierarchy?

If or when *jus cogens* human rights norms are introduced to the battlefield on a par with IHL, this new regime may bring about conflicts with the doctrine of state immunity. It is one thing to bring claims against or prosecute Heads of State, like General Pinochet, or senior state officials, for crimes against humanity or war crimes. These cases amount to a limited number internationally. However, to hold individual soldiers accountable for violations of human rights of a *jus cogens* character could potentially give rise to a very large number of cases. The question we approach is of course the scenario where every single collateral damage incident amounts to a potential human rights violation that should trigger a general legal interest of investigating. We will get back to this issue soon, but for now the question we must consider is this: does the principle of state immunity shield individuals from prosecution even when the norm that has been violated is of a *jus cogens* character or creates obligations *erga omnes*? Do *jus cogens* rules rank higher than the law of immunity?

The so-called 'normative hierarchy theory' seeks to resolve this conflict. The theory emanates from a 1991 US Supreme Court decision, in which the Court found *jus cogens* norms to hold absolute normative dominion in the field of international law. The normative hierarchy theory had considerable impact in practice and on theory until the 2006 UK House of Lords decision in the case of *Jones v. The Kingdom of Saudi Arabia*.[84] In this case the Court discarded the idea of a hierarchy of rules arguing (with reference to the writings of Professor Hazel Fox) that the rules on state immunity are of a procedural character and as such they cannot logically collide with *jus cogens* norms, which are of a substantive nature.[85]

However, in the 2008 case *Ferrini v. Federal Republic of Germany*,[86] which concerned a claim for compensation by an Italian national who had been deported to Germany in 1944 and was the victim of forced labour, the Italian *Corte di Cassazione* found that 'because the act conducted constitutes an international crime, there can be no valid reason to maintain the immunity of the State and therefore to deny that its responsibility can be enforced before the judicial authority of a foreign State'.[87] While the Court did not explicitly mention *jus cogens* norms, it made clear that violations of fundamental human rights encroach upon universal values protected by *jus cogens* norms. Because these norms are at the top of the hierarchy of norms in the international legal order, they take precedence over conflicting law, including state immunity. Immunity should not lead to impunity, is the rationale.[88] With this argument, the *Corte di Cassazione* lifted the state immunity of Germany. The *Ferrini* case unleashed a number of other proceedings against Germany in Italian courts.[89]

Not happy about this, in 2008 Germany filed an application instituting proceedings against Italy before the ICJ. Germany claimed that since 2004 'Italian judicial bodies have repeatedly disregarded the jurisdictional immunity of Germany as a sovereign State' and thereby violated their obligations towards Germany under international law.[90] Germany did not, thus, call upon the Court to decide whether the acts of German officers during the Second World War were illegal. No one contested the illegality of the acts. Germany called upon the Court to decide 'whether or not, in proceedings regarding claims for compensation arising out of those acts, the Italian courts were obliged to accord Germany immunity'.[91]

The ICJ delivered its decision in *Germany v. Italy* on 3 February 2012. The Court found that the practice of the Italian courts did indeed constitute a violation by Italy of its obligation to respect the jurisdictional immunity of Germany.[92] The Court thus maintained the conventional 'restrictive' doctrine of state immunity. The decision in *Germany v. Italy* seems to settle the question of *jus cogens* and jurisdictional immunity of states. For now, it makes it very difficult to imagine that human rights norms may be able to pierce state immunity in national courts, which some had hoped for.

Since incidents falling into the IHL category of collateral damage are very far from the kind of grave international crimes the ICJ considered in *Germany v. Italy*, the chance is slim that outwardly unintentional civilian casualties could ever form the basis of civil proceedings in national courts against other states and their representatives—even in cases with serious damage and obvious misapplications of the collateral damage rule. A normative hierarchy of substantial norms may still be argued to exist, but it has no practical impact on the jurisdictional immunities of states.

Conclusion

Under the current state of international law, IHRL should be considered fully applicable to armed conflicts, not least the kind of low-intensity armed conflicts we have seen in Afghanistan. The lawfulness of collateral damage in armed conflict is, however, unlikely to be affected by the applicability of IHRL. IHRL contains far more restrictive necessity rules in comparison with the IHL conception of military advantage, and it does not accommodate arguments of 'overall military advantage'. The applicability of IHRL to armed conflicts may thus modify the criteria for permissible collateral damage. Civilian casualties may become less accepted due to stricter interpretations of necessity and proportionally. New courts may take action. But on a substantial level, the legal category of the collateral damage rule remains intact. So does the hegemony of the international legal doctrine of state immunity over IHRL norms even if they are of a *jus cogens* character. There is a long way to go before the legality of collateral damage produced by states acting outside their own territories in armed conflict becomes a legal question to be considered under IHRL in national or international courts. Will it ever happen? Probably not.

Yet it may also be concluded that civilian casualties trigger the positive procedural obligations enshrined in IHRL. Practice from national and international courts confirms that parties to the ECHR sometimes have positive obligations to conduct independent investigations when civilians are killed during international military operations. IHL also obliges states to investigate civilian casualties. But on this issue, the rules of IHL are weak. Civilian casualties are only subjected to independent investigation if there is a serious concern that a war crime has taken place. Victims have no possibility of having their cases heard by an independent court. One might say that this epoch of war is now over: the general exemption of collateral damage from legal responsibility, which has long prevailed, may be reformed by the procedural obligations to investigate under IHRL. States bound by ECHR can no longer commence international military operations that involve a high degree of control over territories or persons without also being prepared to conduct independent investigations if civilian casualties occur. If contracting states are unwilling or unable to act, affected individuals of whatever nationality may be granted legal standing by the ECtHR. This does not imply that collateral damage has become unlawful, or that investigations need to be conducted regardless of the security environment. Nor does it in any way imply that the ECHR applies, which will most likely not be the case. We may, however, use ECtHR practice to assess how the duty to investigate in the ICCPR should be applied. Furthermore, to discuss to what extent this duty should be considered *lex specialis* compared to IHL, which contains less detailed rules of investigation. If a human rights duty to investigate arises wherever life has been lost in circumstances possibly engaging state responsibility, then how should we apply this duty in the context of low-intensity urbanised warfare, where the environment often hinders investigation? Who should judge when investigatory duties apply or not, and how these duties should be balanced against security considerations? As I see it, under human rights law, it has become unlawful to not investigate assumed collateral damage incidents if an investigation is possible. And in cases where the ECHR binds member states, the obligation is indisputable. In this way it may be said that incidents falling under the traditional IHL category of collateral damage no longer remain entirely outside the scope of legal responsibility. They are sometimes brought within it, not by way of substantial unlawfulness but by way of the procedural duty to investigate.

The investigatory duties under IHRL will in all likelihood lead to better quality facts about collateral damage incidents and thus an expanded practice of norm application. This may lead to a further development of the IHL principles of proportionality and necessity. In other words, collateral damage seems certain to evolve into a more detailed legal category. What is more, because the choice of applicable legal norms always depends on the available facts, the IHRL investigatory duties may impact on the choice of norms in a given situation, and thus impact on the relationship between IHL and IHRL norms—because the IHRL duty may simply generate better facts than the corresponding duties under IHL. If implemented properly by states, the procedural obligations under IHRL may thus have a direct legal impact on the relationship between the IHRL regime and the IHL regime. The importance of procedure to the relationship between IHL and IHRL should remind us how procedural issues are relatively underdeveloped in international law, both in practice and in scholarship.

Substantial questions about rights and responsibility preoccupy courts, scholars, and legislators. This is unfortunate. Injustice is equally caused by lack of proper investigation. Another good reason for strengthening the focus on procedural rights is that 'it is much harder to make cultural arguments against procedural rights than substantial rights'.[93] People not sharing moral or religious beliefs will probably find it easier to agree on the importance of conducting proper investigations into alleged injustice than on the normative agenda for judging the facts.

3

COLLATERAL DAMAGE AND COMPENSATION

The previous chapter concluded that the substantive lawfulness of collateral damage remains but that a new duty to investigate may sometimes apply for some states. Now, collateral damage presents us with another question of responsibility, which relates to the economic and emotional costs inflicted on victims and their relatives: the question of reparation for damages. In principle, international law has mandated reparations to war crime victims for some time,[1] although individuals only recently started to explore that legal option.[2] In the context of restitution and reparations, collateral damage constitutes a category different from war crimes and non-combat incidents caused by negligence or hazardous behaviour due to the lawfulness and inherent permissibility of collateral damage. Yet collateral damage victims suffer in the same way as victims of war crimes and non-combat related damage. They may not understand the difference of their fate. In countries lacking access to proper medical treatment, minor injuries can easily cause thorny medical situations. A light fracture may throw an entire family into poverty, as may the death or disability of the family's breadwinner. We should not forget that the majority of the world's population live without any form of insurance[3] and that for them, what is lost is lost.

During the Vietnam War, when civilian victims required relief the Americans often cooperated with the Vietnamese to ensure that compensation was available, regardless of the cause of the loss.[4] Recent practice from leading militaries reveals a growing standardisation in such compensation of individuals for losses resulting from collateral damage. This raises the more general question of whether surviving collateral damage victims or relatives of the ones who have been killed should and could expect to receive some kind of redress. Could and should acts leading to lawful and accepted collateral damage trigger an obligation to compensate? Could lawfulness and legal responsibility be married?

I will not here argue for or against compensation. Instead, I will use the question of compensation to walk around some additional aspects relating to lawful collateral damage victims and the question of obligations, which are: 1) Transnational human rights litigation (THRL) practices and developments in tort law, two fields that have been said to influence the question of legal liability for collateral damage; 2) The possibility of expanding non-combat related tort claims to (combat-related) collateral damage; 3) The question of whether it is possible to imagine a 'restorative justice' approach to bring into being an obligation to compensate for lawful damage. Finally, I will reflect on how the recent compensation programmes for collateral damage victims strongly reject any form of responsibility for fear of creating 'wrong expectations', thereby in fact supporting the possibility of the development of legal responsibility for collateral damage.

Transnational human rights litigation

Let us first look at the prospect of seeking damages through national courts. The international human rights movement has put some hope in the emergence of THRL as an alternative path by which to take legal action against alleged human rights violators. THRL refers to a situation where a case is litigated in national courts against persons in other states or even foreign diplomats or state leaders for alleged human rights violations. International humanitarian law (IHL) does not contain effective rules for reparations,[5] but international human rights law (IHRL) does, and hence offers a legal basis for individuals to seek 'reparations', the term used in IHRL for compensation for violations of IHRL. IHRL was not designed to address large-scale violations in international armed conflicts, but, as we have learned, IHRL finds increasing use in such contexts. The question is whether THRL could perhaps penetrate the otherwise responsibility-free category of collateral damage in war with an effective legal claim to some sort of compensation for the victims.

Besides the recent practice of Italian courts, which (as described in the last chapter) was overruled by the International Court of Justice (ICJ), and a handful of cases that since 11 September 2001 have been brought to Canadian and British courts,[6] THRL has only been practised by US courts. This practice commenced with the 1980 landmark decision in *Filártiga v. Peña-Irala*,[7] in which the US Court of Appeals for the Second Circuit endorsed the appellants' argument that '[t]he district courts shall have original jurisdiction of any civil action by an alien for a tort only, committed in violation of the law of nations or a treaty of the US', as provided by the US Alien Tort Statute (ATS).[8] The case thus interpreted the ATS to provide jurisdiction over claims for torts within the US as well as abroad.

In the three decades following *Filártiga*, US federal courts systematically adjudicated responsibility for torture and other violations of IHRL under a 'mixture' of the ATS, the 1991 US Torture Victim Protection Act (TVPA), and (a creative interpretation of) the 1976 US Foreign Sovereign Immunities Act (FSIA).[9] Actions have been filed against sovereign states, heads of states, state officials, political organisations and multinational corporations for acts including torture, terrorism, genocide, war crimes and extrajudicial killings.[10] Since 2001, Iraqi and Afghan citizens have sought damages for torture and other IHRL violations in US courts;[11] aliens subjected to the CIA rendition programme have asserted various constitutional claims;[12] and foreign nationals detained by the US military at Bagram Airfield Military Base in Afghanistan have filed petitions for habeas corpus.[13] Litigations have largely proceeded without any immunity concerns.[14]

The development of THRL in US federal courts under ATS, TVPA, and FSIA, and the tension between universal human rights norms and immunity rules, has been widely discussed among academics and jurists. The debates gained new momentum in 2010 when the US Supreme Court by a unanimous decision affirmed a Fourth Circuit ruling in the case of *Samantar v. Yousef*,[15] holding that FSIA immunity did not automatically apply to foreign government officials.[16] Rather, the Court stated, immunity for foreign state officials is to be developed on a case-to-case basis as common law:[17] '[w]hether petitioner may be entitled to immunity under the common law, and whether he may have other valid defenses to the grave charges against him, are matters to be addressed in the first instance by the District Court on remand'.[18] The decision in *Samantar v. Yousef* should not be seen as endorsing THRL, but rather as affirming that the FSIA offers no general rules with regard to the questions of when and why courts should grant immunity or not.[19] In other words, the Court found, in line with the general theories on the law of immunity, that immunity is not a general rule but a case-specific claim. Hence, there was nothing controversial with *Samantar*. The ruling will not 'open the flood-gates' to unrestricted litigation towards foreign state officials,[20] nor does it impinge on current litigation practice. Instead, the US district courts will now have to develop a 'modern common law' with regard to the question of the immunity of foreign state officials.[21]

No US federal court seems yet to have considered any claims about compensation for collateral damage. The question is whether we should expect to see THRL in US courts in cases where states or individuals are alleged to be responsible for the use of force leading to casualties that fall under the category of collateral damage. Should we in this context expect to see the 'right to life' treated on a par with the prohibition against torture? In many ways, the scene is set for the first THRL case about redress for collateral damage.

THRL—no prospects

Let us assume that victims of collateral damage succeed in filing a case for violations of the 'right to life'. Let us further assume that the court rules in favour of reparations. The question is what kind of impact such a case could have, including whether courts in other states would choose to pursue the THRL practice of the US courts. To answer this question we can look at the output of THRL so far. With regard to impact in terms of holding individuals responsible, it seems that THRL, as developed by the US courts, holds fewer promises than often suggested. No plaintiff has ever collected any substantial damages.[22] THRL has demonstrated no measurable impact on the general human rights culture, and remains for the most part ignored by the international community of states[23]—presumably because of the disregard for the law of state immunity. Further, there are no transnational enforcement mechanisms, which diminishes the practical impact of the cases. What is more, US court practice with regard to THRL suffers grave procedural problems, and demonstrates little knowledge of international law at district court level.[24] Add to this the sturdy tradition of viewing collateral damage as lawful and permissible (as opposed to typical THRL claims of torture, war crimes, genocide), and altogether it seems highly unlikely that THRL will have any legal impact whatsoever on the interpretation of the lawfulness of collateral damage. For similar reasons, and due to the lack of international legitimacy inherent in THRL, it is highly doubtful whether other states' courts will try to follow US court practice in a way that could influence the legal status of collateral damage.

In this regard, it may also be worth noticing that the two most progressive court decisions regarding THRL, immunity and extraterritoriality both contain strong elements of legal activism. In the case of *Filártiga v. Peña-Irala*, which opened the gates for THRL against alien state persons in US Federal Courts, Judge Kaufmann described his judgement in the decision as 'a small but important step in the fulfilment of the ageless dream to free all people from brutal violence'.[25] Similarly, the Italian *Corte di Cassazione* declared that its decision that Italian courts have jurisdiction over claims for compensation against foreign states brought by victims of war crimes and crimes against humanity contributed to the development of international customary law. In both cases, idealistic visions of a new world order paved the way for civil lawsuits against foreign state officials regardless of state immunity principles. They all hit the wall of immunity.

Along the same lines one could point to the International Criminal Tribune for the Former Yugoslavia case of *Prosecutor v. Tadic*,[26] in which the judges famously departed from the decision of the ICJ and candidly stated that their judgement intentionally aimed at replacing the standard set by the ICJ with regard to the relationship between state responsibility and control over non-state groups.[27] This provides us with dramatic cases that can be seen as examples of the so-called 'fragmentation of international law', driven by change-seeking judges rather than actual norm conflicts. To be sure, norm conflict on this level is fairly rare.[28] Legislators and judges mostly aspire for coherence. States that draft treaties and judges who apply them take great care not to contradict existing international law.[29] Accordingly, the court-driven 'fragmentation' stemming from the proliferation of THRL as well as from the drama created by the Italian *Corte di Cassazione* in *Ferrini* will in all likelihood not induce any substantial changes to international law whatsoever, and the fortress of immunity surrounding collateral damage remains intact. In terms of its effect on the legality of collateral damage, THRL may turn out to be just an isolated and controversial expression of idealistic court activism.

Collateral damage and the US Foreign Claims Act

Then how about tort claims under the US Foreign Claims Act (FCA)? In the US, compensation for non-combat damages in war already has a long history. During the First World War, the US instituted a compensation mechanism, the so-called 'Indemnity Act',[30] for noncombat injury, death and damages to property to make amends to the discontented victims of traffic accidents caused by the more than 100,000 US military vehicles roaming the European roads, which were at the time best suited for horse wagons. Of the 51,745 civilian claims that were filed, 38,299 were paid.[31] As the US entered the Second World War, the Indemnity Act was updated and re-labelled the Foreign Claims Act (FCA), which remains in place as the legal basis for claims related to non-combat death and injury. Claims under the FCA are today entirely standardised.[32] Other states (this includes most foreign militaries operating in Afghanistan) also compensate for non-combat injuries, but the FCA remains the only formalised foreign claims system.

The FCA only allows a claim if it did not 'result directly or indirectly from an act of the armed forces of the United States in combat'[33] and thus exempts our category of collateral damage. However, we may notice how the processing of FCA claims and the separation of admissible and inadmissible claims along combat and non-combat lines constitutes a most important legal instrument for demarcating the category of collateral damage. Every time an officer rejects a claim under FCA on the ground that the incident in question is 'combat-related' and therefore inadmissible, the decision reinforces and delineates the scope of the collateral damage rule. This procedural aspect of FCA is tremendously important to the practical fabrication of collateral damage: the day-to-day separation of claims into combat-related and non-combat-related death and injury produces collateral damage by rejecting access to FCA. After all, collateral damage is not collateral damage before the imprint of authority labels it collateral damage, and in this regard, FCA-processes play a key role.

An oft-used example to illustrate the separation of combat and non-combat claims—and its bewildering nature—is a 2005 episode where a US army helicopter fired at and killed a fisherman in a boat on the Tigris River in Baghdad but then failed to moor the boat now drifting downstream. The bereaved family received $3,500 for the loss of the boat but nothing for their lost father and husband: the shooting was viewed as a combat exception, that is, as collateral damage. The failure to moor the boat was not.[34] However, cases also exist where the FCA has been found applicable to combat-like situations. One instance is a 2006 brake-failure accident in Bagram, Afghanistan, where dozens of people where injured by a run-away eight-wheeled military 'Heavy Expanded Mobility Tactical Truck'. The accident ignited the already tense emotions among the locals. The ensuing riot led to a shootout where US military personnel killed and injured additional civilian persons. In this case, claims were accepted under FCA for the shootout injuries,[35] even if a riot against US military personnel could be viewed as creating a kind of self-defence combat-situation and thus blocking access to FCA. The two examples illustrate inconsistencies with regard to the FCA, but perhaps more so the general difficulty with regard to drawing the line between combat and non-combat. Both victimiser and victim may have great difficulties in deciding whether the situation was combat-related or not Do shots need to be fired before we have a combat situation? How about high-speed driving in dense traffic to avoid suicide bombers? When a drone finally fires its rockets after having circled the sky for hours, is that a combat situation? How about anxious checkpoint shootings: combat or not?

In the words of Professor Jordan Walerstein, '[o]ne of the most pressing legal issues facing troops on overseas deployments is the adjudication of claims by civilians against US military forces for damages to real and personal property or for physical injury or death.'[36] Unfortunately, while firm in principle, the FCA regime reportedly suffers from 'distressingly sloppy lawyering', and 'wild inconsistencies' in the administration of claims.[37] In addition, the FCA's refusal to pay compensation for combat-related damage in the face of the need to do so for strategic reasons has been a recurring problem.[38] The difficulty in drawing a legally workable line between combat and non-combat raises questions about the appropriateness of using this dual regime to regulate damages for death and injury inflicted by military forces. It has been suggested that collapsing combat and non-combat damage into a single category of the FCA system could facilitate a more effective procedure.[39] This would allow military organisations to compensate on a case-by-case basis and 'offer further flexibility to cope with combat claims without violating long-standing principles of IHL and customary international law'.[40] In other words, the suggestion is to give collateral damage victims the right to file a claim under the FCA in the same way as non-combat victims.

From a pragmatic perspective, which favours strategic and moral expediency, it may appear practical to collapse combat-related and non-combat injury into a single liability regime that institutes compensation for injurious acts not prohibited by international law. It would indeed reflect better the blurring of combat and non-combat in contemporary armed conflicts. However, the inclusion of collateral damage under an FCA-model would involve a concrete political decision from the US Congress.[41] While inclusion under the FCA may appear as a possible avenue to take, it would imply the acknowledgement of legal liability for lawful acts and thereby change fundamentally the idea and rule of lawful collateral damage. It would require politicians to proclaim, 'Yes, we admit that collateral damage implies our wrongdoing!'

An obligation to compensate for lawful acts: restorative justice

May we then imagine that collateral damage could be covered by a liability rule establishing the right to compensation outside the rules of state responsibility?[42] In other words, an obligation for warring parties to compensate or make amends for lawful acts, where the failure to compensate would not impact on the lawfulness of the act itself but instead constitute an independent breach of an obligation.[43] Such a 'restorative justice' model[44] would meet some of the wants of the collateral damage victims while accommodating military necessity and the strategic goal of winning hearts and minds. It has been argued that such a model would be a 'fair' solution as it would shift some of the burden, including financial costs and risk, from the victims to the victimiser, while not impinging on the military necessity of accepting some civilian casaulties.[45]

I see some controversial moral aspects of such a 'kill and pay' model, including conceivable ways for both victims and victimiser to exploit it. I will not address that here but instead take a glimpse down the avenue of principles of such an approach: both the FCA-model and the restorative justice model raise complex questions about standards. Any formal notion of compensation for collateral damage would have to answer the questions: Whose laws? For what? For whom? How? A formal compensation regime would require procedures for adjusting compensation in accordance with local customs and demands. Local authorities will need to have a say in this process, or else compensation would be futile at best. No universal compensation standard would meet the very diverse emotional and practical needs of the harmed and bereaved. Still, evidence shows that compensation and the implied social recognition in most cases provide at least some kind of emotional remedy, even if the financial compensation or practical assistance may not get close to anything like a fair balance. Yet those who argue that it is absurd to decide a price on death and suffering fail to remember that the law does exactly this all the time. Why should it be different in times of war? It is of course more difficult to calculate the economic loss of death or disability for a person or family in, say, Afghanistan, than in countries with standardised incomes and comparatively stable living costs. In such countries it is relatively easy to estimate what, say, 10 per cent disability amounts to in terms of reduced income. Such calculations are already part of FCA procedure.[46] However, the question of constructing procedures and mechanisms remains a practical matter and not about the principled question of responsibility for collateral damage or not.

Expanding the FCA model or adopting a restorative justice approach seem more realistic than the THRL route but involve controversial political aspects of accepting legal responsibility for collateral damage. Alas, we will most likely not see any progress in these branches with impact on the legal status of collateral damage.

Customary international law

Although states continuously reject responsibility, the latest development in norms and attitudes has extrapolated and squeezed smaller than ever the accepted scope of the collateral damage rule. And warring parties increasingly compensate collateral damage victims and their relatives. It has been suggested that '[t]he evolution of the principle and practice of making amends constitutes a key momentum in international standard setting.'[47] But where is the threshold between this new standard, between the new norms and practices of compensation, and legal obligations? Could we imagine that the sum of new norms and attitudes and compensation practices might eventually give rise to what is know in international law as *opinion juris sive necessitates*: a subjective 'feeling' among states of acting out of a sense of legal obligation to the extent that it gives rise to the body of norms known as customary international law? As set out in the Statute of the ICJ, customary international law is one of the three key sources of international law, which includes also treaties and 'general principles of international law recognized by all civilized nations.'[48] The Statute of the ICJ describes custom as 'evidence of a general practice accepted as law'.[49] Custom involves, in a nutshell, two components: state practice and *opinio juris*.[50] State practice has been defined by the ICJ as 'consistent and uniform usage practiced by the states in question'.[51] In other words, if states behave consistently with regard to certain matters, such practice may be said to constitute a source of customary international law.

Practice, however, cannot stand alone. Also required is a so-called 'subjective element'. In international law this is known as *opinio juris*. *Opinio juris* can be defined as a state attitude that explicitly and unequivocally verifies that the concerned practice is upheld out of a sense of clear legal obligation. *Opinio juris* and concrete state practice may together generate customary international law. Since *opinio juris* is notoriously difficult to identify, its presence is most often derived from a certain state practice.[52] Jean-Marie Heankaerts, who headed the comprehensive 2005 International Committee of the Red Cross (ICRC) study of international customary humanitarian law, noted that: '[i]n the area of IHL, where many rules require abstention from certain conduct, omissions pose a particular problem in the assessment of *opinio juris* because it has to be proved that the abstention is not a coincidence but based on a legitimate expectation'.[53] The ICRC study, the core conclusions of which have been accepted to a large degree by leading states, relied in its exploration of *opinio juris* on military manuals, including teaching manuals, field manuals, state reports, and other similar documents.[54]

The theory of customary international law remains weak. It is not entirely clear what may actually amount to state practice and *opinio juris*, respectively. Both components suffer from conceptual enigmas, and questions such as 'What is relevant state practice'; 'What is the role of treaties'; 'What are the sources of evidence for *opinio juris*'; 'How can it be observed and described'; 'What is the function of state practice'; 'How much and how long should practice and opinion flourish before it may be said to have a law creating effect?' are difficult to answer.[55] It has even been asked whether customary international law can be considered law at all, or whether it should merely be regarded as habitual norms. It has also been argued that international customary law is anti-democratic and therefore illegitimate because it grows out of highest state-level practice and does not consider the broader democratic community. Notwithstanding these difficulties, customary international law is a central and unavoidable source of international law and commonly applied by the ICJ.

Could we imagine a customary international law development with regard to responsibility for collateral damage? Concerning the lawfulness of collateral damage, state practice and attitudes speak loud and univocally: it is lawful. But what about compensation for collateral damage? Could state practice in the form of the compensation practices we have seen in Afghanistan and Iraq, in combination with the changing normative attitudes towards collateral damage have the effects of creating if not a new rule then perhaps the seeds for a new rule of customary international law? What would be the tipping point to where new practices and attitudes start generating a law creating effect? Let us reflect on some aspects of the extensive practice of compensating for collateral damage that has emerged during the past decade with the aim of assessing whether they might contain the seeds of a customary international law development.

The practice of compensation

The practice of compensating collateral damage victims including the injured and bereaved has developed above all as a counterinsurgency strategy.[56] The main purpose has not been a sense of any moral duty but the effort to win (back) the hearts and minds of civilians. The practices developed on estimations of to which degree compensation could save some civilians from shifting loyalty to the enemy. Accordingly, the US military placed their collateral damage compensations in Afghanistan under 'Money as a Weapon System-Afghanistan' (MAAWS-A), part of the Commander's Emergency Response Program (CERP). CERP is a programme funded by the US Department of Defense that allows commanders ad hoc access to financial assets in order to assist 'native people' and facilitate the 'timely completion of their mission'.[57] CERP distinguishes between 'condolence payments' and 'solatia', the former being symbolic gestures and the latter given for more direct combat-related death and injury. Yet both forms of compensation relate to combat-related incidents, and are separate from non-combat-related damage, which falls under the Foreign Claims Act regime.

By mid-2010, the US had in the context of Afghanistan 2001–10 paid out more than $32 million, apportioned to an unnumbered amount of cases.[58] Reportedly, in addition to solatia and condolence payments, the total amount provided by compensation programmes in Iraq, Afghanistan and Pakistan for livelihood assistance reached well above $130 million. Such assistance typically consisted of aid packages 'tailored to meet particular families' needs in close cooperation with the local governing bodies, such as village elders'.[59] NATO countries embraced US practices. In the year to 19 November 2012 the UK Ministry of Defence paid out £537,684, slightly more than the £510,728 paid out for incidents in 2011, but much lower than previous years. In 2010, payments totalled £1.3 million apportioned to 951 cases.[60] Canada paid CA$1,047,946 to 453 people from 2005 to 2011.[61]

These amounts are in some sense comparatively small. Tomahawk missiles cost around $1.4 million a piece. More than 160 were fired in the opening days of the 2011 war in Libya. And the numbers are without doubt imprecise. As an example, a 2009 incident where an estimated 140 civilians were killed in Afghanistan does not figure in the International Security Assistance Force (ISAF) 'CIVCAS' database.[62] And the ISAF countries demonstrated weak coordination on this matter. Commanders in the field mostly settled payments ad hoc and only (it is not too much to say) where it served strategic purposes, i.e. to tranquilise strong emotions among the injured or bereaved. Payments built on operational budgets rather than a centralised fund system. Practices and tariffs varied from cash paid on the spot to help with community matters such as schools or aid during the winter. In 2009, the United Nations

Assistance Mission in Afghanistan (UNAMA) reported that '[t]here continues to be no uniform standard, procedure or even timeline between the different countries who mechanisms [sic] for payment, creating confusion, anxiety and anger amongst affected Afghans'.[63] Not least the Afghans expressed deep frustration over the confused practices. In 2010, the criticism from various sides of the unclear condolence payment practices led NATO to adopt (non-binding) compensation guidelines to improve cohesion and reduce confusion among collateral damage victims and their relatives.[64] While the guidelines came as a response to the calls for a unified and improved compensation policy, procedures remain weak, despite many demands for the mainstreaming of compensation policies and the establishment of a centralised funds system. 2010 also became the year where the term 'making amends' for collateral damage was used for the first time in a high-level UN document, as the 'Annual Report of the Special Rapporteur on Extrajudicial, Summary or Arbitrary Executions' stated that amends for those killed 'even in lawful attacks' is an 'expanding practice, which is not yet being systematically tracked or instituted by the international community'.[65] Later that year, the UN Secretary General's report on the protection of civilians noted 'the emerging practice of several States, one that other parties to armed conflict might consider, of acknowledging the harm they cause to civilians and compensating victims'.[66]

Sufficient or insufficient programmes, flawed numbers or not, compensation for collateral damage developed into a standard practice during the wars in Iraq and Afghanistan. Today, the norm is to compensate for collateral damage—not to deny it. Notwithstanding the confused procedures, compensation presents us with a consistent practice, which straddles a range of states, including some of the most powerful.

Does this practice add up to 'state practice' in the context of customary international law? The formal policies and practices of the armed forces of a state are obviously attributable to the state. The international law concept of state conduct does not require a mainstreamed approach, international cooperation or common forms of action. From an international law perspective, the answer therefore seems to be yes: we see state practice. If the practice of compensating for collateral damage as it has developed during the last decade does not amount to a consistent and uniform practice by the states in question, then what is 'practice' in the context of the laws governing the conduct or armed conflict?

Then again, while we see significant practice, we may not see any profound institutionalisation of it. As of 2013, the US, which pushed hardest to establish civilian casualty mitigation norms and mechanisms, still had no Pentagon officer specifically responsible for monitoring civilian harm.[67] And in 2014 the US had still not codified policies and training to replicate this approach in future operations, although high-level US military divisions recommend such a codification.[68] To assess the effect of the recent proliferation of CIVCAS[69] norms and practice on the deeper institutional structures, including international law, we need to wait and see. It may have been just a blip on the screen in the history of war. In sum, it seems safe to conclude that at this stage we do not see sufficient state practice to talk about customary law development—but what we see may certainly count as a beginning.

Opinio juris

The next step towards identifying the seeds of customary international law is to ask if these practices are expressions of *opinio juris*. Now, the compensating states take great care in framing their compensation practices as *ex-gratia* payments, that is to say not provided out of a sense of legal obligation. For instance, after NATO/ISAF in June 2010 agreed on the non-binding guidelines for dealing with cases of civilian combat-related casualties, NATO's Secretary General reported to the UN Security Council that the '[d]ecisions on making payments in cases of civilian combat-related casualties or damage remain a matter of national discretion. The non-binding guidelines are not intended to alter the legal position and obligations of individual national ISAF forces in Afghanistan, and payments are not an admission of legal liability or fault.'[70] I think it is safe to say that this statement articulates the attitudes of all states—at least I have not come across any disagreement at state level. Hence, we see no expression that the practices of compensating for collateral damage are initiated or sustained out of a sense of legal obligation: no *opinio juris* underpins state practice.

No means maybe

However, the question of customary international law and compensation for collateral damage does not end here. Paradoxically, the concern for law-generating effects, the fear of creating expectations, the fear of setting standards, may be viewed as a response to the power of the idea of customary international law and the possibility of standards tipping into law. In fact, the langauge of *ex gratia* and solatia speaks directly to the possible law-creating effects of compensating for collateral damage in war. It reveals how states and their militaries in fact do consider a law-generating effect as a possible offspring of their compensation practices. Whenever states openly reject any legal obliteration for collateral damage, they compensation, they recognise a possible custom and thus possible law-creating effects of such state practice. If not, then why bother? The more states and their militaries emphasise how compensation is entirely *ex-gratia*, the more they confirm the possibility of legal norm creation. Put plainly, the more they say 'no!', the more they say 'maybe!'

From the perspective of current customary international law theory, it is highly uncertain, some would say unthinkable, that current compensation practices could have a law-creating effect and form the basis of a change in customary international law. This reflects the 'chronological paradox' of international customary law, which is that for a rule to become international customary law, states must express the belief that it is already international customary law.[71] But one thing is the legal questions of obligation and the possible formation of customary rules. Another thing is how the awareness of international customary law affects the way the international community and military powers address collateral damage in war. When it comes to compensation practices, we see how the theory of customary international law impacts on state practice. If states were not worried about the legal effects, there would be no need for states to be so cautious about the political and practical framing of compensation practices, which come at a relatively low cost, compared with the overall costs of military operations. Everyone save the insurgents would benefit from better compensation regimes. The fear of rule-creating effects appears to be the only reason not to unify and institutionalise compensation practices. In this case, the idea of international customary law seems to stand in the way for humanitarian action by constituting a roadblock for the development of better compensation programmes.

4

LIFTING THE FOG OF WAR
AND COLLATERAL DAMAGE

I will end this enquiry into the legal configuration of the collateral damage rule (and thus the collateral damage victim) with an observation on how new technology affects a cornerstone of this rule, which is the international humanitarian law (IHL) rule imposing the obligation to take due precaution in attack. In the recent armed conflicts in Gaza, Libya, Afghanistan, Iraq, Kosovo, and Kuwait, all of which were fought with cutting-edge Western military technology, weak situational awareness was the dominant cause of collateral damage. Military powers continually referred to 'the fog of war' as a plausible and legally accepted reason for applying the collateral damage rule. This chapter peeks into a future where technology enables tremendously improved situational awareness, and where this 'lifting of the fog of war' will affect the collateral damage rule. I am not talking about the surgical precision features of killer drones but the way this technology will mature into an increasingly powerful tool for surveilling and controlling territories and persons, which, for those who possess it, will bring still greater transparency and situational awareness to battlefields and targeting situations. By this means, drone technology offers an effective measure for vetting targets and thus enables a much improved safeguarding of civilians and civilian objects. As the rules of IHL oblige states to do everything feasible to take due precaution in attack, drone technology gets pulled into the list of precautionary measures that need to be exhausted before an attack may be launched. Indeed, drone technology appears to be the greatest hope for reducing collateral damage in future armed conflicts. Not only due to its precision capabilities but also by putting a heavy yoke of precautionary obligations on the shoulders of military commanders and changing some fundamental dilemmas related to targeting in war, thereby shrinking the scope of the collateral damage rule. As I will show in this chapter, drone technology amends or even dissolves classical humanitarian law dilemmas about balancing concerns for personnel and material losses and urgency against military efficiency and collateral damage.

Recasting the drone problematic

Let us recap a few general facts about current drone technology, which in presents us with a major leap in the history of seeing in war; a history that has moved from hilltops, watchtowers and scouts to the use of binoculars, balloons and airplanes and then on to radar, night vision, satellites ... and drones. Drone technology brings us closer than ever to the battleground. As of 2015, the state-of-the-art military drones are remote-controlled, silent, slow-speed planes, which can stay airborne for an extended period of time. Numerous drones can hover over a small area far more easily than conventional planes, thus allowing multiple surveillance platforms, and they may be flown at low altitude without compromising pilot security. As of the time of writing, surveillance accessories include 1.8 gigapixel cameras,[1] infrared cameras, synthetic aperture radars (which means that they can look through foliage), electromagnetic spectrum sensors (which detect sources of energy), biological sensors, chemical sensors, and equipment for eavesdropping on cell phones and radio as well as interceptors for wireless internet communications. But this is only 2015. The history of technology shows us that computer speed and memory, pixels in digital cameras and sensor technology improve exponentially, doubling roughly every two years (this is often referred to as Moore's Law). We can expect drone technology to develop at a similar speed. Soon we will see better sensors and data transfer technologies and better software for analysing drone surveillance material. Eventually we will develop algorithms for biometric identification of persons. And we will see cheaper drones,[2] smaller drones, tiny, beetle-sized drones, whirring around close to the ground; militaries already use hand-sized miniature drones for reconnaissance.[3] Although the range and functions of such 'nanodrones' remain limited they constitute a small revolution in the field of intelligence, surveillance and reconnaissance.[4] Finally, drones will become increasingly robotised. Autonomous weapon systems raise many questions,[5] yet notwithstanding the weapon aspect, the mere surveillance advantage of robotised drones flows directly into this chapter's main argument about how new ways of 'seeing and knowing' in armed conflict impact the application of the precautionary principle in IHL and thereby bear new procedural implications for the use of the collateral damage rule.

The principle of precaution

As surveillance technology matures, the fog of war lifts, and it becomes increasingly hard to excuse civilian casualties by a lack of situational awareness. However, technology also changes other parameters for gauging collateral damage. To see how let us place this concept of drones as flying 'super sensors' in the context of the principle of precaution in IHL. The obligation to take due care in attack to limit collateral damage has been affirmed by belligerents for a long time. According to Article 27 of the 1899 Hague II Convention, '[i]n sieges and bombardments all necessary steps should be taken to spare as far as possible edifices devoted to religion, art, science, and charity, hospitals, and places where the sick and wounded are collected, provided they are not used at the same time for military purposes.' Article 2(3) of the 1907 Hague Convention (IX) established that the commander of a naval force, 'shall take all due measures in order that the town may suffer as little harm as possible'. Furthermore, '[i]f for military reasons immediate action [against naval or military objects located within an undefended town or port] is necessary, and no delay can be allowed the enemy, [the commander of a naval force] shall take all due measures in order that the current town may suffer as little harm as possible.' The principle of precaution was not codified as a rule of international law before the First Additional Protocol to the Geneva Conventions, Article 57(2)(a) in 1977.[6] However, Article 57 did not constitute a new rule but rather codified customary law.[7] Today, it forms a key IHL rule and figures in the military manuals of numerous states.[8] The principles enshrined in Article 57 become relevant when targeting starts. It is linked to both the principle of proportionality—as its formulation 'everything feasible' (see endnote 6) places precaution between military necessity and humanitarian obligations—as well as to the principle of distinction, by obligating attackers to do everything feasible to verify the target. Due precaution may build on years of intelligence or on a sound, split-second judgement. It applies to the immediate situation of a military attack, and not so much to the possible long-term effects of attacks on health, the economy or the environment.[9]

Some scholars have argued that in an armed conflict scenario the principle of precaution is more than often unworkable. Precaution may be impractical since it risks revealing tactics, and pre-operational data collection may be impossible due to urgency and security issues. However, even if it may be hard to satisfy the principle of precaution as reflected in Article 57, it still constitutes a crucial standard governing the conduct of armed force. In this regard, the obligation to use drones if available and feasible is not different from the obligation to use binoculars to check out the target before firing the mortars. Precaution is a natural moral obligation, in armed conflict as well as in all other spheres of life.

Precaution in attack has been treated in a number of scholarly contexts.[10] Here it suffices to note how the obligation to take all feasible precaution when choosing ways and means of attacking, with an eye to minimising collateral damage, stands as an essential rule governing the conduct of armed conflict. If commanders are uncertain about the exact status of the target, they are obliged to exhaust available means for verifying it. This implies that 'a bombing raid that is carried out on the basis of mere suspicion as to the military nature of the target amounts *ipso facto* to a violation of the principle of distinction'—even if the attack produces no damage at all.[11] This also means that if a commander launches an attack without exhausting available means for precaution and as a result harms civilians, we see a war crime and not collateral damage. In that way, the rule of precaution forms another backbone of the collateral damage rule: compliance with the rule of precaution is the *sine qua non* for invoking the collateral damage rule. If military commanders fail to exhaust available and feasible precautionary measures, there can be no collateral damage.

Drones and the principle of precaution

How does our extended concept of drone technology affect the application of the rule of precaution? Like most IHL principles, the meaning of 'everything feasible' in Article 57 is contextual. The primary variables of Article 57 may be identified as 'the time necessary to gather and process the additional information, the extent to which it would clarify any uncertainty, competing demands on the intelligence, surveillance and reconnaissancer system in question, and risk to it and its operators'.[12] In this regard, drone technology removes or alters the classical dilemmas related to precaution, namely 1) precautionary measures versus tactical considerations, that is, the time to gather and process additional information, or the risk of revealing tactics or loss of other military advantages; 2) precautionary measures versus personnel considerations, that is, the risk to the soldiers, the operators of weapon systems; 3) precautionary measures versus materiel considerations, that is, the risk to the weapon systems. The fourth variable is the question of whether additional information would add anything at all to the assessment of a given situation. Here, this aspect may be resolved by limiting our discussion to situations where additional information could make a difference.

Tactical considerations impacting on 'everything feasible'

Regarding urgency, here defined as a military situation in which the need for rapid response decreases the scope of feasible precautionary steps, we may notice how signature strikes and targeted killings more often than not take place in the absence of actual fighting, and mostly rely on careful targeting considerations. Ground operations and bombing campaigns nowadays generally build on minutious planning involving detailed aerial reconnaissance. For instance, the ISAF forces in Afghanistan closely synchronised their operations with the availability of drone surveillance support. Hours, days or weeks of surveillance may lie ahead of attacks. This leaves plenty of time for considering and taking precautionary steps. It has been argued that there is 'strong evidence that UAVs [unmanned aerial vehicles] are better, not worse, at noncombatant discrimination'.[13] That may or may not be true; statistics indicate the latter.[14] My argument is merely that in a tactical landscape void of the kind of urgency we have traditionally associated with armed conflict, such as hectic combat situations or the sudden necessity of protecting strongholds, the 'feasibility' parameter of balancing urgency against feasible precaution changes. In situations of targeted killings and signature killings, urgency does not stem from battle distress. It springs solely from the risk of missing the chance to kill a suspected or confirmed target. Still, the principle of precaution applies. The question drone technology presents us with is what 'everything feasible' may mean in a situation devoid of the kind of military urgency the principle originally envisaged. Furthermore, the availability of drone technology obviously attaches new precautionary obligations to many other weapon systems. In many situations, if the drones are not already hovering, their swift deployment time may simply require the commanders to send them out in advance of bombing or shelling.

Personnel considerations impacting on 'everything feasible'

The same fundamental change in the balancing of precaution versus necessity follows from the fact that the use of drone technology removes the risk for pilots and intelligence, surveillance and reconnaissance staff. According to IHL, it is entirely lawful to balance the protection of own military personnel against the risk of harming civilians or civilian infrastructure. While '[r]ules of engagement designed to protect civilians tend to place soldiers at greater risk; ... and rules that stress force protection usually come at the expense of civilians', this '"duty to reduce harm to enemy civilians ... does not entail an obligation to assume personal life-threatening risks"'.[15] The risk connected with sending reconnaissance divisions into hostile environments therefore has a direct bearing on the scope of 'feasible' precautions. Moral arguments have been made for and against weighting troop protection higher than civilian lives, but the arguments all build on the dilemma of weighing troop protection against the scope of feasible precaution.[16]

Drone technology, however, removes this dilemma since no human lives are put in danger on the side of the drone flying state. Apart from the urgency of military necessity to prevent targets from escaping, the only balancing of 'feasible' precautions we see in the context of drone technology is a balancing of the cost of conducting investigations and deploying sufficient technology and the risk of harming civilians. Today we can get incredibly close without risking any personnel and in an extremely stealthy manner, without even requiring the giving up of any tactical advantage.

Material considerations impacting on 'everything feasible'

The dilemma of balancing feasible precaution against the protection of military material surfaces in situations where necessity requires compromising precautionary measures in order to protect expensive or sensitive military equipment from being destroyed or falling into enemy hands. In the context of conventional airpower, the dilemma dovetails with personnel considerations. Flying jets within the range of surface-to-air missiles endangers the lives of the pilots and at the same time risks the material loss of sophisticated equipment. Drone technology unyokes the personnel and material dilemmas, and since the personnel dilemma has ceased, only the material dilemma remains. The risk of losing civilian lives is inherently difficult to balance against the risk of losing war equipment. Yet the price tag difference between a $3 billion B2 bomber, a $17 million Reaper and a $100,000 ScanEagle[17] alters such calculations significantly. This must affect the legal interpretation of what 'everything feasible' may mean in the context of the rule of precaution under Article 57.

Drone technology and the rule of precaution

The obligation to take all feasible precautions depends on what 'feasible' is balanced against. In this regard, drone technology recasts conventional dilemmas attached to Article 57. Out of the dilemmas related to tactics, personnel and materiel, only the latter remains. This is a good example of how it can be '... hard to talk about morality when it comes to new military technology'[18] because sometimes, as in this case, new technology, upon closer inspection, simply modifies conventional dilemmas.

What then could the international law obligation to do everything feasible to verify that objects to be attacked are neither civilians nor civilian objects mean in the age of drone technology? How much surveillance capability must, if available, be procured and employed to satisfy the rule of precaution under IHL? How will precautionary capabilities be multiplied by new technology, including micro drones, available in the near future? If a commander can fly micro drones through windows and peek into houses, could this become required as a mandatory precautionary measure in the use of armed force? Are states that possess advanced surveillance technology bound to follow higher standards than states who do not own such technology?[19] Will future precautionary obligations include flying a micro drone up to the face of the possible target to record biometric data? Will it be lawful to target with a solitary drone, or will combat drones have to be accompanied by a swarm of scout drones? Where should the line of precautionary obligations be drawn in an age of nearly unlimited surveillance?

Lifting the fog of war

Drone technology represents the avant-garde of intelligence collection and targeting. Drones alter not only the threshold of feasible precautionary measures but also their very rationality, and thereby recast the parameters for applying the rule of precaution, which is a *sine qua non* for invoking the collateral damage rule. Legally viewed, without due precaution there can be no collateral damage. In this regard, the obligation to use drones for precaution is logically not limited to drone attacks. It applies across all weapon systems, to land and ground forces and laser beams from space. If the deployment of drone technology may conceivably reduce collateral damage, the state is obliged to employ the technology. For those military powers that have access to the latest high-tech surveillance gear, armed conflicts are moving pixel by pixel towards ultra-high definition and total transparency. Even in the near future, attacks may no longer be lawful without engaging available drone technology for the purpose of precaution.[20] Drone technology already raises the question of a humanitarian law obligation for states to employ drone technology if available to exhaust all feasible means of precaution if any doubt exists as to whether an attack may lead to 'excessive' collateral damage.

During the Israeli bombing of Gaza in the summer of 2014, this thought kept coming back to me. Clearly, the duty to give warnings to civilians prior to an attack, as codified in Article 57(2)(c) of the First Additional Protocol to the Geneva Conventions, stands independent from the rule of precaution in Article 57(2)(a). In other words, while warning surely aims at avoiding or reducing harm to civilians, it bears no effects to the application of the rule of precaution in Article 57(2)(a). Even if Israel claimed to satisfy the duty to issue warnings with phone calls and warning rockets (so-called knock-on-roof-bombs), it would still be obliged to do everything feasible to take due precaution to spare civilians and civilian objects. As many Israeli rockets hit pre-selected targets with plenty of time to consider means of precaution, and as the Israeli army possesses highly sophisticated drone technology, how should all feasible precaution be understood? As I have pointed out in this chapter, this represents a general question concerning the challenges of technology to conventional laws.

As drone technology lifts the 'fog of war' from critical aspects of the use of armed force it creates foreseeability in a very concrete manner. Put in the context of the collateral damage rule, the procedural obligations related to targeting in combination with new technology drastically narrow the scope of what may be considered unforeseen side effects. We therefore need to think through the application of the laws of war in armed conflicts characterised by total visibility and the effects of this on the application of the collateral damage rule—as well as other parts of international law applicable to armed conflict. We need to look at drone technology not only as a game changer: drone technology triggers obligations and alters some fundamental moral and legal parameters for applying the collateral damage rule.

5

HOW BAD CAN BE GOOD

Eternal lingering of useless pain!
Come, ye philosophers, who cry, 'All's well',
And contemplate this ruin of a world.[1]

I have so far traced the juridical category of collateral damage in the context of armed conflict up to a point in time where doubt has been cast on its moral and strategic appropriateness. On the other hand, my juridical explorations have established how the collateral damage rule endures as a legal construct; Nothing indicates that the lawfulness of collateral damage will ever cease. We should therefore expect to continue to face the moral dilemmas and puzzles associated with having such a rule available to us. The enduring lawfulness of collateral damage in war, however, raises new questions: why does it seem impossible to cover the category with legal responsibility? After all, we are talking about a fairly systematic killing of children and other unknowing, innocent persons. Why is it so difficult for law to handle the kind of incidents we label collateral damage? Why do we need this legal category? If the idea of collateral damage in war is an expression of some deeper ideas, then what are they?

To answer these questions, this chapter delves into the historical legacy of the category of death and suffering we label collateral damage. We will see that collateral damage essentially stands for an enduring historical problem of moral authority. Solving the puzzle of collateral damage and responsibility amounts to resolving the problem that gave rise to the biblical story of Adam and Eve, and which since then has driven our major intellectual traditions, including just war theory, the theological debates about theodicy, and utilitarianism. The intractability of the problem explains, I believe, why it remains so unmanageable in law. This aspect in itself warrants an exploration. Yet I am after something a bit more ambitious. In the final chapters I intend to show readers how the collateral damage problem is perhaps the most fundamental and significant problem of our theories of authority in governance broadly viewed; and that the question of who may claim collateral damage equals the question of who may rule the world

To work towards these arguments, this chapter examines four historical debates that have been of particular importance to the classification and moral perception of collateral damage in war: just war theory, the doctrine of double effect, theodicy, and utilitarianism. Each intellectual tradition has been driven by questions of responsibility, justice and legitimacy in cases where agents of authority have advanced governance in such a way that innocent persons have been harmed or killed. They have been driven by a timeless frustration at the gap between the promise and the performance of a supposedly 'good' authority—a frustration that draws particular attention when authority's visions of the good life are realised in ways that inflict severe agony. It might not be obvious for the victims that it is not evil that has come their way: and so the wind carries a ceaseless cry of 'why?' from the star-crossed. Collateral damage, is our answer.

I will argue that collateral damage is not merely double doctrine thinking, a theodicy, a utilitarian calculus, or a product of just war theory. Rather, collateral damage denotes a fundamental problem of and driving force for these intellectual traditions. By clarifying how this is the case, I will at the same time redefine the problem of collateral damage as a more general problem of authority and governance. However, before we get to just war theory, the doctrine of double effect, theodicy, and utilitarianism, we need to move upstream a bit. We must recollect the two themes that originally called for these discussions: the human experience of pain and suffering, and the universally painful experience of a discrepancy between wishful being and disappointing realities in both human and imagined divine agency.

Collateral damage and the Fall of Man

Let us begin our inquiry into the deeper foundations of the collateral damage rule with a sweeping generalisation about a human inclination: we humans like to 'do the right thing'. In our daily lives we aspire, to varying extents and with varying degrees of success, to live up to private and public ideas of a good life. We try to entertain private ideas of what it means to be a good person. Notions of doing good or doing bad are vital components of individual and collective identity. Humans dream about doing the right thing, alone and together, and the fear of failure haunts our dreams at night. At this level we seem to be essentially equal, even if our various notions of virtuous life may clash head on: some social groupings or societies believe that, say, militant anarchism or female circumcision are indispensable to live the good life while others believe in non-violence and that female circumcision is evil incarnate. From the individual viewpoint, doing the right thing does not necessarily mean to live up to some generally accepted moral standard. In September 2011, an apparently rational person murdered 69 young people at a summer camp in Norway in cold blood and bemoaned that they had to die for what he profoundly believed to be a good universal cause. Similar we have the puzzling case of the Nazi Adolf Eichmann, who did not dispute the Holocaust or his role in it, but to his death denied he had done anything wrong as he had merely followed the decrees of Adolf Hitler, who to him personified the highest cause of the Aryan race and nation. History is full of these figures. Despite their horrific aspirations, they clearly struggled with personal issues related to lack of human perfection.

We all live our respective lives with a highly subjective vision of a virtuous life as a form of underlying categorical imperative. But we keep missing, failing, doing the wrong thing when we meant to do the right thing. Our lack of ability to always hit the nail, and our difficulty when it comes to guessing and gauging the direct and indirect effects of our daily actions, reverberate around the globe. If the flapping wings of a butterfly in Australia may start a storm in the Sahara, as we learn from chaos theory, what kind of storm in the opposite hemisphere might something as big as a small human action create? Some rather significant ones, for sure. We aim carefully, but leave a trail of unintended side effects in our wake; side effects that may have good, but sometimes bad, consequences. We cannot free ourselves from this contingent dimension, which leaves us with an existential gap between what we aspire to do and be, and what we actually do and perceive we are.

The human desire for properness and congruity between dreams, desires, intention and practical virtue constitutes a fundamental issue in all aspects of our intellectual development. The authors of Adam and Eve's eviction from the Garden of Eden built their story on this desire. What gives the fable of the

Fall of Man its timeless drama and universal appeal is the split between man's desire to be good and man's inescapable propensity to do harm—regardless of all good intentions and efforts. The Fall of Man, which provided the opening example for this book, and the idea of original sin present us with something equivalent to a Big Bang of moral philosophy. It left us with two overall sets of problems. First, what does it mean to be good? What is the difference between good and bad, and where should people look for a compass to navigate their actions towards the good? Second, if man is doomed to fail in spite of endless striving, how can he reconcile his failures with his desire to be good? How is atonement possible?

Pain and suffering

Way back in earliest written history and probably before that in the oral traditions, the first speculations on blame and responsibility were far more than an exercise in rhetoric. Then, as now, we speculated on the meaning of the human experience of pain and suffering.[2] We humans are sensitive creatures, by nature not resilient in body or psyche in the face of pain and death. Our flesh is vulnerable. Our nerves are tense. We experience physical pain caused by illness, wounds, cold, heat, hunger and sleep deprivation. We suffer emotional pain from loss of love or loved ones, the fear of losing love and loved ones, worrying about this or that, lack of recognition or feelings of deprivation; and an imbalance in brain chemistry can carry us away. As the philosopher Arne Johan Vetlesen reminds us, 'living involves being exposed to pain every second—not necessarily as an insistent reality, but always as a possibility'.[3] And pain experiences vary. Anyone who has lived through long periods of physical pain knows that pain is not a singularity. It is an experience of shifting intensities and combinations perhaps best analogised in the shifting harmonic tonality, dissonance and volume of orchestral music. Pain experiences remain an obscure enigma to science and tend to isolate individuals because of the impossibility of describing pain to others. Yet humans do have a peculiar empathic ability to suffer pain from the experience of others in pain, even animals, although such pain is still a subjective experience.

Pain does not automatically constitute suffering, which may best be described as a certain intensification of the pain experience. Pain may at first create uncomplicated discomfort or even an enjoyable sensation, but as pain increases in intensity or prolongation it will at some point lead to the experience we describe as suffering. As Buddhists show us, cognitive training may enable us to overcome or at least align with pain and, in particular, the experience of suffering. Humans are capable of sitting still and humming a tune while burning to death. Concentrated cognitive training can trim down the body's physical pain experience and adjust the threshold between pain and suffering. Suffering and the threshold between pain and suffering are individual experiences. Hence we may view pain as a bodily sensation, while suffering deals with spirit; it tends to submerge the person, group or even society, akin to a general condition. It does not invite quick fixes but requires more lengthy remedies, sometimes from extraordinary authorities.[4] Yet pain and suffering remain primary human experiences, a fundamental human condition that constitutes a sturdy foothold for community, as everyone agrees about the undesirability of pain and suffering—particularly meaningless suffering.

Suffering, redemption and authority

The quest for removing pain and suffering forms an enduring vehicle for human thought, creativity, invention and, not least, political struggles for power and authority. We crave gods or leaders who can ease our suffering. It is as simple as that. Persons capable of convincing the community members that they posses the power to reduce suffering have historically been elevated to community's highest posts. Political and divine authority always legitimised itself by reference to its unparalleled power to reduce suffering, to lead us out of the desert and to save our souls, even if this may take a genocide or two. Historically and intriguingly, the same authority 'of salvation' has also been in command of the most destructive and pain-inflicting powers. In Western history, two major figures have occupied this place of rescue and destruction: God and the state. The liberal state project promotes a life without suffering for its citizens as the state's foremost purpose and its very self-legitimisation. A somewhat sweeping claim that lacks nuances, one may claim. Yes. The good life has many parameters. But in the end, we measure the liberal state project by its overall ability to promote the good life for its citizens, whether by interventionary force, as a facilitator or in the form of constitutional restraints on power safeguarding the autonomy of the individual. It has recently been questioned whether a state that cannot or appears unwilling to lift its citizens out of suffering should be recognised as a legitimate state at all.[5]

In addition to God and the state, some of us have nominated capitalist market forces as a mighty authoritative salvation force. Yet market fundamentalists never suggested the market itself as the end goal. Rather, they view laissez-faire as a path to redemption. Despite epochs of market dogmatism, the agents of the market, the private corporations, never obtained formal entitlement on a par with state authority to organise and make use of destructive powers to pursue their goals. We accepted accidents and calculated devastating side effects; and accident laws have historically favoured corporations rather than their victims. But we never formally attributed to private corporations in and of themselves the mandate to inflict intended destruction, become organised military powers and make explicit calculations of collateral death and suffering. One could argue that colonial trade companies such as the Dutch or English East India Companies held such mandates, but they were authorised by state authority. It was delegated power, hosted by state authority.

Destruction and salvation

This doublet of destruction and salvation, incarnated as it is in the figure of the soldier as the violent executive of state authority, presents us with a continuing scheme in the history of ideas of authority and governance. Just think of the twentieth-century discussions of constitutionalism and sovereignty and the question of whether emergency powers should be governed by law or be regarded as the natural prerogative of political authority. From Hans Kelsen versus Carl Schmitt in the 1920s Weimar Republic to Europe versus the United States in the so-called 'War on Terror'.[6] Does the wellbeing of the nation and its people depend on unlimited and unchecked state power, even if such power almost per definition breeds collateral destruction and suffering? Are constitutional rights and plights a barrier or an aid to good governance? How may the liberal state weigh up its sovereign authority against individual autonomy? The problem for theologians and political philosophers has been not so much a matter of balancing destruction and salvation, but more about how we can come to terms with this thorny doublet: how can salvation be destruction, and vice versa? How can bad be good, and good be bad?

Theorising the suffering created by good agency

Historically, the debates were divided between idealistic and apologetic accounts. The idealistic branches strove to capture the truth behind the, by all accounts inseparable, nature of good and bad. The apologetic branches have been driven by political, religious and economic leaders' quest for sustaining public legitimacy in times where their ventures created more destruction than salvation. As is often the case with such matters, a historical oscillation between philosophical idealism and political apology makes it hard to seize hold of what has actually been at stake in the debates. As the political scientist Robert Cox once said, '[t]heory is always for someone and for some purpose.'

For our purpose, it is not so important to find out what motivated the theory developers. What matters is the development and extrapolation of ideas that make collateral damage victims comprehensible as a distinct category of death and suffering—our 'third category' of death in war. Both the realistic and the apologetic contributions added to the discourse, allowing us to comprehend and discuss the delicate problem of how good can be bad, and bad can be good. To be sure, the enduring frustration of the gap between promises of salvation and constantly derailed performance generates conversations and arguments: the problem spurred an extreme productivity in terms of generating intellectual activity.

From this perspective, just war theory, the doctrine of double effect, theodicy, and utilitarianism appear as a family of conversations and arguments that all revolve around the same core: the problem of explaining suffering brought to innocents by a regime of 'good' authority. Collateral damage proves to be a semantic code for the problem that lies beneath the conversations and seizes the crux of the problem. It sanitises the fissure between promise and performance. While this may take the form of a constructivist claim, let me make clear again how it all originates in the very concrete human experience of suffering and the whys, which called forth these theoretical replies in the first place. We are talking about severe physical sensation, humans decomposing in raw pain. Not a social construction. Our need for these theories is, after all, due to a certain nerve impulse, a pain experience stemming from a vulnerable human flesh and mind, the point zero of it all. At the root of these intellectual traditions lies a phenomenology of pain, a sorrow, and the human cry: 'Why?' Why pain? Why suffering? Why me, why us?

As we will see, the category of collateral damage materialises as these debates establish a semantic space for appreciating death and suffering imposed by sovereign authority as something that does not compromise the righteousness and decency of authority. They try to explain under which circumstances good authority may inflict death and suffering on innocents without losing its glory; they seek out a reply to the wretched. Now, let us examine each debate to expose the prominence of the collateral damage problem, and how this has influenced the debates.

Just war theory

Some thousand years of just war theory, which at first was not so much a theory as an answer to practical questions about war and responsibility,[7] fashioned the moral foundation for our present laws of war. The establishment of the United Nations Charter in 1945 expelled morality from the judgement of the righteousness of the international use of armed force by stating that the legitimacy of warfare could and should be measured only in terms of legal and illegal. The post-Cold War era led to a revitalisation of just war theory as the UN Charter fell short in several instances when it came to regulating international attitudes towards the rights and wrongs of humanitarian intervention. Today, in judgements about the use of coercive force, formal legal principles compete with moral opinions. Yet the discursive battle about right and wrong in war still revolves around the two major axes of just war theory and the laws of war. These are: firstly, the triad consisting of the principles of proportionality, distinction and necessity, and secondly, the distinction between *jus ad bellum* and *jus in bello* (concerning the right to start a war and the righteous ways to fight a war, respectively). I will recap here the essence of the principle of proportionality in the context of *jus in bello*, which seeks to establish the parameters for assessing the moral legitimacy of the use of violent force during war.

The principle of proportionality embraces the core dilemmas of just war theory, and thereby also of the laws of war. In short, this principle aims at pointing out a fair balance between the amount of force that is necessary to achieve 'just' military objectives and the resulting damage and suffering. It points to the delicate threshold between doing good and doing wrong. The principle of proportionality is tightly bound to the principles of distinction and necessity. The principle of distinction concerns the bounded nature of the legitimate military target, and thus presupposes a vision of the distinction between friend and enemy, and assessments of why, how, when and where this enemy poses a threat to 'us'. The principle of necessity instructs the assessment of the balance between the perceived threat and what may be proportionate force to defeat the enemy. Take away one of these three keystones and we would lose the prism through which we observe and judge any violent act of military force.

The principle of distinction stands relatively clearly *as a principle* (though difficult to translate into the real world), yet the notion of necessity remains highly disputed, as does its progeny, proportionality, which contains 'all the power and the problems of just war theory'.[8] To be sure, the character and function of proportionality in international humanitarian law remains to be settled and awaits further development,[9] including questions such as what makes a good and just cause; what makes a military target; long and short-term consequences; how short-term situations and long-term obligations and promises relate to each other; what kind of alternative actions or weapon technologies could have been chosen in a given situation; and different interpretations of the meaning of death. These issues present us with problems that threaten to undermine any notion of proportionate acts of war. When we try to apply the conventional scheme of planning and evaluation to situations defined by risk, as discussed in Chapter 1, the muddle only deepens.

For our purpose of seizing the intellectual contours of the problem of collateral damage within the discipline of just war theory we do not need to examine this extensive and innately troubled literature. Some general observations on how just war theory distinguishes death and suffering on the battlefield and how it addresses the question of civilians in war will suffice.

Just war theory and the limits of legitimate violence

For as long as warfare has raised moral concerns, discussion about the principle of distinction has moved beyond the idea of a bounded enemy body, community or nation.[10] It has always been controversial to choose military targets merely according to the background of community attachment or territorial residency. Wars of total destruction occupy a painful chapter in the history of war. Yet even our earliest intellectual treatments of warfare, including the Old Testament, itself steeped in civilian blood, contain evidence that indiscriminate targeting of innocent persons was contentious. The idea of combatant and non-combatant, and of non-combatant immunity, is as old as warfare itself. Yet the criteria for drawing the line in the battle zone vary greatly among thinkers. The same applies to the criteria for when a combatant is a combatant, and the justness of killing non-aggressive innocent persons. Even if Augustine argued for a total war that included both civilians and combatants,[11] or did not care so much about who was killed because he believed in God's divine plan and took in any case more interest in the state of the souls of the killer and the killed and where they went,[12] his philosophy of war nevertheless implied an idea of separation. This separation made it possible, in the first instance, to discuss whether civilians were legitimate targets or not; whether the guilty and innocent dead (soldiers as well as civilians) enjoyed different standings before the Creator; and whether an armed attack or response could be out of proportion due to its impact on civilians and civilian infrastructure, or whether innocent people got killed as an unavoidable side effect of war without rendering the perpetrators guilty. Logically, if we want such a thing as just targets, then we need unjust targets to contradistinguish them.

What is more, traditionally the question of legitimate violence focused not so much on drawing the line between combatants and non-combatants, but more about how hard one may hit the legitimate targets. Similarly, the nineteenth-century conceptions of humanitarian law solely addressed violence towards combatants. As previously mentioned, proportionality measures in war did not really grow out of 'noble' ethical principles of restraint, even if this is today a dominant view. As an international law principle, their role in curbing violence to avert conflict escalation stands more important.[13]

The just war grid of violence

In just war theory, the discussion of the relationship between the principles of distinction and proportionality has been caught up in versions that tend to count 'whole bodies'. Insofar as the principle of proportionality (containing all the power and the problems of just war theory) historically also considers the treatment of the enemy soldier, it would be more correct to treat the principle of distinction as a more abstract separation that organises the entire war zone into go zones and no-go zones. No-go zones may include civilians and civilian infrastructure as well as issues like environment and cultural property in addition to enemy soldiers and military installations. Abstractly viewed, the principle of proportionality organises the body of the individual enemy combatants into a grid of distinctions mediated by the politics of necessity and proportionality. We see this 'division of the enemy body' in all kinds of norms addressing obligations toward enemy combatants: the outlawing of torture, the rights of prisoners of war, the rights of surrendering soldiers, and so on. Altogether, it seems that the principle of proportionality is oriented along two lines: excessive violence towards non-participants and excessive violence towards participants.

One may claim that this further integration of the principles of proportionality and distinction may layer confusion onto already fuzzy categories, yet we need to make this conceptual manoeuvre to capture the role of the problem of collateral damage in just war theory. Non-lethal harm inflicted on enemy soldiers may be counted as collateral damage—just as friendly fire usually gets counted as collateral damage. To readers familiar with just war theory this may sound rather redundant. It seems important, however, to free ourselves from the idea of a just war theory organised around notions of bounded nations and bounded identities of combatants and non-combatants. In reality the discussion always moves beyond such bounded agents. Collateral damage, makes up a highly abstract category, which cuts across bounded identities such as combatant and non-combatant, enemy soldier and friendly soldier. Unintended harm and death to enemy soldiers belong to the same category as unintended harm to civilians and friendly fire. Civilians and combatants inhabit the same moral system.[14] From the view of just war theory, the fields of war comprise one united moral world where civilians and soldiers are not separate moral categories. The more juridified (i.e. legally codified) the battle space becomes, the more clear we see the 'division' of the enemy body and how unintended but perhaps foreseen harm to enemy soldiers belongs to the category of collateral damage as bad, undesired, unintended effects.

Of course, complex proportionality and distinction problems also exist with regard to objects that have both military and civilian purposes—'hard' targets such as infrastructure and industry. The destabilising effects on international relations and environmental consequences of wars also present us with critical proportionality and distinction issues. As already mentioned, we have difficulties deciding on what qualifies as participation in war, and the principle of distinction also singles out places of worship and cultural inheritance as illegitimate military targets. However, all these side effects stir up the same moral problem as the five-year-old collateral damage victim, who merely embodies the problem's most dramatic expression in the form of death to innocent civilians.

Collateral damage: the very heart of just war theory

This broader category of collateral damage stands central to just war theory's discussions of *jus ad bellum* and *jus in bello*. This point arises now and then in the discussion of just war, yet a profound treatment of it seems not to exist. For instance, one of our most influential contemporary just war thinkers, the American philosopher Michael Walzer, writes in his major work *Just and Unjust Wars* (1977) that:

> [t]he war convention rests first and foremost on a certain view of combatants, which stipulates their battlefield equality. But *it rests more deeply* [my emphasis] on a certain view of noncombatants, which holds that they are women and men with rights and that they cannot be used for some military purpose, even if it is a legitimate purpose.[15]

Another important voice in contemporary just war theory, the American philosopher Robert L. Holmes, similarly notes regarding the killing of non-combatants and innocent persons that '[n]othing ... is more central to the moral assessment of war, and this issue is at the heart of the question whether the waging of war can be justified ....'[16] If this is true, the killing of innocent and non-responsible civilians can be said to be the underlying problem of any just war theory.

We can also view it like this: historically, violence directed towards killing the indisputable bad guys did not stir up much moral discussion.[17] Neither would indisputably wrong and clearly immoral use of violent force stirs up any discussion about morality. It could enflame anger and reprisals, but not really moral disputes. Discussions spring from disagreement. Intellectually, the use of violence looks morally uncomplicated in situations where, in the eyes of emperors, kings, priests, presidents or the democratic community, it appears proportionate or disproportionate without a shred of doubt. Clearly just or unjust violence calls for no discussion or morality as such. However, such ideal type situations of just war and justly conducted fighting are, as history has proved, hypothetical. People tend to disagree on these issues. Still, the chief issue of just war thinking has not been the clearly right or the clearly wrong, the clearly just or the clearly unjust. The primary problem has always been about fencing the threshold where just moves into unjust, where right moves into wrong. On one side we see an area of clearly just agency; on the other side we see clearly unjust agency. In the middle, abstractly viewed, we see this third category, the category of collateral damage, where the lines between just and unjust blurs. Structurally viewed, this category is a constant. Yet the range of what we accept as legitimate collateral damage—one or fifty thousand dead— is pushed back and forth by our restless sentiments regarding proportion and necessity. As the category open to negotiation between legitimate and illegitimate force, it is pushed back and forth by arguments about moral superiority in warfare.

In that way, the core concern of just war theory appears to be the innocent, the non-responsible, the civilian and not the soldier or the war fighting agencies. The focus of just war theory is not the antagonists or the military target, but rather the limits of this military core and what lies beyond it and the moral effects of bringing damage to this domain, better know to us by terms such as: 'non-participants', 'innocent', 'civilian', soldiers *hors de combat*. It is the innocent and not the guilty that just war theory is preoccupied with. It is the friend, not the foe; it is love, not hate. Accordingly, at the end of the day, it is not the cause or the means of war or who may be killed that are the prime concerns of just war theory, but collateral damage. Collateral damage constitutes the epicentre and driver for just war theory. In this sense, the otherwise mostly invisible collateral damage victim appears to be the discreet protagonist of just war theory.

Doctrine of double effect

Just war thinking was from the outset troubled by the imperfection of human agency, the frustration about the gap between promise and performance, and the experience of death and suffering that war was notorious for unloading on innocent people. To clarify the question of guilt arising from the harm warfare causes to the innocents,[18] the early just war theorists adopted the 'doctrine of double effect', a moral axiom developed by early Roman Catholic theologians reworking the ideas of Thomas Aquinas. The doctrine's central ideas are as follows. Firstly, that every act has more than one effect and side effects transpire as an inevitable part of human agency. Secondly, that a distinction can be drawn between intended outcome and unintended side effects, and that they can be viewed as two separate categories of moral consequences. Thirdly, that these two categories of consequences imply different forms of responsibility. Fourthly, that the unintended side effects entail no moral responsibility. A person may thus harm and kill innocent people as long as no evil is intended, and as long as the harm is not out of proportion with the projected good of the person's intentions. In this regard, foreseeability is permitted: it is inherent in the logic of the doctrine of double effect that side effects are inevitable and thus foreseeable. They will happen, it is in our nature, and therefore we need the doctrine in the first place.

The proponents of the doctrine composed their arguments on the basis of a range of examples brought into line by 'the distinction between what an agent foresees and what an agent intends'[19] and the belief that this distinction matters to moral evaluation of agency. Consequently, evaluation must ultimately depend on the assessment of inner motivation. Any intention of direct harm disqualifies consideration under the doctrine, and the harm created must not be a means to the good effect. But side effects, even foreseen, stand subordinate to primary goals and intentions. This is the doctrine's ultimate distinction.

In this manner the doctrine of double effect excused unintended excess from conferring guilt. As Professor of philosophy, Alison Macintyre, puts it, the doctrine of double effect 'declares the existence of a class of exceptions to a prohibition on causing harm without defining the criteria for membership in that class'.[20] How the doctrine can be applied and what kinds of criteria one should include has been a continuous problem for consequentialist thinkers, who believe right or wrong depends on the consequences of an act and that the more good consequences, the better the act. Applied to the context of war, the doctrine established our well known category of legitimate, unintended but perhaps foreseen 'bad' side effects of 'good' acts of war.[21] By importing the doctrine into the moral judgement of warfare, a distinction between directly intended and unintended or at least not directly intended damage was established as a key parameter for judging acts of war. Even if the idea of intention constitutes a key component of the laws of war as well as the broader field of criminal law, moral philosophy has developed no consensus over whether intention is morally relevant, or how it should be understood.[22]

Calculating grace and sin

The modern concept of accountability, based on a principal–agent model of governance,[23] finds its roots in this early medieval calculation of grace and sin, and was later elaborated by Jean-Jacques Rousseau and Max Weber among others. Historically and semantically, the concept of accountability is closely connected to 'accounting', in the literal sense of 'bookkeeping', an idea which can be traced back more than a thousand years.[24] For instance in France, at the beginning of the second millennium, the idea of accountability played a prominent role in monastic management. Record keeping and archiving techniques developed with the purpose of documenting the glory of monastery leadership. But the concept of accountability also developed as a powerful tool in the hands of medieval lords trying to erect a hierarchical societal order where power could be delegated but not shared.[25] The emergence of accountability represented a turn to administrative thought,[26] organised around a vision of a single sovereign authority—in these early cases, God. Some medieval historians consider monastery administration to be the birth of modern governance.[27] The concept of accountability involves the question of to whom or what authority the agents governing society are accountable. It was of utmost importance to keep track of the deeds and misdeeds in one's heavenly bank account, and to know how to account for different actions. In this regard, the idea of sin as debt stands as an old Judeo–Christian idea that receives plenty of attention in the Old as well as the New Testament.

It is from this perspective that the doctrine of double effect emerges as a response to the simple question: how do I account for the bad things I have done but that I had absolutely no intention whatsoever of doing? If I have only good intentions, and if I try really hard, do I still hold moral responsibility for the damage that unavoidably unfolds in my wake, in this never-ending cycle of Adamic glitches. I remain disaster-prone, but to what extent should I be accountable and to whom? These sorts of questions found an answer in the doctrine of double effect that can also be seen as representing a turn from the concept of virtue towards a focus on the link between the inner life of man and questions of worship and faith. Intention becomes the deciding component of moral action, and means of judging collateral damage, which by definition necessitates moral intentions.

Contingency rules

The doctrine of double effect contributed enormously to our perception of death and suffering on the fields of war. To this day, we frequently apply it in the debates on warfare, if not accepting the doctrine as a prevailing truth then at least habitually referring to it as a valid point of departure. Yet the doctrine of double effect has never established itself as anything near to a positive science. After some 1,000 years, it remains bogged down in unresolved philosophical questions about the theories of intention, agency and responsibility. Just as the categories of just war theory and the laws of war remain unwieldy, so too does the doctrine of double effect; it has never crystallised into an effective formula.

Whether inconsistent or not, whether legitimate or not, for our discussion of collateral damage it suffices to notice how the doctrine of double effect originally carved out a certain moral space in an interconnected providential universe where questions of sin and guilt were the predominant questions asked of human agency, and where the idea of sin as debt had its heyday. It was a world where humans accumulated sin as a debt to the creator through bad actions, or gained credit through virtuous activity. It was a divine providential economy where surplus in the treasury paid back manifold and accumulated sin could be repaired by God's grace if almsgiving and prayers were adequate. The doctrine of double effect simply removed unintended negative side effects from this economy and ascribed to them a status in their own right. It thereby divided violence in warfare into three sets: legitimate proportionate violence towards combatants; violence which is illegitimate because it brings needless suffering to combatants or non-combatants; and legitimate 'side effect' violence bringing suffering to non-combatants and to combatants—the scheme we today recognise in the laws of war as legal killings, illegal killings, and collateral damage.

The questions of time and duration appears relevant to this tripartite distinction in that suffering caused to non-combatants as well as combatants may happen immediately or may take the form of long-term poverty and disease stemming from destroyed infrastructure, food supply and economy, or nuclear fallout. Also, the 'negative' unintended but perhaps foreseeable side effects may happen before the intended 'good' outcome. The structure remains.

This short section obviously fails to fully reflect the rich literature on the doctrine of double effect. Nevertheless, the bare bones of the doctrine are straightforward and its function and effect on thinking about war and violence evident. For the purpose of understanding the problem and norm of collateral damage, it is useful to note how the doctrine of double effect played an important role in the carving out of the category of death and suffering that we today label collateral damage. The range of the category and its various philosophical and theological underpinnings are not so important. From the perspective of war and governance, we can look at the doctrine of double effect as the emergence of a new classification code that set apart a group of incidents on the battlefield. No matter how low the threshold for the side effects of violence is set—at one or at fifty thousand dead—the doctrine introduces a distinction that allows us to comprehend the killing of innocent people as something other than a criminal act of murder. It suggests that under certain conditions we can find acts of war that are both morally good and (experienced as) bad simultaneously. But if we move upstream, the problem that engendered the double doctrine appears to have been the problem we today associate with collateral damage, and the double doctrine's solution to the problem was to omit this class of incidents from accountability.

As we will see in the next section, not only were human actions subjected to double doctrine thinking; God was put under the decree as well.

Theodicy

Theodicy is the intellectual proof of God's almightiness. It is a theological discipline, *theo-logic*; a reasoning about God and his intentions. A central issue for theodicy is the problem of innocent suffering in a world ruled by a good and almighty God. According to available scripts, the problem of innocent suffering had already emerged as a theme in ancient Babylon, two thousand years before the Christian era.[28] Moreover, there is no reason to believe that people did not discuss it before that. Later, the authors of the Old Testament embodied the theme in the figure of Job[29] and thereby commenced the greatest trial of all time: that of the Judeo–Christian God for innocent human suffering. Why should Job suffer? Why should his family suffer? If God really is omnipresent, omniscient, omnibenevolent and omnipotent, what is then the source and meaning of human suffering? Why have faith in a God who leads us into pain? What is the meaning of suffering in a world ruled by grace? The basic problem of theodicy is the tension between narratives of suffering and anguish on the one hand, and narratives of a supreme divine power on the other. It is an intellectualisation of the experience of suffering vis-à-vis a certain faith-based worldview.

The Manichean response to the problem, formulated by the Persian prophet Mani, was to suggest the concept of 'evil' to ascribe meaning to suffering. According to the Manichean worldview, the world was ruled by two opposing forces: good and evil, light and dark. The New Testament employed this dualism in the figures of God and Satan—a dualism that collided with the Old Testament's image of the all-powerful, all-knowing and all-seeing Jewish God, famously problematised in the riddle attributed to Epicurus:

> God either wishes to take away evil, and is unable, or He is able, and unwilling; or He is neither willing nor able, or He is both willing and able. If He is willing and is unable, He is feeble, which is not in accordance with the character of God; if He is able and unwilling, He is envious [malicious], which is equally at variance with God; if He is neither willing nor able, He is both envious and feeble, and therefore not God; if He is both willing and able, which alone is suitable to God, from what source then are evils? or why does He not remove them?[30]

Whatever answer we choose, we see a God who is either imperfect or who is willingly imposing evil on humans. The paradox calls for an explanation of why God should be considered the almighty good authority if he is not; or why humans should sustain their love for and faith in him if he keeps harming them by intervention or indirectly through passive bystanding. All choices, hence, call for an explanation and justification for why and how God, in the face of evil that is not a radically opposing force but a part of God's Providence, may still be considered omnipresent, omniscient, omnibenevolent and omnipotent.

Augustine criticised early Christian and Manichean dualism. In the course of his inexhaustible work he created a vision of a world where every last action and grain of matter were subjected to God's foresight but where individuals had free will. He suggested a view of evil neither as God's will nor as any opposing force. Rather, he identified evil, the source of the experience of suffering, as the result of a fundamentally wicked error of man's free will—a wickedness that originally resulted from the wrong choice having been made in the Garden of Eden to eat the apple of the forbidden tree and the consequent Fall of Man and expulsion from Paradise. According to Augustine, transgressive will was a human condition and the source of sin. For him, good and bad men were all sinners, and 'sufferers are different even though the sufferings are the same trials [...] the tide of trouble will test, purify, and improve the good, but beat, crush, and wash away the wicked'.[31] Some thousand years later, Aquinas maintained the Augustinian view that evil was not a force in itself, not an entity like Satan or God's will, nor a sanction, but merely an unsystematic and non-purposeful lack of good, the privation of perfect being.

The clash between experiences of suffering and narratives of good almighty authority that is most famous today was sparked on the morning of 1 November 1755 when a cataclysmic earthquake shook Lisbon to pieces before a giant tidal wave swallowed what was left of the city. The inhabitants of Lisbon experienced death and destruction on a biblical scale, a shock that prompted widespread scepticism about the virtue of God. In the intellectual aftermath, the great enlightenment thinkers, including Voltaire, Rousseau and Kant, reopened the trial of God by revisiting the writings of Gottfried Wilhelm von Leibniz on the theodicy problem. His elaboration of the theodicy problem had addressed the resolution of the existence of anguish in a world that is ruled by an almighty and inherently good God.[32] Leibniz's theodicy was another theological and philosophical defence of a God who had already faced severe legitimacy problems amidst the hunger, plagues and wars of the middle ages.

For our enquiry into the problem of collateral damage it suffices to observe the structural organisation of the experiences and claims that have characterised theodicy thinking for the thousands of years it has acted as a defence of an image of good authority in the face of the experience of human suffering. While the concept of evil and the doctrine of double effect are essentially contested ideas, the basic structure or problem that these ideas respond to has a much more positive character. In a nutshell, theodicy may be viewed as a struggle to bridge the gap between promise and performance that has haunted the image of God—very similarly to the way it has, in modern times, haunted the state. To be sure, the structure of theodicy repeats itself in state leaders' quest for legitimacy at times when their blunders threaten to push them off the throne: 'I performed badly, but I am still the incarnation of good; I tell you, what you experience as bad is really not that bad. In the long run it will be good for you. Suffering is not what you think; it is not meaningless. It has meaning, and that meaning is good!' So we tell the bereaved families in Afghanistan. My first point here is that the concepts of evil and the collateral damage norm and rule correspond to each other. Not that collateral damage 'is' evil but that the concepts of evil came into being as an answer to the same problem as the norm and rule of collateral damage. My second point is that previous efforts to come to terms with perceived evil under a good God provide a clear analogue to the apologies of secular state leaders for their misdeeds. They both function as responses to a clash between narratives of good governance and narratives of suffering. Both concepts relate to the same puzzling tension between promise and performance. Every child killed by the international forces in Afghanistan amounts to a small Lisbon earthquake, setting off the need to defend good authority in face of perceived evil.

For this reason, it would be wrong to 'apply' the philosophical or theological notions of evil to describe collateral damage. Rather, collateral damage denotes the same class of incidents that more than two millennia ago created the case of evil. Similarly, the modern military concept of collateral damage is not a 'theodicy'. Our concept of collateral damage and theodicy thinking instead correspond to each other on the level of rhetoric; both are structures of argumentation that are preoccupied with resolving or tranquilising the same irresolvable problem. The solution in both cases has been to carve out a theological or political–legal category for suffering that allows it to happen without obstructing the glory of authority. It is not a question of impunity, which merely means to be unpunishable for otherwise punishable crimes. It is about a theological or political–legal accommodation of a category of seemingly bad and evil acts, now deemed permissible and as graceful, inherently blameless and incurring no responsibility or guilt.

Providence and collateral damage

We can in that way view God and the modern state as two images of centralised 'good' sovereign authority, which in the course of their governing must continuously account for human experiences of suffering. The idea of a division of will, intention and acting into agent and agency is observable in both the concept of a transcendent God who governs through immanent presence in the human world via the Holy Spirit and Jesus, who was put on earth as an interventionary force, and the concept of the state as a centred form of authority, governing through law-based delegated configurations of bureaucracy, courts, police, military, and other interfaces between the public administration and the governed spheres. We can organise a range of other conceptual pairs that are important to Judeo–Christian understandings of God as well as to the modern state, such as God–Providence, God–Trinity, State–Bureaucracy, Law–Order. The idea of God as governor is inherent in the biblical narratives, which habitually portray God as the father, the shepherd, the guide, the sovereign, the leader, the one who offers a promise of salvation: the 'one'.[33] Popular faith and trust in God resemble the political community's faith and trust in their political leaders and their government, or perhaps even more the faith in the state as an entity with no one beside or above: a 'one'. Whether faith in God or the state system is strong or weak, the implied ideas of a centred hierarchical order of authority are well comparable; both are manifestations of faith in a centralised form of governance.

In the Judeo–Christian, Western tradition, God and the constitutional state stand as the only legitimate ways of thinking and organising the larger political community and its governance. Similar to the way in which the political and legal sciences draw a distinction between government and the practice of governing, what the state is and what it does, we distinguish between the conceptions of God's nature and God's actions. This distinction ordains the theological debates on the nature of God as the creator and God as the intervener in worldly affairs: what God is, and what he does; and the difference between knowing God and knowing the actions of God. Our understandings of the modern constitutional state and God both build on this separation between ontology and virtue. The ideas of God's presence in the human world or the state's presence in national and international society have usually been seen as different from their ontological status. Or at least we view the relationship between being and doing as calling for separate theological and scientific examinations.

From an international law perspective, the concept of the state relies on concepts of agency in the form of active political systems. State identity derives from its virtue. Still, the international law definition of the state rests on ideas of what kind of virtue characterises a state. Political science sports a range of criteria for identifying 'the state', drawing not least on the theories of Max Weber, and the tradition of separating studies of public administration and theorisations of the concept of the state. Altogether, there is a strong tradition separating questions of state ontology and of state virtue when it comes to understanding state virtue as governance. The question of the nature of these two historical agents of governance—God and the state—and their attributes and qualities, including their utility for helping people make choices and judgements and transform these into action, is an ontological matter. Questions regarding the form of actions that put these choices and judgements into practice, be it in the shape of God acting though divine intervention, or be it the state's action through public administration, are a matter of governance.

If we accept the comparison of the narrative of God and his providence with that of the modern state and public administration, we can also compare the two principal aspects of these narratives, which are agent and agency. Similar to the idea of God's rule through foresight,[34] the modern liberal Western state employs the idea of an authoritative centre (agent) that enjoys more knowledge than the periphery, and therefore can govern by anticipating the future through laws and regulation (agency). Even the most minimalistic versions of liberal theory have this idea of centralised authority and foresight as the bottom line, in the form of an independent judiciary and a basic legal regime that anticipates future problems. Liberal law and regulations contain, at their heart, an idea of governance through foresight. Both versions of the notion of providence imply, or are shaped by, ideas of centralised, interventionist and anticipatory governance, built on wisdom greater than that which is found among common people; in other words a patriarchal rule with a cause and knowledge base exceeding common man. I am not suggesting that God is an agent similar to the state, but that God and the state are both identified as primary, centred forms of authority governing humans by intervening in their daily affairs in an anticipatory manner. Any further enquiry into agent and agency will throw us into an endless spiral of methodological questions.

We do not need to go there. In our exploration of collateral damage, we merely need to observe the prominence of this distinction in the history of ideas of governance; and, furthermore, how both narratives of God and narratives of the state imply notions of intentionality in the form of the will of God or *raison d'état*—foresight—as their attributes. The will of God and *raison d'état* both present us with fundamental constituencies, whether derived from divine power, the will of the state leader, a natural law notion of the state as a legitimate system in and of itself, or the idea that the state with its political leaders represents the democratic community. When good brings bad, when we face a situation where an ontologically viewed good authority imposes suffering on those innocents who believe or want to believe in the superior goodness of this authority, our gaze implies these divisions. And thus we circle back to the gap between promise and performance. The doctrine of double effect with the treatments of the theodicy problem and present-day apologetic political discourses both bridge the cleft between agent and agency. They reconcile the rift between perceived good and perceived bad.

The concepts of evil, theodicy and double doctrine thinking were originally invented as post-action evaluations of divine power as responses to 'why suffering.' Since God ruled as the ultimate planner, no logical need for calculating good and evil in advance of actions existed. Theology seeks to uncover the mystery of God's way, the logic of his intentions and terror, the logics of God's being and doing, his ontology and virtue. As man gradually replaced God on the throne and imagined themselves the chief officers of the larger, govern-the-world-mission, the category of innocent suffering that these intellectual mechanics tried to accommodate and tranquilise became a strategic component of pre-action planning of governance agency. Unintended suffering became something political leaders needed to take into account in advance, not to save themselves before God, but to guard their seats of power and legacy. The challenge of uncovering the mystery of God transformed into the challenge of prefiguring the tipping point where negative side effects would start undermining the legitimacy of secular rule. In this regard, utilitarianism became a foremost idea.

Utilitarianism and collateral damage

Utilitarianism profoundly shaped modern secular discussions about just war and the permissibility of killing civilians in war. The father of modern utilitarianism, Jeremy Bentham, invented utilitarian theory as a tool of practical governance reform in England. He famously opened his 1789 opus *Introduction to the Principles of Moral Legislation* with:

> Nature has placed mankind under the governance of two sovereign masters, pain and pleasure. It is for them alone to point out what we ought to do as well as to determine what we shall do. On the one hand, the standard of right and wrong, on the other the chain of causes and effects, are fastened to their throne.

Bentham was so weary of natural law theory and religious doctrines that he avoided any engagement with metaphysical questions. His thought was congruent with the popular contemporary belief in 'deism', which held that while the Judeo–Christian God certainly was the 'supreme being', the 'grand architect' and 'divine watchmaker', he was practically absent on planet earth. No divine authority, no intervention and certainly no revelation. God did his thing—the creation and the progamming—and then checked out. According to deist thought, humans held the task of governing the world in their own hands. Providence belonged to them and called for rational choice and sound judgement. Hence, Bentham did not really enter the debates on the presence or not of God. His resistance to metaphysics and theological questions led later scholars to proclaim him an icon of secularism. Most important, for our concerns about collateral damage, Bentham and his utilitarian followers' break with the tradition of pinning the narratives of governance on a centralised divine authority implied different accounts of time and responsibility in governance. In utilitarianism, accountability structures fed right back into the collective's measures of overall utility rather than relying on a final Day of Judgement. The time of governance shrank to the timespan that humans themselves were capable of overseeing; and the measure was a concrete 'greatest good for the greatest number of people', rather than an abstract divine authority.

Bentham wrote his treaties in the early days of the Industrial Revolution. John Stuart Mill and others carried the ideas further. Utilitarianism promoted and was promoted by the elevation of secular state authority, the ideas of progress, modernisation and industrialisation. The bore tide of production and state governance came roaring in, claiming victims as it advanced. It became ever more necessary for state authority to explain and account for the increasing amount of suffering produced by actors endorsed by the state. In this context, utilitarianism offered a convenient formula for calibrating, explaining, and legitimizing good and bad outcomes of the practice of governance. Since Bentham and Mill, utilitarian endeavours to come to terms with the problem of 'egg breaking' and 'the greater good' have filled libraries. Act and rule utilitarianism, hedonistic utilitarianism, deontological utilitarianism, ideal utilitarianism, pluralistic and monistic utilitarianism, Kantian utilitarianism, philosophical consequentialism; all have tried to construct an arithmetic science to measure the overall utility of acts. Utilitarianism became the modern secular state's foremost solution to the moral problem of the bad side effects of good governance. It thoroughly guided modernisation theories and liberalism, and influenced the structures of all kinds of state institutions from legal to economic, while modern warfare became particularly fixated on utilitarian thinking.

From the utilitarian perspective, inequality was fine as long as it was bound up with a notion of overall happiness maximisation. For utilitarianism, inequality exists as the lesser evil in an economy where hardship, suffering and death cannot but be unequally distributed among the population. The immediate relative wealth of the poor can certainly be improved but in the long run it might backfire on the overall utility, including that of the poor; utilitarians argue that it is a matter of balancing. In fact, the utilitarian delimitation problem is that of whether it is permissible to punish the innocent if it serves a greater good. Utilitarian thinkers do not completely agree on this question.

However, similar to the way just war theory, double effect thinking and theodicy never found rest, no utilitarian model has yet succeeded in providing a broadly accepted, coherent model for such measuring. Critiques within political science have called utilitarianism 'a false science' since it fails to offer any concrete, unambiguous, legislative principles.[35] The lack of a clear-cut doctrine has reduced its popularity today,[36] yet utilitarian reasoning still enjoys a strong standing, not least in the war discourse.

Utilitarianism and war

Thinking war without the utilitarian formula is not easy. Our general ideas of killing civilians fit splendidly into the utilitarian scheme, as a trade-off of lives for military utility, as a way of computing and balancing good against bad to find the golden mean. The scheme works well for speaking about the right balance between destruction and accomplished mission goals—between promises and probable harmful consequences of performance. In fact, some of our contemporary thinkers argue that only utilitarian thinking can justify war.[37] Yet a meticulous utilitarian would most likely find the typical use of utilitarian reasoning in war far too shallow. It is a dreadfully complex equation to measure up instant and long-term effects against some greater good. Too many unknowns obstruct the quantifying. A true utilitarian assessment would also need to consider all kinds of positive spin-offs, including how the military–industrial–entertainment complex drives scientific development, impacts on economies, and shapes community feelings. How are such matters to be weighed against immediate death and suffering and long-term negative effects on individuals, societies, the environment, our world? 'The complexity problem', as the philosophers of utilitarianism name it, would be a valid reason to discard utilitarianism as a yardstick for weighing collateral damage in war. We can, of course, as international humanitarian law in fact does, view each isolated incident and see if they, by themselves, fit a local utilitarian calculus. But such 'local' thinking fits awkwardly with utilitarianism, which thinks big. It gauges the larger overall utility balance; but as soon as the micro and macro levels are connected, utilitarianism mostly short circuits.

From a historical perspective, a curious thing about viewing the problem of collateral damage as a utilitarian dilemma of balancing good against bad would be to disregard a long philosophical and theological tradition for seeing good and bad as inseparable. The utilitarian separation, rationalisation and reification of good and bad contrasts with earlier ideas like the doctrine of double effect and theodicy. These ideas did not operate with the same distinction but instead saw the relationship between good and bad as much more intricate and undecided. A really interesting aspect of utilitarianism is thus its suggestion that good and bad can be separated, reified, computed, and measured up against one another.

Utilitarianism, the less affluent, and confusions about sacrifice

But are collateral damage victims not precisely a utilitarian sacrifice of some for the greater good of others? Let us examine this question of utilitarianism and sacrifice—this will also provide a lead-up to the discussion of sacrifice and collateral damage in the next chapter. I will pitch the discussion around French philosopher Paul Ricoeur's reading of American philosopher John Rawls' influential work *A Theory of Justice* (1971), which offered the first systematic critique of utilitarianism. Some two hundred years after Bentham's *Introduction to the Principles of Moral Legislation*, Rawls' key objection was that utilitarianism 'does not take seriously the distinction between persons,'[38] and therefore fails to respect the liberal principle of individual liberty and freedom. He worried about its 'willingness to take from one person and give to another, depending on who will derive the greater net benefit from the allocation.'[39] Rawls argued that this disadvantaging of some for the benefit of others would not enjoy broad acceptance, and therefore utilitarianism could not offer a legitimate principle of justice for ordering society.[40] According to Rawls, a society is only justly ordered when 'its major institutions are arranged so as to achieve the greatest net balance of satisfaction summed over all the individuals belonging to it.'[41] Hence Rawls' critique of utilitarianism is twofold: he indicts utilitarianism for an unethical underprivileging of some, and for engaging a logic that dissolves the integrity of personal autonomy; and he maintains that the prospect of a fundamental willingness to self-sacrifice is an unlikely engine for mutual consent.

In his book, *The Just*, the French philosopher Paul Ricoeur discusses Rawls' critique of utilitarianism, and concurs that '[i]n extrapolating from the individual to the social whole as utilitarianism does, the notion of sacrifice takes on considerable weight. It is no longer a private pleasure that is sacrificed, but a whole social layer.'[42] Ricoeur applies a notion of sacrifice that I will use here to shed light on what I consider a notorious mistake in the common habit of framing the collateral damage rule with a discourse of utilitarianism and sacrifice.

Ricoeur invokes the philosopher René Girard to explain how 'utilitarianism [...] tacitly implies a sacrificial principle that is equivalent to legitimating the strategy of the scapegoat.'[43] Girard builds his theory of the scapegoat on the Jewish Yom Kippur ritual of symbolically saddling a goat with all the sins of the Jewish people and then driving the loaded 'scapegoat' into the desert. The scapegoat carries away the sins, leaving behind a purified and atoned community. Girard views the scapegoat as an allegory of the psychosocial dynamics involved when social groups project their own insufficiency or frustrations on individuals or groups and blame them for all the iniquity, thus marshalling an identity-building bond among 'us' towards 'them', the scapegoat.[44] Girard's theory of scapegoating and sacrifice clearly remains a matter of great topicality to daily politics all over the world (including the current rise of rightwing anti-foreigner sentiments), but it seems not fully adequate to describe utilitarianism's distribution of pleasure and pain. The ritualised quality of the Old Testament scapegoat and its doppelgangers in current identity politics appear fundamentally different from the status of the less affluent in the utilitarian scheme. The scapegoat is sacred. It is bestowed with a spiritual value greater than its physical goat existence. People vest it with meaning and symbolic power, and that's what it is all about. That cannot really be said about the less affluent in utilitarianism. According to utilitarian theory, the less affluent offer no purification or atonement; such concepts are foreign to utilitarian theory. The less affluent entertain no societal myths apart from the practical calculus of striking the balance between pain and gain. Ricoeur furthermore writes that this sacrificial principle of utilitarianism must remain hidden and not public.[45] If we were to see that it allows the use of some for the benefit of others, it would ruin the equality principle of utilitarianism. Well, utilitarianism may of course be used apologetically. It may be used to excuse exploitation, suppression, and brute violence. Yet that has to do with power politics and not utilitarianism as a theory of evenhandedness. To criticise utilitarianism for having a 'hidden agenda' sounds a bit shrill compared to Rawls, who countered utilitarianism on utilitarianism's own terms. What is more, scapegoating presents us with theatrical public happenings: to say public happenings must remain hidden and not public does not make sense. The difficulties of a superior mind such as Ricoeur's in sorting out these aspects tells us something about the difficulty of coming to terms with the standing of the less affluent in utilitarianism and also, I would say, about how the word 'sacrifice' often confuses our semantic takes on various forms of cost-benefit analysis.

The value of the less affluent

We must reject the idea that the less affluent under utilitarian rule should constitute a form of sacrifice on a par with the scapegoat. Now, this does not make the question of sacrifice irrelevant to utilitarianism. But, instead of saying that utilitarianism endorses sacrifice, I will say that utilitarianism's utterly arithmetic dictum of 'the greatest good for the greatest number of people' cannot work in practice without a sacrificial system. By sacrificial system I do not mean the blood sacrifice of individuals, groups or classes. I mean a system for ascribing sacred value to self-sacrifices. Let's remember how utilitarianism does not see any particular value in self-sacrifice. As John Stuart Mill pointed out:

> The utilitarian morality does recognise that human beings can sacrifice their own greatest good for the good of others; it merely refuses to admit that the sacrifice is itself a good. It regards as wasted any sacrifice that doesn't increase, or tend to increase, the sum total of happiness. The only self-renunciation that it applauds is devotion to the happiness, or to some of the means of happiness, of others.[46]

If the principle of equality forms the underlying premise of utilitarian thinking, how can the principle of equality be married with practical inequality? Modern liberal society with its ideals of equality always had difficulties explaining why some people must endure more hardship than others, why some have to give up their freedom for the greater good, why some have to die. This divergence has mostly been solved in the most peculiar way: by adding extra value to different kinds of hardship. As a form of compensation the modern state project developed codes of honour for suffering and hardship, recognising hardship with words, honours and medals. A sweeping look at today's societal core values reveals that giving oneself up for others or society at large gets recognised and honoured as a sacrifice for the greater good. Soldiers, factory workers, farmers, teachers, lawyers, deputies, doctors, fathers, mothers—all of them go through hardship, it is said, to sustain the greater common good. The self-sacrifices of working men and women make society possible, we are told. This narrative of 'our everyday heroes' not only bestows grace on the hardship of the less affluent but also sustains the equality scheme by lifting up the lowest classes. I am not, like Ricoeur, trying to uncover veiled repressive ideologies. I am only pointing at how hardship in modern society has generally been measured against principles of equality, and how such values ascribed to self-sacrifice, rather than a hidden agenda for sacrificing others, seems to provide the prerequisite for the utilitarian machine by restoring a sense of equality. Utilitarian hardship and deaths must be given a value. They must be exposed, ritualised, honoured, and celebrated. Otherwise the utilitarian notion of 'fundamentally equal' standing breaks down. Only sacrificial 'added value' can remedy the rift between norm (all are equal) and necessity (some have to die).[47] Either we must think of utilitarian politics as containing sacrificial thinking in itself, or we must think of utilitarianism as being parasitic upon society's sacrificial systems; utilitarianism cannot stand alone. But it is the surplus value of the deliberate self-sacrifice that utilitarianism hooks on to—and not the Girardian sacrifice of others.

In that way utilitarianism presents us with yet another attempt to come to terms with the problem of innocent suffering: because innocent suffering essentially contains a question of inequality. Why should I and not they suffer? What is the meaning behind this seemingly arbitrary distribution of affluence? Yet the discreet union of utilitarianism and sacrificial thinking presupposes a sort of social contract, a consent to take part in this exchange. Hence, those who resist imposed inequality or those unaware of the exchange make up a residual group. Their questions of 'why suffering?' and 'why inequality?' find no answer apart from a taciturn paternalistic 'because'.

There you have the Rawlsian criticism of utilitarianism, which really founds its scepticism on the problem of collateral damage: no one wants to be someone else's collateral damage; this is a disadvantage that will not enjoy broad acceptance. There you also have the core of the colonial narrative: speaking truth about the worth of collateral damage for the greater good. But the language of power is a one-way argument. Power offers no solution to the puzzle that originally produced this constant one-way dialogue between sovereign power and the less affluent. Rather, the problem of collateral damage, the 'why suffering', came before utilitarianism, and its arithmetic language should be viewed as just another attempt to sort out suffering produced by good authority. If we had not had this problem, why theorise about utilitarianism in the first place?

Collateral damage as a norm and rule corresponds to utilitarian thinking by accommodating a place for innocent suffering within a good governance paradigm. It also resembles theodicy and double doctrine thinking: we could call it a 'family resemblance'. Yet, utilitarianism should not be regarded as a 'secular theodicy' and it would be wrong to consider the collateral damage rule a utilitarian doctrine. Rather, the collateral damage problem came first.

Summing up

If I am right in my speculations, the kind of incidents we today label collateral damage stand at the very heart of just war theory, the doctrine of double effect, theodicy, and utilitarianism, as the primary riddle these theories seek to resolve. In their quest for a sound answer to the problem, the theory builders carved out, in various ways and with more or less mutually borrowed and overlapping ideas, a moral–political–legal form for the category of suffering we today label collateral damage. They provide our times with the cognitive frame and semantics for appreciating and communicating about collateral damage as norm, rules and victims. Yet the problem of collateral damage involves a problem that historically existed before just war theory, the doctrine of double effect, theodicy, and utilitarianism. This problem constitutes a key reason for why we today have these theories. Its heritage cuts back to the core of the narrative of the Fall of Man, a narrative that stands next to these theories as another attempt to ascribe meaning to unintended bad side effects of good intentioned actions. From a scientific perspective however, just war theory, the doctrine of double effect, theodicy, and utilitarianism all represent ultimately failed efforts at solving this problem. Instead they have shelved and sedated the problem, tied it down by faith-based resolutions. After all, there is no apolitical way of 'breaking eggs to make an omelette' nor any positive manifestation of an 'inherent in the nature of war' to which to resort. There is nothing natural about the category we label collateral damage, except for the problem it seeks to resolve or gloss over. Just war theory, the doctrine of double effect, theodicy, and utilitarianism may offer convenient redemptions for our frustration, but they offer no solution.

In that way, collateral damage appears to be just a new word for a historical puzzle that not even the greatest thinkers in the world have succeeded in resolving. Collateral damage is merely our most recent tag for the category of incidents that authority constantly produces due to its lasting imperfection—a restorative claim that patches up the potential blows to legitimacy that a state authority may suffer as its governance activities generate destructive side effects, like when innocent people are harmed or killed in the course of 'good' military operations. The idea, concept, doctrine and international customary and treaty law of collateral damage simply accommodates 'the bad actions of good governance'. They claim an indivisible unity of destruction and salvation—a claim that has always belonged strictly to God or the state. The idea of collateral damage bestows a certain class of imposed death and suffering with an aura of moral grace. Yet the grace falls, and let me be very clear about that, not on the victims, but on the warmonger.

6

A DEATH WITHOUT SACRIFICE

Blood alone moves the wheels of history. (Martin Luther)

War is a bloody, killing business. You've got to spill their blood, or they will spill yours. (George S. Patton, Jr.)

One of the opening claims of this book was that collateral damage in war presents us with a death without sacrifice. To explain and qualify that claim and its implications for our investigations, this chapter contrasts dominant views on the role of sacrifice in human communities with the striking invisibility of collateral damage victims. I will argue collateral damage stands apart exactly due to its non-sacrificial quality. The victims enjoy no medals, limelight, tributes, memorials, songs, heroic narratives, recognition. They contract no surplus value, no glory. In the context of understanding the place and role of the collateral damage norm, rule and victims in the realm of war and governance, its non-sacrificial quality stands central. That aspect may further explain why collateral damage deaths appear unappealing and uninteresting, if not dull and worthless, to popular media and enjoy minimal representation in war culture. Rather, collateral damage deaths remain faceless numbers.

Sacrifice and war

War craves its sacrifices. War offers a place for making the ultimate sacrifice. War is an epic drama revealing and exposing citizens' heroic willingness to sacrifice their lives for their fellow citizens. War illuminates ultimate loyalty patterns, and draws up the social borders of the nation. War puts everything at stake. It reminds us of who we are as individual humans and as a community. These are all long-standing imaginaries of the tie between blood sacrifice in war, the nation and its people. As American journalist Chris Hedges writes in his best-selling book, *War is a Force that Gives US Meaning*:

'The enduring attraction of war is this: Even with its destruction and carnage it can give us what we long for in life. It can give us purpose, meaning, a reason for living. Only when we are in the midst of conflict does the shallowness and vapidness of much of our lives become apparent'.[1]

A renowned contemporary theologian, Stanley Hauerwas, echoes this by writing:

American civil religion (our assumption that we are a 'religious nation') relates to the fact that war for most Americans is unproblematic. War is a moral necessity for America because it provides the experience of the 'unum' that makes the 'pluribus' possible. War is America's central liturgical act necessary to renew our sense that we are a nation unlike other nations.[2]

Shedding others' blood supposedly generates a sentiment of collectivity by drawing up the external borders of community. Likewise, American history Professor John Tirman frames and explains the fate of civilians in America's many wars with what he refers to as the frontier ideology. He argues that the 'taming of the wilderness and the regeneration of the nation through savage wars' in the imagined borderland have made up a fundamental archetype in American history.[3] In this sense, violence in war apparently functions as a type of generative violence, producing and sustaining the sense of national unity. It has been argued that international humanitarian law, by permitting certain forms of violence, in fact endorses 'a form of sacrificial violence that seeks to promote the preservation and cohesion of the international community'.[4] I am not saying these accounts are true or not, but they do represent dominant views about violence in war.

The question is whether the kind of spillover violence that generates this form of death we label collateral damage belongs to this imagined (or not) sphere of generative 'sacrificial violence'? Should collateral damage deaths be viewed on a par with other forms of sacrifice in war, like the soldier's self-sacrifice, or the mother's sacrifice of her sons in war? How do ideas of sacrifice structure the meaning of death on the field of honour, and how does the collateral damage victim fit into these accounts?

Sacrifice and the modern state

In the Western world, during the Middle Ages, sprinkling the blood of beheaded animals on the altar or on each other gradually went out of fashion, and turned into a feature of 'occult' sects and 'backward' barbarian cultures. The 'civilised world' that emerged from the Enlightenment viewed the practice of sacrifice as an irrational behaviour, and it later became a topic of anthropological enquiry. More recently, the question of sacrifice has resurfaced as an entry point for studying the religious undercurrents of modern secular culture.[5] Scholars search for the quasi-religious structures of our everyday political life, and point at how we act in a less secular way than we believe. 'American patriotism is a civil religion organized around a sacred flag', sounds one diagnosis,[6] furnished with Dwight Eisenhower's account of his induction into West Point:

> 'Toward evening we assembled outdoors and, with the American flag floating majestically above us, were sworn in as cadets of the United States Military Academy. It was an impressive ceremony. As I looked up at our national colors and swore my allegiance, I realized humbly that now I belonged to the flag. It is a moment I have never forgotten.'[7]

American law Professor Paul W. Kahn, presents a similar analysis, which he evolves from the idea that '[p]olitical power is present when individuals recognize in themselves the capacity for sacrifice for the state. In the act of sacrifice, polity and citizen, objective power and subjective faith are one and the same.'[8] To be sure, the modern state with its professional, volunteering, non-conscript army does not claim the lives of its citizens. The state does not command sacrifice. It expects its citizens' willingness to self-sacrifice for the nation, as a brave and gracious act of free will. It is a demand, not an order or law. Modern states do not sacrifice their citizens; but citizens sacrifice for their nation. The nation becomes visible through the rituals exposing and amplifying the self-sacrifice of the soldiers.[9] They display belonging, loyalty and love. In that way, the readiness of the citizen to self-sacrifice in the name of the nation constitutes a fundamental glue of the nation state. Multicultural societies accentuate the willingness to sacrifice as an ultimate proof—and problem—of belonging as, for instance, when citizens of foreign descent travel to their country of origin to join fighting against the troops of their new state.

If this bond between sacrifice and belonging deserves primary standing in our understanding of violence in war, it challenges the idea of generative violence as a symbolic killing of others. The primary question is then not who may or should be killed. It is rather: who do you want to risk your own life for, who do you care for, who do you want to show love for? There is an intuitive truth to this account. Enmity and hate clearly come second to friendships and love as a driver for political life.[10] Political groupings and enemy configurations have always primarily built on loyalty. It is not the blood sacrifice of the scapegoat that forms the core of modern political community, but love and loyalty. It is not otherness but selfness. In this sense war and enmity offer an egocentric stage for enacting the medium of sacrifice, a medium for communicating and demonstrating love, loyalty and community.

Sacrifice as the glue of political community

If we want to understand the role of sacrifice in war, and what it means to our analysis of collateral damage deaths, we should turn our attention towards the community rituals surrounding sacrifice. The vast, mostly anthropological, literature on sacrifice finds sacrificial traditions in all cultures throughout history.[11] Some classic anthropologists go so far as to view sacrificial practices as fundamental to human socialisation, as a deep and almost primordial human proclivity placed 'at the very root of true religion',[12] where 'religion as the foundation of a rational sociability, and sacrifice as the foundation of religion for all times and all places'.[13] Others have argued that sacrifice is more local, that is, not an original phenomenon but a product of civilisational processes, or at least a 'domestication' of some more general human inclinations.[14] Whichever is the case, for our present purposes we need look no further than the manifestation of sacrifice in human society for ideas about what it can mean to humans and their shared lives.

Intensive scholarly attention has not led to a general theory of sacrifice.[15] Yet some theories dominate the literature. Overall, sacrifice is thought of as an individual or collective response to a sense of loss,[16] which calls for 'restoration' through some form of generative activity. Such function may be said to be valid for both sacrifices *of* (others) and (self-) sacrifice *for*—the two general modes of sacrifice (in war manifested in soldiers' self-sacrifice and the parents sacrifice of their children who go to war). This experience of a loss calling for closure is mostly theorised as a distance between two modes of existence, like the sacred and the profane (Marcel Mauss),[17] the body and the soul (Claude Levi-Strauss),[18] or the individual and the collective (Emile Durkheim, René Girard);[19] the sacrifice makes it possible to communicate across these gaps and thus repair the sense of loss.

In the Judeo–Christian context, Cain and Abel's sacrifices *of* their sheep and their fruit, the first biblical account of sacrifice, is often used as an example here.[20] So too are Abraham's intended sacrifice *of* Isaac,[21] and Jesus himself, who self-sacrificed *for* humankind. Sacrifice as a way of atoning for the original sin, a communication across the gap between man and God, makes a critical topic in Judeo–Christian theology.[22] In one scholar's opinion:

> The Christian language of sacrifice only makes sense within a context of the Fall and Salvation. It is only intelligible if we recognize contingency and 'fallenness' of the world, its nature as a divine gift, and the joy and the suffering it entails; and love as the form in which we accept sacrifice and suffering as 'making sacred'—a redemptive path.[23]

The sacrifice's tangible manifestations—like rituals, remedies, or sacrificial objects—are generally not viewed as the most important aspect of sacrificial cultures. What matters more is how sacrificial practices preserve the idea of divided spheres, and the capability of communicating across the gap or even remedying the rift. This idea of 'restoration' as a cross-spherical communication, which at the same time reinforces the idea of a difference between the particular and the universal, lies beneath the idea of generative violence: like the particular 'lone' individual versus the universal community of the nation; or the short and brutish profane human life versus eternal divine providence. The different theories about sacrifice leave us with the observation that the restorative, cross-spherical communication referred to as sacrifice features a ritualized character and, furthermore, that the augmented value ascribed to sacrifice through ritual and remedies composes the crucial element of sacrificial practice.

In the context of war, we see how the lack of augmented value for or rituals of collateral damage deaths makes a stark contrast to the value-loaded, heroic, ritualised death of combatants. By rituals, I think of the practices of honours and salutes, the flags, the hymns, the social institution of self-sacrifice, the tradition of taking trophies from dead combatants; the death cultures of military organisations, the individual and collective preparations for death and loss of soldiers, the memorials, the veterans' days, and so on. The ritualised pre-death preparations and post-death social–psychological handling of the soldier's self-sacrifice take place on all levels: from the highest level of the nation and the military organisation down to the spouses, mothers, fathers, children, relatives, and friends. In many ways, war is ritualised killing. It is about taking and giving life, for the sake of conquering or defending particular visions of the good life.

The cuisine of death

According to one dominant account, the many ritualised activities involved in preparing sacrifices form the key aspect of sacrifice while the sacrifice alone holds minor value to the understanding of sacrifice.[24] As one scholar notices, the actual killing 'is often *not* a definitive or culminating activity within sacrifice.'[25] The broader scope of sacrificial procedures comes out more important than the climax of the sacrificial act itself. The custom of substituting the sacrifice—'if we have no ox we find a cucumber and call it the ox'[26]—pays evidence to this idea of the empty sacrifice. From that perspective, the rituals constructing the sacrifice become the heart of the matter. And from a community perspective, what matters most appears to be the nurturing of the imaginaries that in the first place suggest it makes sense at all to toy with sacrifice. Rituals form a collective medium of social codes and practices organized around and culminating in the performance of the sacrifice. Sacrificial rituals and practices may be viewed as merely a medium, an empty form for communication.[27] And congruent with how communities view themselves as bounded, the medium of sacrifice also takes an exclusive form. Those outsiders who find sacrificial practices obscure (like this ridiculous notion of calling the cucumber an ox when it obviously is not an ox but a flaccid cucumber) fail to see how sacrifice also functions to establish exclusivity. By stating that you 'don't get it', these crazy people do ridiculously strange things like celebrating flaccid cucumbers they call 'the ox'', you actually do get it because you are not supposed to get it. You get the message, which is that you should not get it—and this makes you an outsider.

As an age-old community-sustaining practice that works through rituals, the sacrifice conveys a message of exclusiveness by appearing obscure to outsiders. The other way around, the sacrificial community draws up its borders through each individual's understanding of the medium as ritualised procedure. 'The medium is the message', as the famous communication theorist Marshall McLuhan[28] once put it, a dictum that in our context of the sacrifice surprisingly may offer a key to understanding cultures of sacrifice: the sacrifice in itself seems unimportant. It is all the activities that produce and bring forward the 'final' sacrifice that matter. The message of the medium is 'there may be sacrifice', or rather: 'there is community'. We do. We are. And this community is bounded by and limited to those who understand and accept the rituals. The message of the medium of self-sacrificing soldiering with all its spangled rituals is: there is a nation, and the nation is bounded. The absconder gets punished mainly for disloyalty towards the cult of sacrifice and less for not obeying rules. The real crime committed by the absconder is about revealing a secret, threatening option: you don't have to sacrifice yourself. You don't have to put yourself at stake. If you would rather not go to war you can choose to stay at home. There is a choice. That's the real crime of the absconder, I would say, to point to this possibility, to the fragility of the social bonds.

There is nation! Or perhaps not?

Today, the media from the news to Hollywood[29] provides an endless stream of narratives and images of ritualised military performance of self-sacrifice as the sublime moment of nationhood: there is nation![30] At the same time members of the services, veterans and bereaved families experience a lack of recognition from those the sacrifice was made for.[31] This is a paradox in cultures flooded with images of war heroes. Perhaps the truth is that we long for rituals and sacred images to weave together our (existentially viewed) isolated and unattached lives, but that the sorrow and pain of disabled veterans and devastated families offer little fuel for this ride. The calls of veterans and their relatives for recognition indicate how the actual sacrifice stands less prominent than the surrounding rituals. The heroic self-sacrifice of soldiers may perhaps mean less than we pretend. Nevertheless, as a myth and source of rituals, the self-sacrifice stands immensely powerful. We crave the myth and the drama but sheer away from pain and its burden. Fallen soldiers, disabilities and posttraumatic stress do not yoke individuals to any nation state, but the rituals of soldiering may, although this is not a natural given. Nowadays, conflicts are convoluted and the causes we fight for are vague. Humanitarian and drawnout counterinsurgency operations under foreign skies make it difficult to convince soldiers and their relatives that they die an honourable death for their home country. War support is declining.[32] The blood link between the citizens' love and loyalty to their nation and the soldier's voluntary self-sacrifice on the battlefield crumbles; obscure and absurd (though not often admittedly so) policies have removed the clear-cut causes so essential to fighting, violence and sacrifice. The confused geography of violence makes it difficult to demonstrate love and belonging. The fundamental values and goals that made sacrifice in war meaningful have disintegrated. Soldiers and relatives are more than ever left alone to judge whether their sacrifices are real, whether they make a difference, or whether they are hollow, meaningless deaths, communicating only a fading notion of 'there is nation'.

Collateral damage as non-sacrifice

When we consider our three categories of death and suffering on the battle-field—the self-sacrifice of soldiers, war crimes, and collateral damage—we see how the sacrifice in military culture appears strongly ritualised. Killing enemy soldiers involves a similar economy as own casualties, since enemy soldiers, according to the dominant narrative of warfare, also perform self-sacrifice. The reciprocity of self-sacrifice on both sides finds its corresponding codes in the laws of war, which permit the killing of enemy soldiers. Killing of combatants and killing as a war crime are well captured by powerful political–legal narra-tives of moral and immoral agency. We may even say that just war theory and the laws of war govern who may be sacrificed in war and who may sacrifice. We see that killings sanctioned by the laws of war are usually honoured as sacrifice. Apart from collateral damage.

And there is much to say about ritualised sacrifice in war and how it mirrors fundamental sacrificial structures of the religious sacrifice. There is much to say about war crimes and the rituals of the political–moral–legal machinery erected around war crimes. There is so much to say about these two forms of death on the battlefield, such a rich empirical body of material to dig into. So many films, books, narratives, so many laws and court decisions. So many opinions and so much recorded experience. So many medals and flags. So many emotions. So much public culture. My point is that the conceptual architecture of the heroic sacrifice simultaneously encases collateral damage: the more we explore the role of sacrifice in war, the more clearly we see how collateral damage deaths involve no sacrifice. They show no staged *self*-sacrifice and no sacrifice *for* anyone or *for* any value. Collateral damage victims have not, obviously, sought their destiny; they have not thrown themselves in front of bombs. Then they would not count as collateral damage deaths but as pur-poseful self-sacrifice or suicide. Rather, collateral damage comes with no honour, no ritualised value recognition. It stands apart as a category of lawful killings in war that falls outside sacrificial narratives. Collateral damage stands apart exactly by its non-sacrificial character, both in the sense of sacrificing *of* and *for*.[33] It finds no place in national sacrificial systems. No rites or proce-dures go before or follow after collateral damage. Collateral damage deaths carry no display-worthy information about good, evil, love, crime, loyalty or nation. They offer no medium in the way that soldiers' self-sacrifices offer a medium for conveying the message 'there is nation'. They are not inscribed in any symbolic exchange similar to war crimes (carrying all the heavy symbolic value of crimes and justice and legal systems) or the killing of soldiers. No surplus value. No sense of sacredness.

Hence our third category of dying in war, collateral damage, makes a stark contrast to the ritualised deaths of soldiers and victims of war crimes. Their non-sacrificial and non-criminal character adds a distinct quality to the kind of death we refer to as collateral damage. This aspect may explain further why collateral damage deaths appear uninteresting for the war narrative. They are dull deaths. Really, the only response to collateral damage is 'sorry' and 'I may': I am sorry for your loss because I am also a human and death is dreadful whatever may have caused it, so I recognise your sorrow. But I may. I may kill and harm you. I am permitted to inflict this horror on you because I come with this particular grace. I benefit from the laws of war, and thousands of years of the history of ideas are backing up the permission I come with.

The significant insignificant

It looks as if collateral damage deaths stand for nothing but imperfections, glitches and imprecisions, misunderstandings and errors that unfortunately vaporise humans. Yet, as demonstrated in the previous chapter, collateral damage deaths occur in a political–legal space tranquilised by powerful ideas, such as the doctrine of double effect, theodicy, just war theory and utilitarianism. These schools of thought carve out a space for legitimate bad action stemming from good governance; the bombed-out school in Kandahar finds its political–legal category alongside that of the traffic victim and of the percentage of patients who die from the unintended yet foreseen negative consequences of medical treatment. Collateral damage stands for a permissible category of death and injury in the larger field of public governance. As soon as we establish the connection between this original problem of the doctrine of double effect, theodicy, just war theory, utilitarianism and collateral damage, the insignificant symbolic value of the collateral damage victims themselves appears quite peculiar: the most significant form of death in the history of moral philosophy and theology remains mostly invisible. Every time the US military, or any other military, turns down a compensation claim with reference to 'combat death', the rejection letter carries with it this pattern of intense intellectual drama and symbolic indifference.

117

7

COLLATERAL DAMAGE OR ACCIDENT?

In war reporting, from Kosovo to Afghanistan, Iraq, Libya and Gaza, civilian casualties have increasingly been labelled accidents: accidental bombings, accidental casualties, accidental killing of civilians, accidental harm to civilians. The notions of 'collateral damage' and 'accidents' are used interchangeably and randomly. As a reply to the question of why civilian casualties have occured, both notions are invoked to make sense of violent incidents. They sort things out. Critics claim that the rhetorical shift to 'accidents' should be viewed as a political strategy to avoid responsibility by blaming technology malfunctions and coincidences as opposed to state authority and human decisions. Others consider it a minor semantic shift. To be sure, 'collateral damage' and 'accidental killings' both denote imperfect incidents, yet the concepts imply very different virtues. This chapter aims at illuminating this aspect, thereby qualifying a further distinction for understanding the problem of collateral damage and its answers. We will see how the concept of the accident comes out of an Aristotelian tradition originally preoccupied with questions of causality and the fundamental order of things. In contrast, the category of death and suffering we today label collateral damage originates in Judeo–Christian intellectual wrestling with questions of guilt and responsibility. It comes with a profound tie to the moral domain of sovereign authority and governance. When we view the two concepts from this angle an opposition between pluralism and unity also comes into focus: Aristotelian accidents bear an aura of pluralism, since the accidental connotes singularity, non-repetitive, exceptional, infinite unboundedness. In contrast, collateral damage deaths come bestowed with a discreet

119

aura of unity, by their pointing to a vision of centralised authority, common causes and bounded forms of moral or divine order. And, not least, the idea of collateral damage is a product of the problem of explaining pain and suffering. For Aristotle, accidents embodied glimpses of beauty and perpetuity.

No-fault accidents are today looked upon as isolated incidents, void of organised causation and intention. Blame and guilt, therefore, do not apply here. If the same legal person keeps repeating the same accidental harm, its accidental quality usually ceases due to the seeming lack of will to adjust behaviour. This moves the case into the category of criminal negligence and moral responsibility. However, in the same way that we disremember the semantic heritage of collateral damage, the accident has also been secularised and detached from larger visions of world order. The accident today stands for nothing but imperfection, perhaps with a dash of foolishness. I do not see any problems with that. I am not suggesting any 're-enchantment' of the accident. My aim is solely to elucidate the substantial historical difference between incidents we refer to as accidents and those we call collateral damage, and thereby expound further our contemporary idea of the collateral damage norm, rule and death. By so doing, I will gradually shift attention away from the category of collateral damage as a generative puzzle of our history of ideas toward the 'moral grace' that the claim to collateral damage asserts, and its connection to visions of sovereign authority in governance.

The accident

The accident is the glitch of everyday life. It is the mid-air plane collision, or the building that collapses due to truly unexpected metal fatigue. It is the impossible rat that sneaks into a power plant and chews at the wrong cable causing a short circuit that shuts down cities. It is the *Titanic*, which due to a number of independent causalities and miscalculations ended up being the foremost accident of the twentieth century; it is the spaceship *Challenger*, which exploded due to unpredicted malfunction in a small piece of rubber insulation. As the postmodern accident thinker par excellence, the French philosopher Paul Virilio, noticed, the accident resides as a potentiality in all kinds of constructions—from the cup spilling hot water to the spacecraft. Virilio's point is that the invention of the car simultaneously invented the car crash; the invention of the train, the train crash; the invention of gene technology, the mutated crop that runs amok; and so on. Also nature has its 'built-in' accidents, from forest fires to hurricanes that build up under certain weather conditions. Virilio talks about the original accident as an inherent part of any design, be it human or an outcome of nature's evolution. It could be tempting here to see collateral damage as a product of the invention of warfare but that would be a mistake. The mere isolated accidental killings of civilians may fit into this scheme as war's 'built-in' accidents but the collateral damage problem stands both primary and pervasive as the frame through which we appreciate certain accidental killings of civilians.

Now, Virilio is interested in politics, and in particular the imagined possible accident. And the potential accident does not really become an accident to Virilio until it enters the social as something that individuals and society relate to: 'The accident is invented at the moment the object is scientifically discovered or technically developed',[1] To Virilio, 'accident' is something we attribute to things or the world we live in. We see a perceived risk that may never happen, such as how, now we have detected that the earth floats in space, we watch out for giant meteors that could collide head-on with us. There is today a whole science, safety science, occupied with how to extrapolate human behaviour, constructions and machines so as to minimize the risk and cost of accidents, including how to fend off meteors.[2] But we are stuck with the risk of accidents. Any extrapolation only alters possible accidents or invents new forms of accidents; and the study of possible accidents discovers new potential accidents, like the medical research on vaccination that produces the risk of developing new pandemic viruses or collateral damage-reducing weapons bringing new forms of hazard to the battlefield.

From essence to miracles

Philosophy in our current age habitually remodels classical philosophical puzzles, and Aristotle often appears as the original puzzle creator. This is true for the accident, a critical concept in Aristotle's philosophy.[3] Aristotle used the term 'accident' to distinguish the inessential quality of things from their substantial essence: like the distinction between, say, the essence of 'apple' from the infinite number of actual appearances of this particular fruit. On a molecular or atomic level, there have never, ever been two identical apples: each apple presents us with a unique and, according to Aristotle, accidental constellation. However, Aristotle also used the term to refer to unexpected events without clear causality. His double understanding of the accident points at an intriguing link between accident and essence in the beginning of the concept of the accident. That is, between accident and world order.

Famously, Aristotle announced, 'there can be no philosophical speculation [with regard to accidents]. No science, be it theoretical, practical or constructive, investigates accidents. He who constructs a house does not construct all the accidents or concomitants of the house; for these are endless and indeterminate'.[4] For Aristotle, the source of all creation and mutation of life and thought was accidental, yet the accident, the unusual and unexpected, occupied a secondary quality compared with his notion of a permanent essence of things. The accidents of a house cannot be known in full because one cannot know every aspect of the house: one cannot know infinity, the Platonic plane of reality. A science of the accident would therefore imply an ambition to triumph over infinity, something Aristotle deemed unachievable and meaningless.

Aristotle found food for thought about accidents in the Greek tragedies, in particular the work of Sophocles, who cultivated fear and awe of accidents. Consider how the story of Oedipus Rex enacts the theme of accidents and guilt as Oedipus kills his father and marries his mother not as collateral damage but through tragic accidental mistakes.

Aristotle's philosophy of the accident became a discussion point in Christian theology, started by Augustine and advanced further by Aquinas. Deeply informed by the Augustinian idea of a providential cosmos where every last hair or flower is subjected to the divine foresight of God, the unexpected and unforeseen incident was here thought of as God's intervention. (Human carelessness and clumsiness were different, and deserved punishment.) On the one hand, medieval Christian theology collapsed essence and accident by subjecting everything to God's foresight, a gaze that transcended place and time so that everything, at all times, was instantly visible to God's eye. On the other hand, accidents were granted status as an exceptional set of incidents believed to be proofs of God's direct intervention. They were viewed as heavenly signs, wonders, that could be collected and deciphered. The accidental event 'was subsumed into evidence of providential design'.[5] What, for the Greeks, had been a fundamental unpredictability of essence escaping any rationalization now became subject to meticulous and creative inspection and speculation. Religious authorities recorded, systematized, and scrutinized accidents to substantiate the presence of the creator. In the monasteries and convents, the concept and practice of bookkeeping (that was later to develop into the modern state archives) was invented in part as a means of keeping track of those signs that manifested in cloister life. Overall, the medieval masters of the church swung the essence of the Holy Spirit from the thurible of their administration across the uncertainties of earthly life—the accident became the miracle. The quest for essence or for miraculous manifestations of divine presence was a search for a fundamental order of things. It was about world order—and not about attributing and resolving experiences of suffering and pain by placing blame, guilt and responsibility. This sits in contrast to the collateral damage problem, which sprang from such questions of responsibility; it rose from the experience of suffering and an anxious 'why?' and 'who has responsibility for our agony?' The puzzle of the nature of the accident sprang from a curious 'how?' and not from a miserable 'why?'

The bond between substance and accident, between divine order and miracles, remained an intellectual controversy throughout the Reformation and the Enlightenment, from Montaigne and Pascal to Descartes and Spinoza. What Aristotle, Christian theology and the later Reformist and Enlightenment thinkers all desired was to make sense of the coincidence. They struggled to understand the meaning of non-causality in the light of ideas of cosmic order. Aristotelian substance theory and the medieval theologians were a bit more ambitious than the Reformist and Enlightenment thinkers by ascribing a central place to the accident in comprehensive, all-inclusive, models of the universe. The Reformist and Enlightenment thinkers' deistic rejection of any direct divine intervention in the human world expelled the miracle and stripped away the very possibility of bestowing accidents with divine grace. The object of deistic science was to read accidents not as hidden divine messages but as expressions of an original divine plan. By observing nature and its processes we could hope to get a glimpse of the deific design of our creator. Romantic art was very much about capturing the sublime moment of nature where it all 'comes together' and cracks opens up through which we may catch a glimpse of the underlying divine beauty of the world.

The accident and contingency

Accidents continued to present a metaphysical problem to more modern philosophers, now as a problem of contingency, i.e. the speculation about the lack of any true causality and the fact that everything could have turned out differently. Their meaning was now detached from ideas of governance and authority; in the absence of a grand design accidents were treated philosophically as dispersions in the regularity of historical progress, as manifestations of the impossibility of repetition, and thus as a kind of imperfection in nature which, through such mishaps and evolutionary processes produced an identity between now and then. In this version of the philosophy of the accident, accidents became the 'real' norm, the slight dispersions inherent to any social and biological development, which continually creates a difference in identity between now and then. Postmodern philosophy traded in the great divine watchmaker and the Aristotelian idea of essence for a realism of abyssal 'radical' contingency. Now the accident took on an almost reverse role to what it held in the Aristotelian plane of essence, as it became celebrated as a manifestation or proof of the complete lack of any metaphysical content in the world: the essence of the world was fragmentation and dispersion. The accident was now the sign of the lack of any all-including sign.

The romantic (in search of God in nature) and metaphysical accounts of micro-change are different from the philosophy of Virilio, who writes about the politics of accident and risk. Virilio, in fact, opposes Aristotle's dictum that there is no science of the accident. But Virilio also diverges from Aristotle in that Virilio is primarily interested in the social. He does not, as Aristotle does, aspire for a larger philosophy of the order of the universe. Aristotle's science is about the essence of the world; Virilio's is about politics. Like many of his contemporaries who discard former unifying theories of the world as gibberish born out of longing, Virilio also loses sight of the accident's providential heirloom, its theological or world order-explaining legacy. What was for Aristotle a problem of world order, cosmos and the place of the gods and the individual in eternity, what for medieval theology was a sign of the creator, became to Virilio a question of the irony of politics in a time of contingency.

Accidents and technology

Another significant part of the history of the profaning and delinking of the accident from grand moral schemes follows the history of technology.[6] Concurrently with the growth of modern metaphysics and industrialisation, the age of mechanics had begun. The accident developed into a risk associated with exploding steam engine boilers, buildings that collapsed, ship collisions, train wrecks, car crashes, and so on. At the same time, in the early days of mechanisation, the many and sometimes large-scale accidents that came with new technology stirred up intense discussions.[7] People feared being on the next exploding steamboat or derailing train. At this time in history people were not used to machines, which were seen as mechanical monsters. Accidents were a subject of intense discussion, rumours and media coverage. A 'mass audience for accidents' was created,[8] and accidents grew into a collective experience, since everyone was potentially in the risk zone. A latency of risk was born that implied the paranoid *unheimlich* feeling of our immediate surroundings, our homes, turning against us.

The more complex society grew, the more dependent society became on all sorts of mechanical installations and the more prominent became the issue of the accident, the strategies employed to avert it and its financial consequences. It became important to identify causalities and regularities that could explain the emergence of unexpected events. The name of this science was statistics and its aim was to create human foresight of possible future events. But the more complex the societal functions became, the more difficult it became to predict accidents and to establish accountability *post factum*. The age of mechanics and industrialisation produced a societal reality where the sources of accidents involved many different and independent actors. The accident paradigm for the modern hyper-complex society was soon in place. We had cities cramming together hundreds of thousands, even millions of individuals with no direct social obligations toward each other, or which at best were very vague. We had an accelerated movement of things and persons making various forms of direct and indirect collisions more likely. And we, the humans, grew into cyborgs whose bodies were increasingly entwined with and dependent on all kinds of accident-bearing technology. With numerous direct and indirect factors involved, it became impossible to decide the roots of many accidents. High-tech society's intensification of this simultaneous concentration and dislocation of agency exploded the multiple actor problem of early accident law into something almost unintelligible. Functions turned into multiagency assemblages and responsibility relations diffused among a haze of many hands. The problem of establishing liability is now that accidents often involve numerous parties who are strangers to each other and do not have any contractual ties or any other form of duty toward each other.

A modern accident paradigm

Compared with accident cases of former times involving individuals, which by and large had been treated more like criminal cases with a clear separation between perpetrator and victim, collision cases now often involved the responsibility of both parties.[9] Establishing and balancing the duties and possible faults and carelessness of each party could be very difficult, especially if the accident involved multiple factors on each side. Who was to blame when ships collided in open sea? Who or what was to blame for boiler explosions? The captain who operated the engine too fast or the construction of the boiler?

What also happened was that corporations soon started to feel intimidated by insurance claims as their ships, trains and cars were involved in accidents. Large compensation sums were paid out for the numerous, relatively small, accidents due to juvenile technology, such as people falling in trains due to bumps from jerky coupling and uncoupling of wagons, cows hit while crossing tracks, people falling off trams, and so on. Compensation costs became a real burden for industries. Early accident law was heavily influenced by a number of court decisions that altered the estimation of corporate neglect of safety in favour of risk-taking industrialists.[10] The project of modernisation thus began by striking an attitude of legal realism whereby accidents were seen as an unavoidable aspect of the technology that held the promise of modernisation, yet were not, like collateral damage incidents, omitted from legal responsibility.

Accident law

During the twentieth-century, accident law, or tort law, developed as a branch of civil law with a very practical focus on the problem of the economic costs of accidents. The idea of liability in accident law today regulates the legal status of and our general attitudes towards accidents in society, and to this we will turn now in order to further contrast accidents and collateral damage. Tort suits for accidents are not criminal cases. They will not result in a penalty sentence. Criminal cases function as a justice-seeking mechanism for the whole society, and the prosecutor is the state, the sovereign authority. Criminal law is public governance. Tort is not about governing society; it is about resolving issues between legal persons. It is civil law, and the plaintiff is the injured person who is seeking redress from their injurer. The prosecutor in criminal cases says, 'no one is allowed to do this', whereas the premise of tort cases is, 'you did damage and you should pay'. The concept of legal liability/ responsibility in tort law is predominantly outcome focused: intention is less often directly an issue.[11] It is about allocating costs of loss and damage, and not about attributing justice and moral wrong.[12] In most legal systems, apart from common law, criminal law is governed by statute, whereas tort law builds on past cases. Tort and criminal law do not exclude each other; nor do they necessarily follow each other. The infamous O.J. Simpson case is illustrative here. In this case, the civil court found enough evidence to hold O.J. liable for damages in the wrongful deaths of his ex-wife and her friend, while the criminal case against him collapsed due to lack of evidence.[13]

One can be a morally impeccable but terribly clumsy person, or inept at predicting the consequences of one's actions. The fundamental problem of tort law 'philosophy' is the question of who will carry the financial burden of accidents and how tort should be calculated. Tort law 'is among the most practical and least high-falutin areas of law',[14] and the notion 'philosophy of tort law' therefore has a sort of 'comical ring'.[15] Tort pushes the question of moral blameworthiness somewhat to the background and exchanges it for fortuity and chance. Inattention does not create an outcome of damage *per se*: it needs some accidental occurrences as well.[16]

Overall, tort law distinguishes two forms of liability: strict liability and fault liability. Strict liability applies 'automatically' without a need to prove negligence. Most legal systems have legal rules providing for strict liability. One of the common areas to apply strict liability is traffic due to the risk of causing harm by simply driving a car. Therefore, in some countries, it is illegal to drive a car without a proper bodily injury and property damage insurance coverage. Fault liability arises from the breach of a legal duty to take care, or negligence, understood as 'the omission to do something, which a reasonable man, guided upon those considerations, which ordinarily regulate the conduct of human affairs, would do, or doing something, which a prudent and reasonable man would not do'.[17] Examples could include throwing rugby balls in a full car park, running on a busy pavement without taking care, or skiing way too fast on a beginners' slope. In such cases, liability applies due to risky behaviour, but the lack of intention to harm others excludes it from criminal law—unless we talk about really serious negligence.

Fault liability is based on the idea that when people act they fail, despite all good intentions. Tort may be viewed as a practical economic response to the theological problem of Adamic imperfectness, emptied from notions of sin, guilt, and theological world order. Fault liability's lack of moral weight stands strong today. So strong that persons 'involved' in traffic accidents tend to view themselves as unlucky victims of accident statistics, even if they held the wheel as their car smashed into the child. Notice the semantic difference between killing and 'being involved in'. If not totally blame-free for the fatal second of inattention, the road designers, car engineers, traffic legislators, and the general misfortune of the situation typically receive their part of the blame. Accident law today is extremely well developed, yet we are constantly faced with situations where application appears really difficult.

In contrast, under international humanitarian law, negligence and carelessness resulting in civilian deaths constitute a crime, and legal responsibility applies.[18] One could view the collateral damage rule as a sort of reversed strict liability: by employing ultra hazardous military force in combat, states exclude themselves from liability for collateral damage in accordance with international humanitarian law. If precautionary obligations are satisfied, the full economic burden of the incident falls on the victim (who, in less developed countries, typically has no insurance).[19] However, the concept of negligence in international humanitarian law belongs to discussions of proportionality and precaution. Here we notice the power of mainstream tort law over our attitudes towards accidents; that tort law focuses on outcome; and how modern accident law has promoted an image of the accident; as being detached from the greater concern of morality. Discussions of accidents and accident law are now mainly about economics and legal matters, the cornerstones of liberal politics: 'the cost of accidents' is framed in terms of economy, tort, insurance, and risk management.[20]

Divesting the accident of religion and morality

In the history of ideas underpinning Western governance traditions, the accident played a prominent role in the development of broader theories of society, cosmos and God. The accident was, in the understanding of the Aristotelians as well as of medieval theologians, a constituent of the rules and powers governing the cosmos: it comprised a vital constituent of the idea of sovereign authority and rule of the world, not least when perceived as a sign from the creator. We no longer have such a providential framework available where we can lodge the accident. The 'de-enchantment' of the accident and modern accident law's conceptions of negligence, tort and liability, are something that emerged from the deism of the Enlightenment and the mechanisation of society. Tort and negligence very much owe their existence to mid-eighteenth century problems with collisions on land and at sea involving ships, trains and cars.[21] Yet, the acceptable death and injuries stemming from the use of new technology were never given a higher moral (or immoral) quality. And accidents were never inscribed into the sacrificial systems of the modern nation state project as honourable sacrifices of modernisation.

I am not insinuating that no-fault accidents should be covered by moral responsibility; that is beyond my competence to judge. I am just noting that from the perspective of the history of human civilization the contemporary view of accidents is atypical in not attributing them with any meaning in themselves. Legal philosophers are challenging this dominant perspective by arguing for moral philosophical perspectives on obligations on tort.[22] It remains to be seen whether these arguments will find their way into our general attitudes towards accidents.

Emptied of any loftier values, the accident stands for the glitch, the annoying statistical incidents that we cannot get rid of. There is an epistemological uncertainty connected to the modern accident, which over the years has led to an erosion of responsibility through the idea of blamelessness.[23] Blamelessness has perhaps also grown partly out of necessity, because clear-cut unambiguous fault is so seldom the case. And maybe accidents are just accidents, and therefore, rationally, without moral implications. I am here merely observing how moral blamelessness for accidents is today a real possibility, even for major accidents with devastating human and environmental consequences. It is a solid political-moral idea, readily available to political and economic leaders, some of whom have, over a short period of time, inflicted so much damage on human beings and on the planet that the general conditions of life on the planet soon may become painful to the degree where a midair passenger plane collision will be considered worthy of nothing more than an insignificant news brief. Tort may apply, yes. Damages may be very high. But society's moral codes for wrongdoing will not necessarily apply. Morally viewed, we believe today that accidents just happen detached from any larger force or cause. One of the implications of the de-enchantment of the accident for the understanding of collateral damage incidents is that accidents today remain connected to governance only through statistics and tort. Governors have a moral duty to take care, yes. But as long they take due care, we believe morality has no say.

The moral dividend

In contrast, as we have already learned, the collateral damage rule embraces a certain category of incidents belonging fully to the domain of governance. Collateral damage involves intentions, grand plans and sweeping models of what the moral life is all about. It involves a notion of sovereign authority, a higher cause, and a political programme. The difference between collateral damage incidents and contemporary notions of accidents may thus be said to be a certain moral codification, a certain moral framing of expected repetitive incidents. It is the difference between making the excuse, 'I did my best, this will hopefully not happen again', and claiming 'I may, and this will happen again'. What moves accidents into the subset of collateral damage is a certain political claim that inscribes the accidents into the domain of governance. It involves a certain politics of accidents, a decision and a foresighted balancing of desired outcomes against accident proneness, and an awareness of repetition, which belongs to a deep-seated Judeo–Christian governance tradition.

Hence it makes sense to understand collateral damage more as a claim than a descriptive term, a norm or a rule. The collateral damage label assigns value, implies decisions, and spells out a bond to sovereign authority, the ultimate holder of the 'I may'. In contrast, the accident label expunges value. The notion of the accident points at glitches, individual errors, unforeseeness, uncalculatedness, and rejects the involvement of sovereign authority. Collateral damage points at notoriousness, general decisions, foreseenness, calculatedness, and authorisation from sovereign authority. Hence the idea of collateral damage confirms a link between the incident and its larger moral and political context. The language of collateral damage is global, or at least national: the language of accident is local. Collateral damage implies a contextualised and collective experience, whereas the accident is individual and does not point to the collective. The languages of accident and of collateral damage thus also imply two different ways of being a subject in the world; they involve different ways of being a soldier in war, as the statement 'I caused an accident' rings fundamentally differently from 'I claim collateral damage'.

In that way it becomes clear that we started this chapter assuming the somewhat false premise of a 'difference' between collateral damage and accidents, as if they were analogous concepts. They are not. The concept of 'accident' is a descriptive concept. 'Collateral damage' is more than anything else a claim, implying an 'I may create notorious accidents without liability'.

Evacuating moral complicity

The academic establishment has analysed the rhetorical turn to 'the accident' to explain civilian casualties in current military operations as a 'physical' part of today's high-tech, zero-deaths, clinical-humanitarian war. In other words, high-tech high-precision weapons, clinical warfare with zero civilian deaths as the ideal, humanitarian goals that invoke civilians in the war zone as the good cause of the war, together with the accident culture of the modern risk society have disposed the political discourse towards the language of accidents. I believe there is some truth to the critics' claim that the concept of accident may be invoked with the aim of evading responsibility.[24] To label civilian casualties in war 'accidents' involves a depoliticisation of the casualties. And the language of accidents definitely makes life easier for the troop-sending Western political communities. Instead of talking about decisions, we talk about chains of coincidences, unlucky circumstances and regrettable outcomes. We talk about isolated incidents, which do not in the same way call upon our shared responsibility. The language of accidents implies no such link. If they should notice the difference, the average American person is perhaps also more likely to identify with the language of accident, which is such an ingrained and up-front part of American 'tort' life. The idea of collateral damage is too complex. If we talk about collateral damage, we imply state action, we imply national responsibility for taking decisions leading to collateral damage. It implies politics. It implies that we as citizens, voters and friends and relatives of persons in service must reflect morally on the situation. They represent and act on behalf of us and our needs and fears. As warring nations, collateral damage is our collective claim.

8

A PRIVATE CALL FOR COLLATERAL DAMAGE?

'Everyone must submit himself to the governing authorities, for there is no authority except that which God has established'.[1] (Paul, Romans 13: 1)

As argued in the previous chapters, to regard collateral damage as the 'sacrifices of civilians', as 'generative violence', as an accident, or as a euphemism, a theodicy or a utilitarian calculation obscures any attempt to see clearly the social phenomenon, the deep-seated and irresolvable puzzle, and the sturdy tie to our visions of centralised sovereign authority in governance, which collateral damage stands for. This intriguing connection will be the topic of the rest of the book, and the premise builds on an observation, which reframes our topic: in the entire Judeo–Christian–Western intellectual history of, or ideas, of governance, only two entities have held the legitimate claim to collateral damage: God and the state. Only the spokespersons of God and the state have succeeded in making a legitimate claim to collateral damage; and it is this claim, which today finds a code in international humanitarian law. The doctrine of double effect, theodicy, just war theory, and utilitarianism are all preoccupied with explaining ultimate authority in governance in the form of either God or the state. In other words, the legitimate claim to collateral damage only sits with a centralised form of authority. Whether the seat of authority has been inhabited by divine power or representative democracy does not affect the overall scheme. The linkage between a centralised superior form of authority and the people, between the governor and the governed,

133

remains in place; a relation characterised by top-down governance and bottom-up legitimacy. The legitimate claim to collateral damage as a particular rightful, justified, reasonable, and natural element of governance and claim of authority stands tremendously potent as the last non-contested attribute of centralised authority in governance. Collateral damage communicates the presence, the singularity and the outstanding status of sovereign authority. In contrast, formally viewed, private individuals, organisations or corporations may not by themselves weigh desired outcome against death and injury. They lack access to such proportionality accounts and, it seems intuitively, the right to it. We usually distrust corporate definitions of public goods and call for the state and its democratic base to decide. We have our reasons to prefer it like this, but we really have no naturally given justifications for our misgivings.

Collateral damage's tie to authority in the realm of governance interests us for two reasons. Firstly, as we have established, the link between collateral damage and sovereign authority quite simply defines collateral damage as a claim, norm, rule and category of victims. Secondly, if its yoke to authority constitutes collateral damage, and if we really are heading towards a world order ruled by private 'decentralised' authority, as claimed by many commentators, then we must ask what will become of collateral damage if or when authority 'fragments'? What happens with the claim to collateral damage if our time-honoured model of centralised authority transfigures into a centre-less world order? The key question to ask in that regard is whether private corporations may eventually succeed in making a legitimate claim to collateral damage. I will argue that the legitimate claim to collateral damage constitutes the very tipping point towards a truly decentralised world order. I therefore suggest placing the claim to collateral damage at the very heart of the discussions about privatisation and outsourcing of public governance. And, in the same vein, that the claim to collateral damage provides a better entry point for understanding the state than the claim to the monopoly on organised violent force. In other words, I see the collateral damage victim, our forgotten victim of war, as a gateway to something that appears to be an overlooked first philosophy of war and governance.

To root this argument we need to look at some of our earliest visions of centralised authority, and examine what was originally at stake in terms of public and privately organised violence. Max Weber did not invent the public–private division and its significance to the historical organisation of violent force. He merely provided a modern conception of an old separation. In the following, we will explore this separation by using a straw man: the figure of the mercenary, which I shall use to capture some deeper ideas of legitimate violence and its connection to authority, governance, and notions of community and idolatry. But let us first frame our inquiry with some illustrative examples: the legal cases of *Grimshaw v. Ford Motor Company* of 1981, also known as 'The Pinto Case', and the *Anderson v. General Motors Corp* of 1999, also known as the 'Malibu case'—cases that stand as modern myths about private corporations getting bashed for balancing corporate profit against human lives.

Ford Pinto: A failed claim to collateral damage

The Ford Motor Company started to build the Ford Pinto car in the early 1970s. When a road accident with a Pinto in 1972 led to a fuel tank explosion, Ford was sued. According to the plaintiff, the Pinto's rear-end placed and poorly shielded fuel tank, combined with error in the design of the carrosserie that prevented the doors from opening after collision, made the car a death trap. As the law suit developed, a memo from Ford appeared that indicated that the company had been aware of the Pinto's safety issues, but decided not to correct these due to the extra production costs. The memo contained a calculation of these extra costs versus a set value per lost life. Ford estimated that it would cost $11 per car to fix the problem. With a run of 12.5 million vehicles this would mean $137 million in additional production costs. Ford also estimated that the design error would probably lead to something like 180 deaths and 180 severe injuries. Setting the value of a life at $200,000 and injury avoidance at $67,000 this would add up to $49.5 million—which meant $87.5 million cheaper than correcting the safety issues. The memo, which became known as the 'Ford Pinto Memo', was viewed as proof of how Ford had cynically calculated death and injury against the dollar value of human life. The court ruled that Ford should pay $580,000 in wrongful death damages, $2.5 million in compensation damages, and additional punitive damages of $125 million because Ford knew about the faulty design and had consciously weighed up the financial implications of likely deaths. That $125 million was reduced to $3.5 million (as a condition for denying a new trial), thus leaving Ford with a total fine of $6,580,000. The court mostly took an interest in the Fort Pinto memo as a proof of Ford's cynical corporate mentality and not the problems stemming from the faulty design.[2] Similarly, the public condemned Ford strongly. The indignation lived on. A 1991 film, Class Action, starring Gene Hackman, based its plot on the Pinto case; and to this day the Pinto case gets taught in law classrooms.[3]

However, by closer inspection, the facts of the case bear little support to the allegations.[4] The Ford Pinto Memo was not, as mostly conceived, an internal document. Rather, Ford produced it as a response to the charges. It was '(...) not prepared with tort liability in mind, but rather for the purpose of submission to the United States National Highway Traffic Safety Administration'.[5] Moreover, Ford's Value of Life figure of $200,000 per victim was not something Ford came up with, but the statistical value used then by the National Highway Traffic Safety Administration when they balanced state investment in road safety. And while the Pinto design suffered some flaws, the car performed quite well overall. Ford apparently felt the corporation had nothing to hide as they wrote up the memo.[6]

Nonetheless, the Pinto case grew into a real myth—a myth about cynical corporate mentality. In this regard, Professor of law, Gary Schwartz, suggested that the case 'shows how disturbed the public can be by corporate decisions that balance life and safety against monetary costs.'[7] To him, the case expressed the public's dissatisfaction with corporations' confidential cost-benefit analysis. And the Pinto myth replicated itself: in 1999, a jury ordered General Motors Corporation to pay a staggering US$4.9 billion to the six persons who survived but were severely burned when the fuel tank of their 1979 Chevrolet Malibu exploded after a rear-end collision.[8] They were compensated with $107 million for their pain, suffering and disfigurement plus $4.8 billion in punitive damages because, the Jury believed, GM acted out of fraud or malice. The proof for this was an internal 'value analysis' memo,[9] which measured the value of preventing fuel-fires with extra production costs.[10] The $200,000 value for human life it relied upon was, as in the Pinto case, derived from government numbers. According to the lawyer for the accident victims, 'the jurors wanted to send a message to General Motors that human life is more important than profits.'[11] The punitive damage award was subsequently reduced to $1.09 billion but the Court reaffirmed that punitive damages were warranted to punish GM for designing a fuel tank 'in order to maximize profits, to the disregard of public safety.' As the Pinto case, this case also rested on weak evidence. The memo was less than a page long. No clear evidence existed that the memo was ever used to guide corporate decisions.

These are merely two examples of a larger tendency. The fact is that courts lean towards penalizing corporations for balancing money against human lives, even in cases where such balancing appears perfectly sound.[12] The calculation itself seems to be the despicable act. No doubt, public mistrust in private corporations runs deep. Indeed, the punitive damages awarded against

Ford, GM and other corporations for weighing replace with production costs against safety merely reinforce a regulatory regime laid down by the US federal government during the steamboat era. Bursting steamboat boilers created a dilemma 'as to how far the lives and property of the general public might be endangered by unrestricted private enterprise',[13] and the federal government's answer was to claim authority over this matter and enforce regulation. Since then, public law has increasingly codified the responsibility relations between state authority and its legal subjects, including corporations. This regime is mirrored by and large by all states, although states usually have more or less effective mechanisms for accommodating and effecting accountability and transparency for private actors. State authority also backs up civil suits: the authority to judge whether a corporation's harmful activities amount to misconduct falls on the courts, which interpret the laws of the legislators. And, it is the government, at least in the eyes of the public, who decides national motor vehicle standards.

Of course, we see a world littered with reckless and incompetent political leaders and bureaucrats. Even so, we attach an ideal to the image of state authority about care for the public good. Public policy should embody the spirit of the public. Failures to do so, we believe, stem from systemic challenges or imprudence among politicians or civil servants. In contrast, we tend to view big business as incarnating an egocentric drive for profit. Furthermore, the necessity attached to value of statistical life and cost-benefit analysis in public policy comes from the necessity of accommodating both safety and efficiency within a limited budget. For corporations, profit appears to be the limit.

I here see sentiments and attitudes rather than a factual reality. In our liberal world order, private corporations do make up the economic pillars of wealth and health, and they often behave responsibly. As a thought experiment: what if Ford planned to reinvest the $87.5 million identified by the memo as saved by not fixing the Pinto in general road safety and thus created a statistical surplus of lives saved? Would this have been an acceptable calculation? It probably would have been if state authority had made it—or if state authority had sanctioned it. What I am aiming at is the imagined divide between our ideas of state authority and our ideas of private corporations when it comes to ultimate aims and accountability. At face value, the Pinto and the Malibu cases fall into the category of product liability cases. However, as I see it, the question of who may balance efficiency against human lives stands at the core of the resentment. Who could and should be the custodian of value of statistical life calculations and applications? I am asking these questions because collateral damage estimations in the context of military force equal value of statistical life calculations in civilian life. Whether we compute the cost per life in road safety investments or weigh military necessity against civilian losses, we not only compute statistical deaths. We exercise a claimed right to make such calculations. If this is true, the resentments that generated the Pinto and the Malibu cases expose the tie between the claim to legitimate value of statistical life calculations and the distinction between public authority and private agency. The question is who may use value of life calculations and for what purpose. Here, I take the Pinto and the Malibu cases as prefiguring the coming of an era where corporations start assuming and enjoying the entitlement to claims and conventions traditionally belonging solely to state authority and, before that, to God. According to some commentators, we are approaching this situation. If true, this implies an inversion of a paradigm of governance that has defined our view of authority since ancient times. At the centre of this possible transformation stands the question of who owns the claim to collateral damage.

The Old Testament: mercenaries, centralised authority, and the good cause of governance

The figure of the mercenary as an historical ideal type embodies the idea of privately organised violent force. The private military and security firms of today stand poles apart from the mercenaries of times past, although a certain polemic endures. I argued in a previous chapter that the use of armed force appears morally uncomplicated if everyone agrees that its deployment is based upon absolute right or wrong. By 'uncomplicated', I simply mean a lack of conflicting opinions. That seems not to be the case with private agents of violent force. The current debates about private military and security companies reveal a concern even in cases where states contract private force for righteous causes. We do not entirely trust non-statutory forces, which, we believe, ultimately engage for private gain (money or adventure) rather than the public good. Killing for money or for fun just does not seem right.[14] 'At least the civilian casualties served some corporate interest or satisfied some adventurous souls' will not work as a legitimating narrative.

It means a lot to us whether blood gets spilled for a public cause or for private interest. We make a deep distinction between soldiers of fortune and national soldiers. To be sure, the private military and security industry, which today merely refers to itself as a branch of 'International Stability Operations',[15] struggled during the 1990s to free itself from the 'dogs of war' mark of mercenarism. They mostly succeeded. Yet private guns still have an aura of egocentricity, a stigma, which excludes them from the national community of self-sacrifice. Speculation about private sentiment always sneaks in as an alertness to any undercurrent of dubious motivations, even in situations where contractors 'work' for causes generally viewed as just. Public and private agents of violent force today operate side-by-side or interwoven in complex hybrid partnerships. Yet the fantasy of a separation lives on. Although not an example from the domain of armed conflict, the Ford Pinto case and the Malibu case illustrate the issue perfectly.

The state's thus far unbeaten claim to the monopoly on organised violent force adds a sturdy element to the nation state. Not surprisingly, most academic treatments of commercial security start off bemoaning the erosion of the state's monopoly on force. But the Weberian idea of the monopoly of force is a fairly recent idea. The prominence attributed to the monopoly on legitimate violence and the focus on technical issues such as political control, legal accountability and social norms, however, blinds us to the deeper normative structures that shape our emotional attitudes towards private force. I would say our obsession with the monopoly of force prevents us from seeing clearly what is actually at stake in the privatisation of violent force which is, essentially, a Judeo–Christian vision of centralised authority, including the connection between authority and the claim to collateral damage. It is this connection that we will trace here.

A world of private authority and the force monopoly

The Old Testament can be viewed as the largest political manifesto ever written.[16] It is our first comprehensive text that systematically tries to come to terms with fundamental societal issues such as power, authority, political rulers, community, loyalty, violence, sacrifice, and also mercenaries. The depiction of God in the Old Testament repeatedly draws on metaphors, political dilemmas and figures from everyday life, and thus gives us insight into the issues that preoccupied society during the time when the Old Testament was authored. There is reason to believe that the issues addressed in the Old Testament, including that of private force, are even older. And many remain the same today. We will see in the following how the legacy of the mercenary in the Old Testament implies questions of power, authority, governance, political faith and loyalty, and images of self, society, and governance, which are still relevant today. The discourse of the mercenary appears not to have changed drastically during the last 3,000 years.

The 1,000 year perspective: international norms

In her book, *Mercenaries: The History of a Norm in International Relations*,[17] the political scientist Sarah Percy gives an account of what she calls the norm against mercenary use, which she traces from the early medieval period to today's discussions on marketised security. Throughout the years, she explains, this particularly strong and durable norm has influenced the attitudes of state leaders and the opinions of the general public. Percy traces the origins and impact of the norm to a period that predates the idea of the state and its monopoly on force. She argues that the well-established academic discipline of international relations theory, for the most part, fails to capture the constructivist nature of the anti-mercenary norm. Consequently, international relations studies fail to notice how the norm has shaped and still shapes our attitudes towards privately organised force, and thereby also fails to see what role this moral position played in the process of shaping the modern state. To illustrate her point, Percy draws attention to how existing scholarship on private military companies approaches its topic in the light of the state's ability to control force. The dominantly rational and institution-focused perspective contains little sensitivity towards the irrational content of our attitude towards mercenaries. For instance, she points at how historians fail to explain why state leaders in the mid-nineteenth century decided to abolish mercenaries instead of developing the institutional capacity to incorporate mercenaries in their armies. This would have been the rational choice. At that time, standing armies were just as ungovernable as mercenary armies and suffered from bad management and desertion, and conscription had not yet been proved to be a driving force for nationalism. So why not take both? There was no clear explanation as to why state leaders at that time thought of the regular army as the preferable solution.[18] No historical evidence exists that mercenaries were less cause-oriented or that they led to tyranny. And no one could know in advance that the nation state project would produce such a strong sacrificial relationship between the soldier and the nation. The idea of an army based on sentiments about homeland and self-sacrifice for the nation did not emerge until after mercenarism was abolished. Instead, irrational and apparently illogical normative feelings played a crucial role in the abolition of mercenaries in the late eighteenth and nineteenth centuries. State leaders' use of mercenaries was looked upon as a sign of weakness. Only the weak state leader would experience a lack of loyal citizens willing to die for him, and honour thus seems to have played a major role in the turn to citizen armies.[19]

We may make a counterfactual speculation about how our world would look today had this irrational insistence on public armies not led to the delegitimisation of mercenaries. Maybe the state project would have taken a different path. If it is true that there really was no rational cause to abolish mercenaries, then we must rethink the monopoly on legitimate force as a fundamental institution of the modern Western state and all the concepts that flow from it. Perhaps the political-legal status of today's private security firms would then have been different. Percy's analysis, in fact, puts an end to the absolute centrality of the monopoly on force in modern political thought, and calls for further theorisation of the historical attitudes towards private force. Perhaps the tie between collateral damage in war and public authority would have been different? I think not. And I will explain in the following why not, by tracing the figure of the mercenary back another 1,500 years, to the Old Testament stories of David the King of Israel in the books of Samuel.

The 2,500 year perspective: political theology

Samuel I and II heavily influenced later ideas of kingdom and state monism, and are considered to be the motherboard for Western ideas of monarchy and centralised authority. But the Old Testament also offers insight into issues, problems and dilemmas that, at that time, were considered prominent in contemporary social, political and religious life. The configuration of the image of God in the Old Testament more often than not utilises customary norms, above all concerning sexual morality, in areas like marital relations, adultery, jealousy, and betrayal.[20] This, the original narrative of God and monotheism, also contains the first historical documents we have about sentiments towards private force. In the political–theological space of the Old Testament, its 'world within the text,'[21] stretched out between earthly and divine power, the biblical mercenary appears as an ambiguous figure located outside the moral matrix of society in a way that connects him to fundamental puzzles of governance and authority still prominent today. They form a distinct category of fighters, one which did not come with the same divinely derived righteousness as the king's own troops. In fact, it is an established theory that the covenants between God and Israel were copies of the forms of covenants that the superior kings made with their mercenary vassals—small communities or nations selling their armed capability to other states—in particular with regard to the obligation to political loyalty that was a foremost issue of these contracts.[22] The practice of contracting and regulating vassals and mercenary factions for military support and the question of loyalty posed by such contracting, not least the implied distinction between contractor and contracted, played a crucial role in the construction of core issues of the Old Testament's account of God, monotheism, kingship, and nation. Kings and vassals apparently had a fundamentally different status in ancient Israel. The biblical text makes it obvious how this difference played an important role in the early development of political community and the obligation and loyalty of its members towards a centred higher authority.

A distinction was thus accordingly drawn between 'troops and warriors',[23] and the biblical text informs us about various uses and forms of mercenary activities, from kings' contracts with vassals to their employment of gangs of bandits.[24] An often cited passage is Jeremiah 46:21, which talks about 'her [Egypt's] mercenaries in her midst are like fattened calves. For even they too have turned back and have fled away together: they did not stand their ground. For the day of their calamity has come upon them. The time of their punishment.' While this presents the biblical mercenary in a way similar to our present-day notion of 'the dogs of war', he was, as will be demonstrated below, a far more ambiguous figure.

King David and Ittai the Gittite

In the Old Testament, the most famous mercenary is David, King of Israel, who in his 'outlaw period' during King Saul's rule served as a mercenary in the army of the Philistines. He also drifted around as the leader of a gang of mighty warriors[25] who '[made] their own rules and cynically form[ed] shifting political alliances for the interest of survival alone'.[26] But David later proclaimed the virtue of cause attachment when he turned down Ittai the Gittite, who wanted to join him with 600 men to fight against David's rebellious son Absalom:

> Why should you go with us? Go back and stay with the king. For you are a for-eigner, and you are also in exile from your own place. Just yesterday you came, and today should I make you wander with us, when I, myself, am going wherever I may go. Turn back, and bring back your brothers. Steadfast kindness to you.[27]

Ittai, however, insisted on joining David, even though he had limited finan-cial or political interest in doing so. He replied to David that '[a]s the Lord lives, and as my lord the king lives, whatever place that my lord the king may be, whether for death or for life, there your servant will be.'[28] And so Ittai the Gittite evoked the self-sacrifice, the willingness to die for a certain cause, as the gesture that verified his cause attachment. Some 3,000 years later, the self-sacrifice, as discussed in the previous chapter, as the ultimate gesture or verification of loyalty and commitment, remains central to the idea of national belonging. It has even been argued that the borders of the modern nation state are defined by the willingness of its citizens to sacrifice themselves in the name of the nation.

Ittai eventually advances to troop leader after David has defeated Absalom.[29] David's initial scepticism indicates that the form of loyalty Ittai came with was not easily understood at that time. Ittai demonstrates a form of loyalty that moves beyond the ethnic, tribal or telluric, and instead directs its piety to a cause laid down by other than 'earthly' demarcations. One can thus read the episode with Ittai the Gittite as thematising an idea of centralised authority, which not even David yet understood fully. The idea of self-sacrifice for authority runs deep, and the figure of Ittai the Gittite stands as one of its first literary expressions.

This story illustrates how military engagement in the biblical narrative was mediated by three general modalities of engagement: ethnic/tribal/political loyalty bonds, mercenary interests and loyalty towards the King of Israel. There is a binary at play here between two mutually exclusive modalities of military engagement: cause-oriented, whether political or religious, and self-serving profit or power-oriented aspirations. The biblical paradigm of power reorganises this binary along monotheistic lines so that the 'serving of other Gods', including serving those leaders who worship other gods, and mercenary activity become one driver of military engagement. The other driver follows 'the right' cause, which is the loyalty to the king of Israel, who embodies the call of God. The jealous Jewish God allowed no other cause than his. And God primarily gave Israel a kingdom with a throne, and Saul and David as individual kings were only secondary. The Israelites asked for a King, not a specific king, and God gave Israel a form of regime with a centred point of authority. Loyalty to the King was, foremost, loyalty to the monarchy of Israel as a regime that pointed to God as its exclusive authority and ruler.[30] We see here an early formation of 'the king's two bodies' in medieval political theology, which Ernst Kantorovich analysed as a duality of the flesh and blood person of the king and the abstract and enduring political–theological figure of the King. I will not unpack this large discussion here, where it suffices to notice how the mercenary functioned as an important figure in the construction of the Judeo–Christian paradigm of power, which paved the way for the political theological order that Kantorovich later analysed, and which eventually greatly influenced the idea of the modern nation state.

Even if mercenaries in the Old Testament narrative are guilty of pursuing causes other than God's, they also sometimes appear to be more reliable than formal troops, as exemplified by one occasion where David was let down by his own people while the mercenaries stayed by his side. This happened as David was returning to Jerusalem as king, when a meeting committee could not decide whether they had the obligation to accompany him over the Jordan River and home.[31] David thus worked as a mercenary and later, as a king, employed mercenaries himself.

Doeg the Edomite

It is important to notice how mercenaries in the story of David are not presented as being either good or bad. Their ambiguity does not render them inexplicable, but rather ascribes to them a certain status and function within the Old Testament's political–divine order. This becomes clear through the figure of Doeg the Edomite, who was a mercenary in the employ of King Saul. Doeg's position in the societal order became evident when Saul turned to him to execute a group of priests conspiring against him, as Saul's own servants 'did not want to reach out their hands to stab the priest of the Lord'.[32] As Robert Alter comments in his translation of Samuel II, 'his identity as Edomite reflects the enlistment [among the servants of King Saul] of foreign mercenaries in the new royal bureaucracy. It also marks him as a man who will have no inhibitions in what he does to the Israelites, even Israelite priests.'[33] Doeg the Edomite thus exemplifies how the mercenary in the Old Testament constitutes a figure who resides outside the divine community ruled by the king and his priests. Doeg could kill priests, an act that within the community would have been strictly taboo.

Interestingly, it was Doeg who in the first place informed King Saul that the priests were conspiring against him by giving the fleeing David swords and bread. The text insinuates that Doeg not only witnessed this situation but also seemed to have known that the priests were not being disloyal to Saul in that they believed that David was still fighting under him (at this point in the story, David had just broken away from Saul's camp). If this is the case, Doeg creates a situation that he could benefit from since he, due to his status as a mercenary, was the only one who could carry out the job of executing the believed traitors.

Does this not provide us with an allegory of how modern private security companies construct security scenarios that serve their own business?

Doeg the Edomite cuts a complex figure and has been subjected to various interpretations,[34] yet his status as a mercenary appears central to his role in the biblical narrative. And through his figure it becomes clear that the biblical mercenary is more than a derogatory name but, in fact, designates a distinct figure whose category of belonging is structured by a vision of a jealous God, a centralised sovereign authority. By singling out what kind of actions fail to worship God, the Old Testament simultaneously erects the image of God. The theological distinction between worshipping and serving 'God and mammon,'[35] or anything else, serves as a fundamental logic in the construction of God and the world of the Old Testament.

In the biblical paradigm of power, the divine cause was a fundamental split in all human action, the delicate line between God's salvation and Hell. This binary coding of all human virtue, which is the main preoccupation of the Bible, also gave rise to the biblical form of the mercenary, which finds expression in the idea that divine worship and personal gain cannot go hand in hand. As we have noted, the issue of personal gain should be viewed a stand-in for the worship of other causes than the jealous God. Similarly, priests who preached for their own gain and not for serving God, mercenary priests, were also looked upon as immoral, as were such judges and prophets, as implied in Micah 3:11: 'The heads thereof judge for reward, and the priests thereof teach for hire, and the prophets thereof divine for money: yet will they lean upon the LORD, and say, is not the LORD among us?'

Good and bad causes

These observations suffice to conclude that the tradition of perceiving mercenaries as different and if not immoral per se then at least as fighting for causes other than community, is at least 2,500 years old insofar as the Old Testament was written down somewhere between the twelfth and second centuries BCE. The monotheistic rearrangement of the cause of action as the fundamental fabric of community attachment was the vector that singled out the biblical place for mercenaries. The exact political–theological dilemmas of particular historical times are not so important to us. And some recent scholars even suggest that the figure of David is pure literary fiction. The point to be made here is that the mercenary soldier was a distinctive figure in the most important text ever in the creation of the idea of centred authority, which simultaneously hints at the legacy of this particular figure in ancient society.

It is evident that the mercenaries in biblical times were powerful players along with political–religious and tribal leaders, and therefore naturally became included in the biblical narrative. To be sure, mercenaries found good business in the ancient Near East. We know that they were an integral part of the socio-political landscape in ancient Mesopotamia from the Amarna Letters,[36] which contain political communications between the pharaohs of the Amarna period (1386–21 BCE) and their contemporaries in Canaan, Mesopotamia, Anatolia and the Aegean. In other words, privately organised force has been a part of the landscape of coercive power since the birth of warfare. Their normative status in the ancient political landscape has not really been addressed by scholars, but there is no reason to believe that the problems treated in the biblical texts were not central to even older societies, and that the Bible merely 'represents a sacralization of phenomena that were originally political'.[37] One could also say that the use of metaphors, political dilemmas and figures from common political life to establish an image of God has led to confusion over what was sacred and what was not sacred according to the Bible. After all, in addition to the question of sacredness, a core problem was that of rival political authority.

Mercenaries and idolatry

The biblical mercenary was a normative figure structured by ideas of community and attachment to causes that, with the invention of the monotheistic God, were transformed into questions of belonging and loyalty to God. The story about how the separation of mercenary force and the kings' own force came about in the first place has been lost in history. But the Old Testament's preoccupation with the question of a God-given, hierarchically ordered world, and rival political authorities funnels the discussion of a biblical mercenary legacy into the debate on idolatry. Let us read the following bearing in mind the question of why the Ford Pinto case created such an outrage, and thus the question of who may claim collateral damage.

Idolatry, the worshipping of other gods, is the most serious charge in both the Old and the New Testaments.[38] It is usually understood as 'an attack on God's exclusive right to our love and trust'.[39] In the Old Testament idolatry was a demonstration of disloyalty. The sin of idolatry was a sin of betrayal.[40] The prohibition of idolatry is typically thought of as demarcating the virtual frontiers of the City of God: idolatry means the opposite of faith. Yet there is no easy definition of idolatry that, if examined properly, appears to cover all of its meanings. These can, broadly, be categorised under at least four headings: idolatry as betrayal and rebellion; idolatry as (even if good willed) a wrong conception of God (metaphysical error); idolatry as 'alien worship', that is, the worship of other Gods or incorrect ideas of God, or the wrong practice in worship; and idolatry as the belief in worlds other than the hierarchically ordered world of God.[41] Within these overall categories myriad discussions and inconsistencies exist. Historically, exegetically, and theologically, idolatry is a far more complex concept than simple prohibition of worshipping other gods. It includes the idea of 'greed as idolatry',[42] and reaches as far as potentially subjecting the Torah in the synagogue to a charge of idolatry, as its material focus of devotion may steal attention from the practice of worshipping God. On the other hand, not all idolatrous activities were radically banned, and some even had a positive function in society. The idolatrous categories of the Old Testament later found a form in philosophy, for instance in Kant's theories of cognition and systemic error as the root of all evil, and Descartes' conception of the role of the human will in the creation of error.[43]

Idolatrous but useful

From the perspective of idolatry, I see an evident theological–political paradox to be found in the mercenary figure of Doeg the Edomite. He illustrates how idolatry, even if banned, could have a certain value for the ancient kings. He could, because of his idolatrous disposition, do things otherwise forbidden under the divine laws of the community. The perspective on biblical mercenary action as a case of idolatry and the ambiguity of the mercenary figure in the Old Testament shed new light on a much later and widely cited passage from Machiavelli, who invokes a passage from David's killing of Goliath to substantiate his scepticism towards relying on auxiliary arms:

> David offered Saul to go and fight Goliath, the Philistine Champion, and Saul, to inspire him with courage, gave him his own weapons and armour. Having tried these on, David rejected them, saying that he would be unable to fight well with them and therefore he wanted to face the enemy with his sling and his knife. In short, armour belonging to someone else either drops off you or weighs you down or is too tight'.[44]

Machiavelli used this allegory to underscore how mercenaries, the arms of others, were useless and unfaithful. Yet, Machiavelli failed to see the iconoclastic legacy of the biblical mercenary, who despite his idolatrous disposition nonetheless finds a place in this order as an instrument of power. He failed to see the mercenary legacy of David; and he surely could have given emphasis to other less black-and-white biblical allegories. Maybe he consciously opted for an image that supported the image of his sovereign Prince; or maybe he failed to see the convoluted nature of the topic.

We find the theme of idolatry and governance in the political philosophy of Plato, who in the fourth century BCE argued in *The Republic* that desires for personal gain and advantage were not suitable for the job of governing. At the time of Plato, in the ancient Greek city states, mercenary armies composed an integral part of the state system, and they were often organised like small cities outside the polis.[45] Most written sources about Greek mercenaries are from the fifth century BCE and later, that is, in the period of democratic Athens. The context of the discourse, without doubt, played an important role in the construction of the image of the mercenary as a less than honourable figure. However, no existing evidence supports a general critical stance against mercenaries in ancient Greece. Scholarly research demonstrates there was nothing shameful about mercenaries as such, as long as they did not undermine the ideal of the city-state. Rather, mercenaries were conventional and accepted players in international and domestic society and politics.[46] Still, there was a clear conceptual separation of mercenaries and city-states, where the city-states were seen as primary agents to which mercenaries were only auxiliary. What bothered the authors of the Old Testament, and later the Greeks, with regard to mercenaries, was not so much the use of violence (or efficiency, as in Machiavelli) as it was the problem of authority and governance: what governance was, who could govern, and, most of all, for what cause was governance to be conducted.

Governance in our time and private force

By drawing upon a large number of examples, allegories and narratives, the Bible's various texts contribute in various ways to the image of a monistic form of centralised authority. The issues raised are typically everyday ones such as marriage, sex and friendship. This gives us insight into what kinds of matters preoccupied society at the time of King David, including the moral standing of privately organised violent force vis-à-vis centralised authority. The tradition of perceiving mercenaries as agents of force residing outside the main political–religious community runs as deep as our first accounts of political life on earth. The Old Testament authors as well as the ancient Greeks all considered mercenaries if not immoral and idolatrous then at least separate and potentially troublesome actors. This observation reveals that the anti-mercenary norm is the expression of an idea of separation that is as least as old as our earliest treatments of the problem of governance. The figure of the mercenary stands for a primary tension in the Judeo–Christian notion of monotheism and nationhood so essential to later Western ideas of state and nation. This tension may be directly translated into the tension that animates the Judeo–Christian notion of idolatry, which basically means to pursue a greater good than God—that is, to put a form of authority other than God at the highest reference point for acts of governance.

The figure of the mercenary, the figure of private force, thus brings into our sight a fundamental figuration of Judeo–Christian–Western–Liberal models or paradigms of governance. What is ultimately at stake in the current privatisation of security and other core governance functions is the idea of centralised authority. What is at stake is a certain configuration of the relationship between authority and visions of good governance, and the use of violence force. Realising this, the modern idea of the state's claim to the monopoly on the use of organised violent force evidently provides only a superficial point of departure for discussing the place of private force in modern society. The constant framing of the problem of privatised force in relation to the state's monopoly of force leaves the discussion in a somewhat shallow condition. The focus on the monopoly of force, transparency, accountability, and regulation is clearly of high importance, but we must also see that the puzzle of commercial, organised, violent force goes back much further and connects to core aspects of our ideas of authority and political community.

The point to be made here is that mercenaries throughout the history of our ideas of centralised authority and governance have constituted a somewhat unchanging category. The question of relationship between the cause and idolatry remain the crux of matter—from Ittai the Gittite to Blackwater in Iraq.

Violence in our time

By tracing the puzzle of private force as far back as pre-biblical times, I do not claim to have identified any 'hidden' religious core to today's liberal attitudes towards private security. I am not after a disclosure of a veiled political theology. I suggest, rather, that we think in terms of a cognitive contemporariness: regular people from then and today, at least in the near eastern areas, meeting across a 3,000-year time gap, would most likely find some common opinion with regard to mercenaries. If we can talk about a concept of 'our time' straddling millennia, and if 'in our time', private force has a distinct (im)moral aura compared to the delegates of (moral) centralised authority, then it makes sense to say that 'in our time' stretches from ancient times until today. If the culture of community rises out of shared attitudes and beliefs, then it makes sense to think of our attitudes towards private organised violence, which connect ancient time with the twenty-first century, as a form of community. And I mean very literally a form, an idealised epitome, which formats cultures or, remembering the preceding chapter on sacrifice, the cult of governance around a vision of centralised authority.

Looking at the debates on governance and political and religious rule throughout 'our time' reveals the common theme of centralised authority. It is an idea implying that final judgements about good and evil reside with some centralised authority, which at the same time gives structure to community. And that the centre is wiser than other parts or members of the community. Of course, the locus of brute power may shift as it always has done. All that is important is the idea that community has or should have a reference centre in the form of something that represents the community's ultimate cause, a reference for sacrifice. This is, not least, valid for liberalism, which recirculates old Judeo–Christian narratives regarding governance, including a vision of anticipated governance through expert guided foresight, embodied by the legislative power of the state. 'In our time', the idea of governance has a certain structure that Judeo-Christian Providences as well as the liberal state model fit into. Since some of the key problems of this model, such as images of private authority and military force, apparently are older than our Jewish–Christian traditions, the structure is most likely even older.

Monotheism was originally a war against polytheism, and the Old Testament's image of God was articulated in opposition to 'idolatrous' human practices. Similarly to how God's unity could not be compromised, liberalism also asserts uncompromisable principles of unity. Even autonomy-guarding liberal principles of freedom of faith, speech and lifestyle contain in themselves an idea of unity. The Judeo-Christian visions of monotheism and providential rule, and the later ideas of the centralised liberal state are products of the same matrix of governance that defines 'our time'. I do not here suggest any critique of liberalism. There are many good reasons for insisting on centralisation. We should not, however, disregard how liberalism recycles a governance paradigm first articulated by the Old Testament, if not before. 'In our time', we desired a centre.

One of the implications of this contemporaneousness is that it challenges the popular idea of a sort of relationship between 'secular' models of the liberal state and 'theological' models of God and Providence, as a matter of the Christian remnants in secular politics. As often suggested by the discussion on political theology, history presents us with a linear progression of political ideas with an observable rupture between Christian theology and secular politics. However, political theology's use of Carl Schmitt's mantra that 'all political concepts are secularized religious concepts' appears less persuasive if the so-called secular and religious concepts are, as I argue, carved out of the same piece of wood.[47]

Who will be our last king?

If it is true that our notions of political community evolve primarily around notions of centred authority, then it also becomes clear to us what is actually at stake in a 'flattened world' where even security management, once the main sacrificial institution of the nation state project, increasingly dovetails with non-state agencies with all kinds of interests and purposes. In such a world, the question of why some may govern others, and why governance should be like this and not like that, gets fuzzy. This current debate on a 'new world order' (see next chapter) mostly addresses the norms and forms of global organisations, institutions, communication, and issues of transparency and accountability. Alas, the form of authority in governance holding hegemony over 'our time' does not provide many answers to the challenges of pluralism and fragmentation. In our increasingly 'flattened' world, the organised means of violent force has been one of the last bastions of centred governance. Yet the critical issue of the privatisation of security seems to be not the force monopoly as such, but the underlying ideas of centred authority that it presupposes. The neoliberalisation of security and organised violence not only exasperates the force monopoly: it contests a paradigm of governance that has held hegemony over our political life over a period of some 3,000 years, and which accommodated both monotheism and the liberal state. The neoliberal reversion of this paradigm suggests implications for notions of community attachment and loyalty similar to those with which the Old Testament struggled.

At the heart of the trajectory of this idea of centralised authority in governance stands the tie to the claim to permissible collateral damage. As the real problem of organised violent force is not its organisation but its use, and as the real problem of using violent force is not the clearly just or clearly unjust use, but the grey zone where just and unjust and good and bad merge into each other, we see how the claim to collateral damage emerges as the real

9

WITH OR WITHOUT A CENTRE

There will, in this day and age, always be three claims involved in counting collateral damage. One claim declaring there is such a thing as collateral damage. One claim judging the fact in question as belonging to the category of collateral damage as laid down by norms and rules; and the third claim stating 'I may claim collateral damage'. These dimensions of collateral damage have been addressed in previous chapters. I found the last claim to belong only to God and the state: our two overall centralised forms of ultimate authority in governance. At least, I have not been able to identify any other claimholders. I urge the reader to consider this account critically. If I were wrong on this one, our contemplations would take a different but perhaps no less interesting path. However, following my premise, if authority in global governance is disintegrating, fragmentising, or fracturing, this transformation will logically affect the availability of the claim to collateral damage, and, I will argue, vice versa: Any changes to the scheme we use today to account for the killing of civilians in war necessarily imply a change in the form of authority laying down this scheme.

My main point, which I have already aired, is that collateral damage should be viewed as a concept that limits and is limited by our vision of ultimate authority in governance and, as such, it constitutes the threshold between centralised and decentralised authority. The successful claim to permissible collateral damage in governance defines the very tipping point toward disaggregated or decentralised authority. In other words, to define, explain and justify collateral damage deaths and harm involves an answer to the question of who should rule the world. Not in terms of actual presidents, emperors, kings or priests, but in terms of the very form legitimate rule may take and how we may legitimately take military action to realise our hope for a better world. The question is, 'who may claim collateral damage?' In a world of truly decentralised authority, collateral damage is set free, or unleashed, depending on how one sees it. But, can collateral damage be decentred, fragmentised, atomised, and fractured? Can we imagine collateral damage at any level in a world governed by private authority? Can we imagine a world where Ford in and of itself successfully claims the right to count and inflict statistical deaths on a par with the state if it serves what Ford considers a common good? Where, in their standard operating procedure, Ford, Volkswagen Group, General Electric, Exxon Mobil, Wal-Mart, Royal Dutch Shell, PetroChina, Chevron and Gazprom, to mention but a few of the world's most powerful private companies, publicly but on their own account calculate and list production-generated human casualties alongside other budgetary items, as a trade-off for what they consider a better world? Can we imagine a world where private military firms might legitimately claim collateral damage deaths—for instance, when intervening in humanitarian crises? The purpose of asking these questions is to explore collateral damage as an entry point for understanding the supposed fragmentation of authority in global governance, not to make moral judgements about who should rule our world. I am interested in exposing some cognitive constraints with regard to imagining an untying of collateral damage, and what these constraints may tell us about the centrality of collateral damage, as a problem and a norm, to our understanding of authority in global governance.

Current visions of the decentralisation of authority

For millennia, God, emperors, monarchs and presidents have incarnated a vision of the indivisibility of authority, which today organises all images of the modern state and establishes connections among its practices, agents (civil servants, legislators, judges, citizens, etc.), and discourses. The idea of centralised authority holds our conceptions of governance in a firm grip. Call it epistemic hegemony, a paradigm of governance, a figuration of authority, whatever. Statehood and statecraft, as well as God's being and doing, plus all derived ideas of hierarchy, commission and delegation, and thus also the collateral damage rule, all rest on an image of a centre, a singularity that is akin to an eternal 'one' of our visions of governance.

Yet the end of the Cold War, the progress of neoliberalism and the acceleration of globalisation generated a political milieu allowing for the growth and consolidation of what was labelled non-state authority.[1] In this regard one can think of neoliberalism not just as economic liberalism, but as a more sweeping transformation of the vision of the locus of authority in governance.[2] One scholarly account puts it like this:

> [B]y the late 1980s a second understanding of neoliberalism had emerged, one that is surely the dominant interpretation today. It is not an academic position within international relations that this understanding names but a particular political–economic project. This time it is defined in opposition, not to realism, but to projects of domestic governance—most notably the post-war regime of Keynesian welfare. Here neoliberalism is associated with a series of developments across the fields of economy, society, politics, and culture. These include policies such as privatisation, deregulation, trade liberalisation, and marketisation; economic phenomena such as the rise of transnational corporations and the power of global financial markets; institutional developments such as the growing prominence of international economic institutions (IMF, WTO, etc.); and ideological shifts such as the valorisation of the market over the state. Today, neoliberalism is used to denote nothing less than a fundamental restructuring of the world political economy over the last 30 years [...] it is a rationality of government [...] a mutation within liberal political reason'.[3]

According to this account, 'neoliberalism' implies a certain political–economic ethos underpinning market dogmatism, which acclaims decentralisation and competition as the solution to stiffened markets and rigid production structures as opposed to classical liberal economic theory of exchange. This idea of competition builds on an anthropology of the individual as 'one who strategizes for her or himself among various social, political, and economic options, not one who strives with others to alter or organize these options'.[4] Neoliberalism forefronts individual desire, creativity, expertise and local ownership. The overall idea is that we need to get planning, decisions and responsibility 'out there', in the midst of the everyday practices of economic and related societal life.[5] The source of world salvation is now believed to reside within the individual rather than with a centralised authority.[6] Hence a break from millennia of thinking governance though the prism of a centralised authority that governs through federal expertise installed by foresight-based interventions. (Compare here our discussion in chapter one about decentralised decision-making in military organisations.)

Practical transformations followed. The end of bipolarity, the growth of neoliberal ideology and globalisation opened the field of governance to new actors. Even wars no longer seemed limited to the bureaus of state authority. The proliferation and consolidation of so-called non-state authority in global governance has led, so we hear, to the formation of a multi-centric world order, 'as a sometime partner, sometime rival, and sometime co-equal of the long-standing state-centric world'.[7] In today's 'flat' world, as Thomas Freidman called it, authority seems no longer to come with a throne or sceptre that can be appropriated: there is no sceptre representing any singularity of authority. As a counter strategy, Michael Hardt and Antonio Negri's grassroots bible, *Empire* (2000),[8] tried to locate potent sites of resistance in such a centre-less world order, where the opposition finds itself without castles to vanquish or plazas to raise their protest flags on. Instead, they claimed, we see numerous sites of authority that overlap, pulsate and reverberate to the extent that the time-honoured model of centralised authority no longer describes properly our economic and political life.

Certainly, many commentators view decentralisation and the alleged consolidation of private authority as a most critical topic, and they swarm to study its metamorphosis: 'These developments [globalisation and the privatisation of power] lead us to question the nature of the boundaries between public and private authority, both domestically and globally. They suggest that we need to reconsider our notions of authority and governance more generally'.[9] We see great efforts on all fronts—political, legal, philosophical, sociological, and anthropological—to come to terms with a world in which the state may no longer be the *terminus a quo* for thinking and organising authority in global governance. Analyses of decentralised authority, however, suffer from the fact that '[n]otions of authority mainly derive from theorizing about domestic political authority, where the tendency to associate authority with the existence of a public realm is almost irresistible.'[10] We also see an enduring insistence on the public sphere as the only one entitled to prescribe behaviour for others, as, it is held, only 'public authorities are accountable through political institutions'.[11] To be sure, the idea of centralised authority really remains the prism through which we observe decentralisation: popular diagnostic labels such as post-Weberian, post-Hobbesian, post-national, post-territorial, multi-level governance, disaggregated, decentralised and empire, all refer back to the idea of centralised authority. Do these conceptual prefixes not come with a nostalgic desire to notionally subject the alleged new forms of authority to our conventional schemes? Be that as it may, the analyses mostly warn us that the governance paradigm based on centred forms of authority is on the verge of tilting into becoming something fundamentally different. But what may happen to our image of authority in governance, as we eventually get tired of calling it 'post'-something, 'beyond' something, or 'fragmented?' What kind of political–legal order is lurking around that corner?

The maturation and consolidation of a powerful private security industry that, with obvious self-interest, shapes our perceptions of peace and security and how threats could and should be met, has brought this question of decentralised authority and 'global causes' to a head. Not that private military firms necessarily create more harm than, say, extractive industries or medical companies, but their violent acts and side effects tap more directly into the scheme of governance, public order, authority and organised violent force. How could profit-driven, private companies be trusted with protecting a critical common good such as global security? And with what means? Much of the arguing about private security concerns these issues, which put at stake all the anxiety and worries of the global governance debate. That is the prospect of a world where the extreme expression of authority, organised violent force, lies in the hands of callous private interests. Privatisation of security is not only 'part of a broader restructuring and reconfiguration of public–private and global–local relations'.[12] It provides us with the most radical case of decentralised authority by suggesting that organised violent force and its unavoidable spillover effects in terms of collateral damage may have other masters than the nation state as the container for the common good. In this regard, as aforementioned the Weberian force monopoly as the defining mark of the modern state comes out somewhat shorthanded. The real question is not about the legitimate claim to institute violent force. An unengaged army raises no principled questions. It is only the practical operation of force—hands-on as well as for its deterrence effects—that stirs up the issues, and in particular the problem of collateral damage, due to its nature of being genetically disputed ground.

Global common goods: fixing Humpty Dumpty

We mostly picture the post-nation state order as chaotic, ruled by untrustworthy private corporations, finance, and networks. One commentator coined the term 'the new middle ages',[13] with its connotations of chaos, intransparency and power abuse, to describe this 'new' (dis)order. Debaters worry about how private authority may be tamed and subjected to democratic control. Who can set the standards for global regulatory regimes? What kind of institutions do we need? Who will run them? How may they be normatively legitimised?[14] Should they be comprised of states, global trade law regimes, or other supranational setups?

We try to glue together our cracked Humpty Dumpty. New forms of regulation, legitimated by new principles of highest order, are suggested as a way of preserving the traditional model of centralised authority.[15] Take the idea of global public goods. The idea is to identify non-rivalled and non-excludable common goods valid for anyone anywhere on earth, and derive from these a unifying cause for global governance.[16] Topics such as health, environment, peace and security, and effective management of global resources stand high on this agenda. Already, the poles are melting. Regions starve. Pandemics roam. It is a quest for a new source of authority to amalgamate our disintegrated world and unite the forces in common action. The United Nations Millennium Goals builds on such notions of common public goods, and the United Nations Global Compact may be seen as an attempt to align and unite business corporations ('private authority') on a voluntary level in a global compliance regime.[17] The idea of global common goods suggests a solution to a situation of 'the tragedy of the commons', where independent and self-maximising agents eat up our shared limited resources and so throw us all into calamity.[18] The idea appeals to a vision of an overall unifying cause in a world of fragmented, diverging political and economic power, a notion of unity and singularity, a centralised cause, which could drive a reintegration of global governance to secure common goods and, ultimately, mankind. The questions are: 'What and who should such authority be for?'[19] Who should finance and provide for such a securing of global goods, and how could global public goods be accounted for in authoritative global institutional designs?[20] What kind of authoritative claims to global common goods can legitimise coercion and military force? Who could and should swing its sword? And what kind of common public goods warrant collateral damage?

Private sacrifice and saints

It has been argued that in the hands of non-state actors, sacrifice potentially loses its meaning.[21] This becomes clear as the deaths of private contractors on the battlefield draws little attention or recognition in comparison to the 'cult stagings' of soldier self-sacrifices—even if the contractor and the soldier may work side by side. As of June 2010, more than 2,008 contractors had lost their lives in Iraq and Afghanistan and contractor deaths thereby made up over 25 per cent of all US fatalities since the beginning of these military actions.[22] Add to this above 44,000 injured, of which more than 16,000 seriously.[23] In Iraq in both 2009 and 2010, and in Afghanistan in 2010, contractors exceeded the US military in losses.[24] US Congressional Research Service reported in June 2010 that the Department of Defense (DoD) was employing about as many contractors as military personnel in Iraq. In Afghanistan, the number of

DoD-employed contractors surpassed military personnel by 30,000.[25] But military contractors and their families receive little formal recognition for their losses. Uniformed casualties were listed seven days a week in *The New York Times* and other media, but contractor casualties are hardly counted. Rather, they are excluded from the American sacrificial tradition and 'their deaths are, for a national audience, banal and insignificant events, not sacrifices'.[26] To honour their dead, some private military companies built their own memorials at their training facilities. Viewed in the light of the earlier chapter on sacrifice, the legacy of the mercenary in the Old Testament, and the debates on idolatry and authority, we see how these questions of sacrifice and private security cut to the heart of our nexus of authority and common causes and thereof derived claims to collateral damage; if there is a hollowness or even nonsense made of sacrifice when solely in the hands of private actors, the same applies to the claim to collateral damage.

However, in a truly global order, redemption no longer flows solely from centralised authority, and we hear competing claims to sacrifice and the use of force in the name of common causes. I heard someone argue 'whoever claims the right to sacrifice—one's own or others—acts not as a soldier but as a saint'. This might be true under a coding of global politics where the self-sacrifice in war still belongs to the state, and where claims to sacrifice outside this system appear dissenting. When private security companies present themselves as paramount experts in the global public good of 'peace and stability', they make a claim to be counted as comparable or higher authorities than the state. They proclaim a vision stating conventional notions of authority should be loosened to provide room for their morally matching agency. They come out as saints preaching a common good beyond the state, beyond time-honoured forms of centralised authority in governance. Intriguingly, their claim belongs in the same camp as those of humanitarians who argue that international law, with its institutionalisation of state sovereignty and principle of non-intervention, acts as a roadblock to protecting and assisting civilians caught up in conflicts and catastrophes. From their perspective, state leaders' struggle to preserve the state's formal sovereign integrity and principles may make them guilty of inhumane consequences.

This claim to humanity organises action beyond the state system: humanity becomes a powerful reference, a commanding cause, and mirrors a world envisioned by one of the founding fathers of international law, Hugo Grotius, in which all kinds of actors, state or non-state, were permitted to use organised force as long as they were driven by the common good.[27] Hence the claim is by no means new. The more the imaginary of global common goods becomes a cause in itself, the more the claim to permissible collateral damage beyond state authority resonates in the global political discourse. In the world of flat authority, the saints walk hand in hand with humanitarians, private military firms and the states. Glory is everywhere, or nowhere.

It is at this level of the political discourse that I suggest locating the concept of neoliberalism: it is about making a claim to self-sacrifice and collateral damage beyond the centralised state as the ultimate incarnation of political authority, ranking above claims to state and nationhood. Now, the private call for self-sacrifice has never been particularly problematic. Calls have been made but they draw relatively little public attention. You can run out and shout self-sacrifice and throw yourself in front of lions and tanks as much as you want as long as you don't harm anyone. Private corporations may create their own honours and medals. It is not a big deal. The private claim to collateral damage is much more controversial: when private companies leave a trail of unintended but perhaps foreseen death and suffering in their slipstream, no formal claim to collateral damage is available for them to excise charges of maliciousness from their otherwise decent acts. Hence, I will argue that the problem of private companies participating in armed conflicts is not the mere use of violent force, but more about justifying the collateral damage that flows from its use.

Authority and autonomy

As a paradigm of governance that embodies a vision of decentralised authority, neoliberalism stirs up another key puzzle of political theory: the authority–autonomy dilemma. Hobbes famously pointed out that if humans did not consent to a coercive authority and traded in some personal autonomy for societal stability, they would end up killing each other. Utilitarianism measured the balance between authority and personal autonomy by means of a notion of overall utility. The kinds of autonomy and authority and their respective values and mutual relationships—these are the issues. Autonomy may here simply be viewed as the right to self-determination—including the right to not to be someone else's collateral damage victim. The claim to collateral damage asserts the right to delimit others' autonomy. Here, neoliberalism insists more sturdily on individual autonomy by elevating the autonomous expertise of the private individual as the critical site of judgement about proper governance. As it relocates the appropriate source of authorship in governance affairs from the centre to the periphery, individual autonomy emerges as a threshold. From the perspective of our Judeo–Christian–Western–liberal world order, private authority ultimately appears as a problem of non-hierarchical steering,[28] and thus cuts to the heart of the modern Weber-inspired[29] visions of a governance regime organised around an authoritative centre. The instruments of rule in decentralised governance regimes are not law and commands, for these are all tools of centralised authority, but standards and guiding principles. The challenge of governance is to herd the horses into common action without straining their freedom.

In the first chapter, this shift was identified in the context of network-centric warfare as a shift from orders of generals to general orders. We see a shift in the idea of planning, which is now looked upon as something that takes place *in media res* and in the immediate and local context, rather than something that flows from above in a top-down command structure. From the perspective of centred notions of authority, this implies a profound transformation of the idea of the locus of authority. If pushed to its *ultima Thule*, it actually collapses the distinction between authority and autonomy. Now, only few anarcho-liberalists endorse the more radical neoliberal standpoint, and they remain without real influence on policymaking. We may, however, utilise neoliberalism's idea of decentralisation to capture theoretically the implications of the tectonic mutation of authority we are presently living through, which is pushing our modes of governance on all levels step-by-step towards the decentralised scheme of neoliberalism.

The eternal One

Consider the important role of mercenaries in the construction of God in the Old Testament, our earliest comprehensive image of centralised authority. Isn't it striking to notice how private force re-emerges today as a sort of limit figure now that the regime of centralised authority seems, by all accounts, to be disintegrating? Private force embodies the drama of the centre-less world, a drama that the poet W. B. Yeats referred to in his legendary 1919 apocalyptic poem 'The Second Coming': 'Things fall apart; the centre cannot hold; Mere anarchy is loosed upon the world'. Yeats' metaphor of the falcon that cannot or will not hear the falconer and therefore turns in a 'widening gyre' depicts the centrifugal societal forces of the 1920s, which Yeats saw as decaying common causes and shared moral codes. He feared a move from a centred world order to a multipolarity of free flying falcons; a state of bewilderment, where 'the best lack all conviction, while the worst are full of passionate intensity'. Yeats' image articulates, I will argue, the common duality of holding centralised authority in the face of multiple belief systems, a dualism that presupposes an ontological difference. By ontological I mean the most fundamental distinction of our idea of authority. My point is that before we can even talk about authority, we must agree that there is such a thing as authority. Only then can we draw a distinction between monocentric and polycentric visions of authority. This distinction is all I refer to when I talk about the ontology of authority—one or many. If authority is singular it cannot at the same time be multitudinous. It is not possible to have one king and two kings, one president and two presidents, one emperor and two emperors, within the same governance regime.

From a power perspective, either the centre holds or it doesn't. From a normative perspective, however, either we believe authority to be per definition centralised, supporting ideas that there can be only one king, one president, one god, one demos; or we believe authority can per definition be decentralised, fragmented, split, divided, shared. If we believe that authority in governance can and should remain undivided and unshared, the phenomenon that commentators label 'decentralised authority' must be understood merely as unchecked power: anarchy. On the other hand, if we believe that authority in governance can be shared and divided, multiple sites of authority may be recognised as legitimate. The first attitude rejects decentralised authority as something that may exist in its own right. The second attitude depletes the notion of authority. Logically viewed, the acceptance of 'setting free' authority leads to a process of disintegration, which comes to an end only when there is no hierarchy left whatsoever, no separation of authority and autonomy, no concept of the subject as a subject of governance. The regression may be brought to a halt only by some authority stepping in to decide the limits to decentralisation—but that would bring us back to the centralised authority regime. In that way the conceptual and structural implications of the notions of centralised and decentralised authority come out as mutually exclusive. They represent fundamentally different visions or figurations of authority in governance.

The incompatibility is located at the level of ontology, at the level of the question of the fundamental nature of authority. The ontological foundation of authority 'colours' the perception of events, actors, discourses, practices, and objects differently. Elements of centralised authority in governance fall into one category; elements of decentralised authority in governance fall into another. It can be argued that any notion of decentralised authority in governance only makes sense in the light of the tradition of viewing authority in governance as 'One'.

From such a viewpoint, it is not the tension as such that is puzzling; it is the very presence of decentralised authority and its relation to the centralised forms of authority. It does not fit, and appears controversial and ungoverned. Conversely, it can be argued that the vision of centralised authority in governance only appears so significant because there may be alternatives. The two figurations of authority in governance are thus conceptually intertwined, and neither would make any sense without the other. Monotheism requires polytheism. Yet the tension between centralised and decentralised authority may be experienced only as a tension from the perspective of centralised authority. Monotheism may feel threatened by polytheism, but to polytheism, the monotheistic assertion sounds just like another self-confident voice in the plural world of polytheism.

In fact, it poses tremendous difficulties to imagine a profound prototypical model of decentralised authority in governance—if we do not just call it anarchy, as Yeats did. We lack a cognitive base for such thinking. There simply is no available political philosophy of decentralised authority. From the perspective of political theology—which we can view as the study of how political and theological programmes order the subject and visions of the good within the larger context of society and the cosmos[30]—a possible emancipation of the subject from hierarchies of authority appears groundbreaking. From providential ideas of a cosmos ruled by an omnipotent, omniscient and omnibenevolent God who rules through divine foresight to modern liberal political theory, the individual has always been viewed as subjected to, or the subject of, a divine or political–legal order. In fact, the etymological meaning of the word 'subject' ranges from 'a person under control or dominion of another', and 'a person or thing that may be acted upon' to 'that which lies beneath' (Aristotle). Its verb form, 'to subject', has etymological roots, such as 'to make (a person or nation) subject to another by force', 'to render submissive or dependent', and 'to lay open or expose to (some force or occurrence)'.[31] Etymologically, the subject is always under the influence of some larger force, some authority: something bigger than the subject. Historically, in Western narratives of political and theological order, the individual has always been subjected. 'To be' has never been in and of oneself but by the force or figuration of something else. The stairways to grace and grandiosity have always primarily been laid down by larger institutions and their causes such as God or the state. And does the etymology of the subject not also imply that a subject is someone who may be subjected to authority's collateral damage calculation in the name of the greater good? I think so. In the light of my reflections so far I see how the etymology of the word 'subject' suggests a partial solution to the collateral damage problem by placing its burden in the hands of authority.

By elevating the private individual to the highest and wisest figure of governance, neoliberalism inverts traditional Jewish–Christian–Western–modern ideas of the place and the role of the subject in the world. This may sound a bit abstract, but from the point of the subject's self-understanding it obviously makes a real difference whether one is recognised as a part of a whole governed by a distinguished sovereign, or whether one is recognised as the (distinguished) centre of the world. Neoliberalism comes with a certain way of understanding the subject, a certain form of subjectivity that situates the subject and its agency in relation to other subjects and society at large—and to authority's access to collateral damage calculations.

The neoliberal subject is a different way of being in the world. It is a different form of political life. Taken to its *ultima Thule*, the claim of neoliberalism is, in fact, that there is no subject(ed) anymore. The neoliberal subject is, in theory, emancipated from hierarchies and bestowed with similar responsibilities as the providential authority of the state and Judeo-Christian God. As a contrast, neoliberalism offers an alternative vision of the subject as a certain form of subjectivity, situating the individual as the highest point of authority. The elevation implies that the private individual is left with some of the core responsibilities that formerly belonged to the centralised authority, including responsibility of governance: neoliberalism turns the private individual into governor. In a neoliberal world, we are all governors; we must all act as governors, we are all 'responsibilised'. We are all saints, yoked to the task of salvation. The critical question is the private access to claiming collateral damage for private visions of salvation and what it takes to get there, and what it means for others to be subjected to such self-contained collateral damage calculations. Furthermore, what it means to the subject to carry the burden of explaining and justifying collateral damage deaths.

These reflections may help us explain why concepts of decentralised authority are mostly constructed as prefixes to concepts of centralised authority, as in the concepts 'decentralisation', 'post-national', 'disaggregated', and 'post-Weberian'. It certainly looks different on an empirical level, where monistic regimes continue to impose their versions of authority and their discreet but devastating cost-benefit calculations on others less powerful than themselves;

and where private 'decentralised' actors decide with great influence over state, market, society, and nature. The classical dilemma between authority and autonomy is present at all levels of liberal governance politics, as the image of 'flat' governance with strong local ownership will mostly not correspond to the actual allotment of power.[32] But what is clear is that the newfangled forms of decentralised governance clash with our conventional ideas of governance that, since biblical times, have been built on notions of centralised authority and planning. Even the most minimalistic versions of liberal theory have this idea of centralised authority and planning as the bottom line, in the form of an independent judiciary and a basic law regime that anticipates future problems. Also, as previously discussed, liberalism comes with this built-in idea of foresight (through regulation) that corresponds to Judeo–Christian theological ideas of providence and its split between common people and the planner. In Greek antiquity, providence was the arrangement that provided the rational structure of the world. In Christianity, providence was the idea of God's rule through foresight.[33] Both versions of the notion of providence imply, or are shaped by, ideas of centralised, interventionist, foresight-based and anticipatory governance, built on wisdom greater than that which is found among common people; in other words a patriarchal rule with a cause and knowledge base exceeding common man.

The accumulation of arguments in this book suggests that commentators and analysts of global governance would be wise to supplement their persistent talk of authority and the monopoly on violent force with the question of the claim to collateral damage. Static organisations and structures spur little scepticism with which to meet claims of authority. Agency does. Agency affects people. It may create glorious worlds; but as we have learned, good willed agency also creates pain and suffering, It stirs up the 'why' that sparked off the quest for a solution to the moral problem of guilt and responsibility for the unavoidable bad side effects stemming from goodhearted agency. My key point is that this problem and moral puzzle of spillover violence runs much deeper than the relatively new idea of the legitimate monopoly on organised violent force as the defining state attribute. It runs much deeper than questions of political, social and legal control. The legitimate claim to collateral damage quite simply constitutes the threshold between centralised and decentralised forms of authority in governance: it constitutes the tipping point between a liberal and a truly neoliberal world order. The implications of setting free, or unleashing, the claim to collateral damage would turn most political theory upside down. In that way the problem of collateral damage offers

10

A PLACE BETWEEN IT ALL

I suggested in the introduction that if there is any transcendence in our social world, we should not look for it in the grand explanations hypothesised by theology or philosophy; but that some kind of transcendence may perhaps rather be found in the core puzzles and dilemmas, which led to the initial need to formulate these ideas. Our Adamic failure-proneness does challenge us with a thorny human condition. Yet our belief in a category of 'collateral damage' void of responsibility lacks a deeper substance. The international treaties and customary law underpinning the collateral damage rule largely grew out of practical solutions to practical problems. They merely express the prevailing view that 'collateral damage' is void of responsibility. While acceptable in courts, a circular reasoning haunts the rule: we assumed collateral damage was void of responsibility so we acted as if, and little by little, a 'legal truth' materialised that justified our beliefs and practices. But neither claims, agreements, practice or law produces moral or philosophical substance. The truth is that the ideas and philosophies usually invoked to support the collateral damage rule all suffer from the same gap between promise and performance that they aspired to bridge. The only cogent substance may be the collateral damage problem itself; not our many confused attempts to resolve it.

Hence the collateral damage rule comes with a secret: collateral damage free from responsibility is not a naturally given, but an invented claim. It is just an idea we have invented to make it easier for ourselves. Despite its anchor in international customary law and treaty, it embodies just another attempt to rationalise, contain and tranquilise the seemingly bad, sinful, evil, wrong, erroneous, wicked, and immoral acts we humans are prone to bring forth whenever we move ahead in life. The rule incarnates our deepest desire for a meaningful world and thus also contains an image of what it means to be human and crave a meaning that keeps escaping. Every dead person we label collateral damage epitomises these problems and desires. Tranquilising the dilemma, exorcising the shame, and hushing the bereaved by proclamations of law will not save us from the problem's deep-seated power over our ideas and visions of governance and authority. As a timeless problem, the problem of collateral damage synchronises or connects the experience of and attitudes towards collateral damage victims on the battlefields of the twenty-first century armed conflicts with key debates about authority and rule from across time—ranging from the Old Testament, ancient Greek philosophy, medieval theology, just war theory, utilitarianism, modern accident law to, as I argue, the debates about the locus of authority in post-nation-state global governance. The noble yet ultimately failed exertions to resolve the problem evolved in tandem with the historical narrative of centralised authority, driven by a yearning to vindicate the suffering inflicted on the innocent by acts of governance. This historical trajectory explains to us why the question 'Who may claim collateral damage' today corresponds perfectly with the question, 'Who may govern the world?' For the same reason, the collateral damage norm and rule, as we know them today, would lose their meaning without the paradigm of centralised authority: the axiomatic and accredited character of this paradigm bestows on collateral damage its aura of grace. Hitherto, only spokespersons of God and the state have succeeded in making the claim to collateral damage. For combatants, the collateral damage rule offers some degree of redemption from speculating about the morality of killing civilians. For the victims, the suffering and bereaved, the rule offers nothing apart from an international stamp of approval.

Where reason fails, only faith offers redemption. In the case of our collateral damage problem, faith in the *raison d'être* of some authority, whether democratically installed or divinely derived. Now, the writing is on the wall: Traditional structures of authority creak and bend under the ascendency of non-state hegemony. Anxiety flourishes about the future forms and loci of authority in governance: will it be multi-level governance, post-Westphalian, post-territorial, post-Hobbesian, post-national, post-Weberian, a new empire, multi-level governance, soft sovereignty, or a disaggregated world order. Global law without a state, hybrid authority, reconfigured sovereignty, or will it perhaps be multi-layered governance? These concepts all derive their semantic vigour from the same shock of the new: the looming truth that the constitutional state may no longer be the sole carrier of ultimate authority in global governance. The falcons depart. The issues at stake are not only about non-hierarchical steering and accountability issues. We are confronted with a more basic problem: why steer? For what cause and reason and towards what ends? The real challenge is the fragmentation of the very cause of community, the reasons we hold together and that hold us together, and thereby of the very legacy and configuration of the collateral damage rule.

The purported fragmentation of authority in global governance sends us back to the quandaries of the Book of Samuel: should everyone follow the same ultimate cause, embodied by the same authority, or could we entertain a plurality of authorities? Is monotheism as a form of centralised governance really the best model for organising political life on earth, or could polytheism prove just as good? In this regard, the successful claim to collateral damage emerges as the threshold of decentralisation. If everyone became entitled to define a local notion of good governance, if everyone, or any corporation, was entitled to derive a claim to collateral damage to maintain the 'goodness' of his or her respective governance project, how would this change our notions of good and bad? How can we then settle the questions of justice that arise when good governance steams ahead and knowingly but 'unintendedly' leaves a trail of death and suffering in its wake? What name warrants collateral damage? How could we evacuate evil from ourselves, how could we explain how bad could be good and good could be bad? What name could be invoked?

The polycentric answer to our contemporary difficulties with authority in governance will throw most of our moral–political theories overboard. It could lift the balloon a bit. Many feel burdened by the institution of centralised authority. Yet the fragmentation of authority will also leave us unable to respond to general questions of responsibility, accountability, and justice. If we plan to 'go polycentric', be it by choice or by systemic pressure, then we had better start beating our brains to find ways to deal with these issues, specifically the problem of collateral damage. In this context, the relatively invisible victims of collateral damage offer a means of understanding the deeper implications of decentralisation.

The fact that questions of guilt and justice have rarely focused on the victim constitutes a historical puzzle in itself. This is equally true for the history of the crime victim. I have provided some explanations for the absence of the collateral damage victim in our culture. Double-effect thinking, just war theory, theodicy, and utilitarianism as well as contemporary popular culture have all focused primarily on the moral standing of the aggressor. Alas, in our culture, collateral damage victims function mostly as a mirror for reflecting back the moral footing of the victimisers. They lack a dramaturgy, sacrificial value, or a moral or legal scandal and therefore enjoy little public interest apart from in their role as chips in this process of moral self-reflexivity or in strategic games. Will we ever be able to establish eye contact with the wretched? I see little indication of this. The idea and rule of collateral damage are a hardwearing institution. Due to the lack of legal recognition, a related profession, strong advocacy groups, movies and media coverage, collateral damage victims will probably remain unscrutinised and consequently never receive much public attention. If the alleged fragmentation of authority in global governance continues, the problem of collateral damage will without doubt revive, but I really wonder whether this would shine any additional light on the victims themselves. Time will show.

How peculiar it is that this anonymous category of death and suffering at the same time constitutes the protagonist of our key historical debates about authority, governance, human agency and morality. Now, what would happen if we were to accept this evident circumstance, and use the problem of collateral damage as a kind of first philosophy of political and legal theory, not forgetting just war theory? What if we revisited our political theories of authority and responsibility in times of war by taking, first and foremost, the perspective of the wretched? To do so would mean a huge sacrifice. The idea that there may be such a thing as collateral damage seizes and sets aside the moral ambivalence of warfare and governance more broadly. It carries out our shame, and it allows us to be perfect. We would have to give all this up.

I try to imagine how the war coverage, and the narratives of war, governance, and responsibility would look if we were to put an end to the collateral damage option. What kind of moral universe comes into view beyond the option of collateral damage? It would mean an exit from a guilt-free world, wouldn't it? A second exile.

NOTES

INTRODUCTION

1. While Augustine is mostly viewed as the key originator of the idea or "doctrine" of original sin, it is unclear whether Augustine was the inventor of the idea of merely "played the role of faithful interpreter of the tradition." See Pier Franco Beatrice (2013): *The Transmission of Sin. Augustine and the Pre-Augustinian Sources*. Oxford: Oxford University Press, p. 8.
2. Ibid., p. 7.
3. For a historical examination of the idea of sin and its various forms, see Gary Anderson (2009): *Sin: A History*. Yale University Press.
4. For a history of the 'forgotten victim', see Richard Shelly Hartigan (1982/2010): *Civilian Victims in War. A Political History*. New Brunswick: Transaction Publishers. For an account of the lack of focus on civilians in American war culture, see John Tirman (2011): *The Deaths of Others. The Fate of Civilians in America's Wars*. Oxford: Oxford University Press.

1. THE THIRD CATEGORY OF DEATH

1. F.H. Russell (1987): '*Love and Hate in Medieval Warfare: The Contribution of Saint Augustine*', *Nottingham Medieval Studies*, Vol. 31, pp. 108–25.
2. Thucydides (1972): *The History of the Peloponnesian War*. London: Penguin Classics.
3. Judith Gail Gardam (1993): *Non-combatant Immunity as a Norm of International Humanitarian Law*. Dordrecht: M. Nijhoff Publishers, p. 5.
4. Jean Jacques Rousseau (1762, 2007): *The Social Contract or Principles of Political Right*. Thousand Oaks: BN Publishing, p. 7.
5. Instructions for the Government of Armies of the United States in the Field, General Order No 100.
6. Martti Koskenniemmi (2001) *The Gentle Civilzer of Nations: The Rise and Fall of International Law 1870–1960*. Cambridge: Cambridge University Press, p. 11ff.

7. See Antony Anghie (2005): *Imperialism, Sovereignty and the Making of International Law*. Cambridge: Cambridge University Press.
8. Hugo Slim (2008): *Killing Civilians*. New York: Columbia University Press, pp. 19–20.
9. Ibid.
10. Alex J. Bellamy (2012): *Massacres and Morality. Mass Atrocities in an Age of Civilian Immunity*. Oxford: Oxford University Press, p. 132; pp. 132–59.
11. Sahr Conway-Lanz (2006): *Collateral Damage. Americans, Noncombatant Immunity, and Atrocities after World War II*. New York: Routledge, p. 1; Ronald Shaffer (1985): *Wings of Judgment: American Bombings in World War II*. New York: Oxford University Press, p. 64, 67, 128–36.
12. Daniel Barenblatt (2004): *A Plague upon Humanity: The Secret Genocide of Axis Japan's Germ Warfare Operation*. New York: HarperCollins Publishers.
13. Mark Grimsley and Clifford J. Rogers (2002): *Civilians in the Path of War*. Nebraska: University of Nebraska Press, p. ix.
14. W. Hays Parks (2007): 'Asymmetries and the Identification of Legitimate Military Objectives', in Heintschel von Heinegg and Volker Epping (eds): *International Humanitarian Law Facing New Challenges*. Berlin: Springer, pp. 65–117.
15. Alex J. Bellamy (2012): *Massacres and Morality. Mass Atrocities in an Age of Civilian Immunity*. Oxford: Oxford University Press, p. 133.
16. Ibid.
17. Conway-Lanz, *Collateral Damage*, p. 13.
18. Ibid.
19. James Turner Johnson (1999): *Morality in Contemporary Warfare*. New York: Vail-Ballau Press, p. 126.
20. R. Charli Carpenter (2006): *Innocent Women and Children*. Hampshire: Ashgate, p. 29.
21. As codified in 1977 First Additional Protocol to the Geneva Conventions, Article 44, para 3 and 4.
22. Judith Gardam (2004): *Necessity, Proportionality and the Use of Force by States*. Cambridge: Cambridge University Press, p. 86.
23. David Kennedy (2006): *Of War and Law*. Princeton University Press, p. 143.
24. Bellamy, *Massacres and Morality*.
25. John Tirman (2011): *The Deaths of Others. The Fate of Civilians in America's Wars*. Oxford: Oxford University Press.
26. See Thomas Franck (2008): 'On Proportionality of Countermeasures in International Law', *American Journal of International Law*, Vol. 102, pp. 715–67, p. 715.
27. US Department of Defense (2001): *Department of Defense Dictionary of Military and Associated Terms*. US Department of Defense, Joint Publication 1–02 (As Amended Through 19 August 2009), p. 102.
28. Air Force Pamphlet 14–210 Intelligence, 'USAF Intelligence Targeting Guide',

1 February 1998, http://www.fas.org/irp/doddir/usaf/afpam14–210/part20.htm [last visited 2 March 2015].

29. US Department of Defense, *Dictionary of Military and Associated Terms*, p. 632.

30. Steven C. Gordon and Douglas D. Martin (2005): 'Modeling and Simulation for Collateral Damage Estimation in Combat', *Proc. SPIE*, Vol. 5805, pp. 309–17; see also Christopher Morton (ed.) (1999): 'Minimizing Collateral Damage During Peace Support Operations Main Report', NATO Technology and Research Organization, Study no. RTO-TR-023 AC/323(SAS)TP/13; Amanda Humphrey, Judi See and David Faulkner (2008): 'A Methodology to Assess Lethality and Collateral Damage for Nonfragmenting Precision-Guided Weapons', *ITEA Journal*, Vol. 29, 4, pp. 411–19.

31. Robert Mandel (2004): 'The Wartime Utility of Precision Versus Brute Force in Weaponry', *Armed Forces & Society*, Vol. 30, 2, pp. 171–201.

32. Patricia Owens (2003): 'Accidents Don't Just Happen: The Liberal Politics of High-Technology "Humanitarian" War', *Millennium. Journal of International Studies*, Vol. 32, pp. 595–616, p. 603.

33. Neta C. Crawford (2013): *Accountability for Killing. Moral Responsibility for Collateral Damage in America's post-9/11 Wars*. Oxford: Oxford University Press, p. 77, 82.

34. Gian P. Gentile (2009): 'A Strategy of Tactics: Population-centric COIN and the Army', *Parameters*, Vol. 39, 3, pp. 5–17, p. 5.

35. See Frederik Rosén (2008): 'Commercial Security. Conditions of Growth', *Security Dialogue*, Vol. 39, 1, pp. 77–97, p. 80ff.

36. Yee-Kuang Heng (2006): 'The "Tranformation of War" Debate: through the Looking Glass of Ulrich Beck's World Risk Society', *International Relations*, Vol. 20, 1, pp. 69–91, p. 71.

37. Joellen Perry (2005): 'Checkpoint Chaos', *Die Zeit*, 10 March http://www.zeit.de/2005/11/checkpoint_englisch [last visited 2 March 2015].

38. Chris Hedges (2009): *Collateral Damage: America's War Against Iraqi Civilians*. New York: Nation Books, p. 29ff.

39. Richard A. Oppel (2010): 'Tighter Rules Fail to Stem Deaths of Innocent Afghans at Checkpoints', New York Times, 26 March, 2010.

40. Martin Shaw (2005): *The New Western Way of War: Risk Transfer War and Its Crisis in Iraq*. Cambridge: Polity Press, pp. 98–9.

41. See Tracey Dowdeswell (2013): 'How Atrocity Becomes Law: The Neoliberalisation of Security Governance and the Customary Laws of Armed Conflict', *Journal of Critical Globalisation Studies*, Vol. 1, 6, pp. 30–56

42. Discussions of the moral and legal aspects of the force protection/collateral damage dilemma can be found in: Thomas W. Smith (2008): 'Protecting Civilians … or Soldiers? Humanitarian Law and the Economy of Risk in Iraq', *International Studies Perspectives* Vol. 9, 2, pp. 144–64; Ziv Bohrer and Mark Osiel (2013): 'Pro-

portionality in Military Force at War's Multiple Levels: Averting Civilian Casualties vs. Safeguarding Soldiers', *Vanderbilt Journal of Transnational Law*, Vol. 46, pp. 747–822; Noam Neuman (2004): 'Applying the Rule of Proportionality: Force Protection and Cumulative Assessment in International Law and Morality', *Yearbook of International Humanitarian Law*, Vol. 7, pp. 79–112; David J. Luban (2013): 'Risk Taking and Force Protection', in Yitzhak Benbaji and Naomi Sussman (eds): *Reading Walzer*. London: Routledge, 2013.

43. Prominent just war philosophers have cast doubt on the moral permissibility of letting civilians bear the burden of risk; see Avishai Margalit and Michael Walzer (2009): 'Israel: Civilians and Combatants', *New York Review of Books*, 14 May.

44. David Kilcullen (2014): *Out of the Mountains. The Coming Age of the Urban Guerrilla*. London: Hurst, p. 50, 52, 232ff.

45. Ibid., p. 232.

46. Ibid., p. 26.

47. Congressional Research Service (2007): 'Network Centric Operations: Background and Oversight Issues for Congress'. Washington DC: Congressional Research Service, summary.

48. David Alberts (2002): 'Information Age Transformation: Getting to a 21st Century Military'. Washington, DC: Department of Defense Command and Control Research Program, p. 7.

49. David S. Alberts and Richard E. Hayes (2003): Power to the Edge: Command and Control in the Information Age. CCRP Publications Distribution Center.

50. Ibid., p. 5.

51. Ibid.

52. Eric J. Dahl (2004): 'Too Good to be Legal? Network Centric Warfare and International Law'. *Journal of Public and International Affairs*, Vol. 15, pp. 38–58, p. 47.

53. David Udris, Michael Udris, James Der Derian (2012): *Human Terrain, the Movie*.

54. Deputy Judge Advocate General at the US Air Force Headquarters of Washington (2006–2010)

55. Charles J. Dunlap (2007): 'Collateral Damage and Counterinsurgency Doctrine', *Small Wars Journal*, http://smallwarsjournal.com/blog/collateral-damage-and-counterinsurgency-doctrine [last visited 1 September 2011].

2. COLLATERAL DAMAGE AND THE QUESTION OF LEGAL RESPONSIBILITY

1. NATO (2010): Letter dated 11 October 2010 from the Deputy Secretary General of the North Atlantic Treaty Organization addressed to the Secretary-General/Quarterly Report to the Security Council on the Operations of the International Security Assistance Force, United Nations Security Council S/2010/548.

2. See David Luban (2012): 'Military Lawyers and the Two Cultures Problem', http://scholarship.law.georgetown.edu/cgi/viewcontent.cgi?article=1964&context=fac

pub; L. Dickinson (2010): 'Military Lawyers on the Battlefield: An Empirical Account of International Law Compliance', *American Journal of International Law*, Vol. 104, 1, pp. 1–28.

3. See Yves Sandoz, Christophe Swinarski and Bruno Zimmermann (eds) (1987): *Commentary on the Additional Protocols of 8 June 1977 to the Geneva Conventions of 12 August 1949*. Geneva: Martinus Nijhoff Publishers, Commentary 1863, p. 598.

4. Protocol Additional to the Geneva Conventions of 12 August 1949, and relating to the Protection of Victims of International Armed Conflicts (Protocol I), 8 June 1977, Article 51, paras 5b. and 57(2)(a)(iii).

5. It matters a great deal whether proportionality is measured against the overall aims of war or in terms of the military advantage gained from an individual attack. To be sure, there is a vast and burgeoning literature on the basically undetermined principle of proportionality. However, from the perspective of law, the substantial lawfulness of collateral damage remains the same regardless of the kind of proportionality assessment that is applied.

6. *Prosecutor v. Kupreskic and Others*, ICTY Case No. IT-95-16, 14 January 2000, para. 524.

7. H. Heintze (2004): 'On the Relationship Between Human Rights Law Protection and International Humanitarian Law', *International Review of the Red Cross*, Vol. 86, 856, pp. 789–814; R. Kolb (1998): 'The Relationship Between International Humanitarian Law and Human Rights Law: A Brief History of the 1948 Universal Declaration of Human Rights and the 1949 Geneva Conventions', *International Review of the Red Cross*, special issue 324, pp. 409–17; H. Robertson (1984): 'Humanitarian Law and Human Rights', in C. Swinarski (ed.), *Études et essais sur le droit international humanitaire et sur les principes de la Croix–Rouge/ Studies and essays on international humanitarian law and Red Cross principles, en l'honneur de/in honour of Jean Pictet*. The Hague, Martinus Nijhoff; D. Schindler (1979): 'The International Committee of the Red Cross and Human Rights', *International Review of the Red Cross*, 208 pp. 3–114.

8. A. Orakhelashvili (2001): 'The Position of the Individual in International Law', *California Western International Law Journal*, Vol. 31, pp. 241–76; K. Parlet (2010): *The Individual in the International Legal System: Continuity and Change in International Law*. Cambridge: Cambridge University Press.

9. See G. Draper (1971): 'The Relationship between the Human Rights Regime and the Law of Armed Conflict', *Israel Yearbook on Human Rights*, Vol. 1, pp. 191–207; G. Draper (1973): *The Implementation of the Modern Law of Armed Conflicts*. Jerusalem: Magness Press.

10. L. Doswald-Beck (2006): 'The Right to Life in Armed Conflict: Does International Humanitarian Law Provide All the Answers?', *International Review of the Red Cross*, Vol. 88, 864, pp. 881–904.

11. ICJ, *Case Concerning Armed Activities on the Territory of the Congo (Democratic Republic of the Congo v. Uganda)*, ICJ Reports (19 December 2005).

12. ICJ, *Legality of the Threat or Use of Nuclear Weapons*, (Advisory Opinion of 8 July 1996—General List No. 95, 1995–1998) para. 25. See also ICJ, *Legal Consequences of the Construction of a Wall in the Occupied Palestinian Territory*, Advisory Opinion (9 July 2004); M. Dennis (2005): 'ICJ Advisory Opinion on Construction of a Wall in the Occupied Palestinian Territory: Application of Human Rights Treaties Extraterritorially in Times of Armed Conflict and Military Occupation', *American Journal of International Law*, Vol. 99, 1, pp. 119–42.

13. ICJ, Legality of the Threat or Use of Nuclear Weapons.

14. The first case that set this out was *Loizidou v. Turkey* (1995), in which the Court was faced with the question of access to private property in occupied territory (*in casu* northern Cyprus). The Court found that the jurisdiction under ECHR Article 1 is not restricted to the national territory of the High Contracting Parties and that jurisdiction may arise when a Contracting Party exercises effective control of an area outside its national territory, for instance through military operations. *Loizidou v. Turkey*: App. No. 15318/89, *Loizidou v. Turkey* (Preliminary Objections), 23 March 1995, 20 EHRR (1995) 99, at para. 62.

15. Inter American Court of Human Rights (2000): *Bamaca Velásquez v. Guatemala*, Judgement (25 November 2000).

16. International Law Commission (2011): 'Draft Articles on the Effects of Armed Conflict on Treaties' 63. Session (2011) Article 3; See also Annie Bird (2010): 'Third State Responsibility for Human Rights Violations', *The European Journal of International Law* Vol. 21, 4 pp. 883–900.

17. F. Coomans and M. Kamminga, (eds) (2004): *Extraterritorial Application of Human Rights Treaties*. Antwerp: Intersentia.

18. See M. Gibney and S. Skogly (eds) (2010): *Universal Human Rights and Extraterritorial Obligations*. Philadelphia: University of Pennsylvania Press.

19. ECtHR, App. No. 52207/99, *Banković v. Belgium*, Grand Chamber, 12 Dec. 2001, 44 EHRR (2001) SE5, paras 59 and 61.

20. *European Convention for the Protection of Human Rights and Fundamental Freedoms*, 4 November 1950, 213 UNTS 221, 3 Sept 1953, Art. 1.

21. *Banković v. Belgium*, para. 61.

22. In a broad sense, the term 'jurisdiction' may be said to describe any authority over a certain area or certain persons. According to Article 1 of the ECHR, the member states 'shall secure to everyone within their jurisdiction the rights and freedoms defined in Section I of this Convention'. Accordingly, member states are only responsible for acts and omissions falling within their 'jurisdiction'.

23. *Banković v. Belgium*, paras. 59 and 61.

24. Ibid., para. 82.

25. European Court of Human Rights Press Unit (2012): 'Extra-territorial jurisdic-

tion of ECHR Member States. Factsheet—Extra-territorial jurisdiction'. Strasbourg.

26. ECtHR, *Issa v. Turkey* [2004] ECtHR 31821/96 (16 Nov. 2004).

27. ECtHR, *Öcalan v Turkey* (Grand Chamber) [2005] ECtHR 46221/99 (12 May 2005).

28. S. Miller (2009): 'Revisiting Extraterritorial Jurisdiction: A Territorial Justification for Extraterritorial Jurisdiction'. *European Journal of International Law*, Vol. 20, 4, pp. 1223–46, p. 1233.

29. *Issa v. Turkey*, para 74.

30. Ibid., para 75.

31. Miller 'Revisiting Extraterritorial Jurisdiction', p. 1228.

32. ECtHR, *Al-Skeini and Others v United Kingdom* [2011] ECtHR 1093 (7 July 2011).

33. *Al-Skeini*, pp. 18–26.

34. Ibid., paras. 149–150.

35. Marko Milanovic (2012): 'Al-Skeini and Al-Jedda in Strasbourg', *The European Journal of International Law*, Vol. 23, 1, pp. 121–39, p. 123.

36. Ibid.

37. See P. Kessing (2011): 'Den Europæiske Menneskerettighedskonventions anvendelse under internationale FN-operationer', *Juristen*, 10, pp. 307–16, p. 309ff.

38. A note could be added here on how the human rights driven recasting of legal authority over military affairs from military justice systems to civilian justice systems is entwining military justice and civilian justice systems. In so far as the theories and studies of civil–military relations have not yet addressed the juridical dimension of civil–military relations as a subject in its own right, this entwining suggests a new subject in the study of civil–military relations, straddling the institutional entwining and the sociological dimension of practical cooperation. I have elaborated on this topic in Frederik Rosén (2013): 'The End of Military Justice in Europe: An Agenda for Juridical Civil–military Relations', *Small Wars & Insurgencies*, Vol. 24, 2, pp. 335–48.

39. House of Lords, Session 2006–07 [2007] UKHL 26, para. 78.

40. *Al-Skeini*, Concurring opinion of Judge Bonello, para 37–38.

41. US case law on extraterritoriality is dominated by the approach that citizenship above anything else determines the constitutional protection that individuals are entitled to. Consequently, foreigners cannot expect to enjoy the same standards of protection. See M. Milanovic (2011): *Extraterritorial Application of Human Rights Treaties*. Oxford: Oxford University Press, p. 67ff.

42. C. Droege (2007): 'The Interplay Between IHL and IHRL', *Israeli Law Review*, Vol. 40, 2, pp. 310–55, p. 345.

43. ICJ, *Nuclear Weapons*, para. 25.

44. ICJ, *Wall*, para. 106.

45. M. Milanovic (2010): 'A Norm Conflict Perspective on the Relationship Between International Humanitarian Law and Human Rights Law', *Journal of Conflict and Security Law*, Vol. 14, 3, pp. 459–83, p. 462ff.

46. ICJ, *Nuclear Weapons*, para. 25.

47. ICJ, *Wall*, para. 106. This approach is reflected in a United Nations field guide on the International Legal Protection of Human Rights in Armed Conflict from 2011, which concludes that 'cases involving the killing of civilians in an attack by a party to a conflict imply the application of the international humanitarian law principles of distinction and proportionality as *lex specialis*, with the relevant provisions of the Covenant being applied as complementary norms'. United Nations (2012): *International Legal Protection of Human Rights in Armed Conflict*. New York: United Nations Publications, p. 61.

48. G. Gaggioli and R. Kolb (2007): 'A Right to Life in Armed Conflicts? The Contribution of the European Court of Human Rights', *Israeli Yearbook of Human Rights*, 37, pp. 115–63, p. 138; A. Gioia (2011): 'The Role of the European Court of Human Rights', in Orna Ben-Naftali (ed.), *International Humanitarian Law and International Human Rights Law*. Oxford: Oxford University Press, pp. 201–45.

49. European Convention for the Protection of Human Rights and Fundamental Freedoms, Art. 15, 3 Sept. 1953, 213 U.N.T.S. 222. Article 15(1) of the ECHR reads: 'In time of war or other public emergency threatening the life of the nation any High Contracting Party may take measures derogating from its obligations under this Convention to the extent strictly required by the exigencies of the situation, provided that such measures are not inconsistent with other obligations under international law.'

50. International Covenant on Civil and Political Rights, Art. 4, 23 March 1976, 99 U.N.T.S. 171. Article 4(1) reads: 'in time of public emergency which threatens the life of the nation and the existence of which is officially proclaimed, the States Parties to the present Covenant may take measures derogating from their obligations under the present Covenant to the extent strictly required by the exigencies of the situation, provided that such measures are not inconsistent with their other obligations under international law and do not involve discrimination solely on the ground of race, colour, sex, language, religion or social origin'.

51. Droege, 'Interplay', p. 318ff.

52. For instance, in *McCann v. UK*, the ECtHR found that death caused by a blunder in the application of lethal force does not necessarily constitute a breach of Article 2. *McCann v. United Kingdom* (1995) 21 ECHR, para. 97.

53. See Juliet Chevalier-Watts (2010): 'Effective Investigations under Article 2 of the European Convention on Human Rights: Securing the Right to Life or an Onerous Burden on a State?' *European Journal of International Law*, Vol. 21, 3, pp. 701–21; Alastair Mowbray (2002): 'Duties of Investigation under the European Convention on Human Rights' *International and Comparative Law Quarterly*,

Vol. 51, 2, pp. 437–48; See also United Nations (1989): 'Principles on the Effective Prevention and Investigation of Extra-legal, Arbitrary and Summary Executions' (Economic and Social Council Resolution, 1989/65, 24 May 1989); United Nations (1999): 'Principles on the Effective Investigation and Documentation of Torture and Other Cruel, Inhuman or Degrading Treatment or Punishment' (United Nations, 1999); Michael N. Schmitt (2011): 'Investigating Violations of International Law in Armed Conflict' *Harvard National Security Journal* Vol. 2, pp. 31–84, p. 49ff.

54. ECtHR *Ergi v Turkey* 1998 23818/94 (28 July 1998); *Rod v Croatia* 2008 47024/06 (18 September 2008); ECtHR *Ulku Ekinci v Turkey* 2002 27602/95 (16 July 2002).

55. *McKerr v. United Kingdom* ECHR 2001–111 Eur. Ct. H.R. 475, para. 111.

56. Ibid.

57. Ibid., p. 113.

58. European Commission of Human Rights, Application No. 18984/91 Margaret McCann, Daniel Farrell and John Savage against the United Kingdom, Report of the Commission (adopted on 4 March 1994)

59. Schmitt, 'Investigating Violations of International Law', p. 54.

60. *McKerr v. UK*, p. 111.

61. Droege, 'Interplay', p. 345

62. The situation I attempt to represent is the fact that decision-making in governance is increasingly decentralised, including within the state and military organizations. See S. Sassen (2006): *Territory, Authority, Rights: From Medieval to Global Assemblages*. Princeton: Princeton University Press, p. 168ff.

63. L. Caplan (2003): 'State Immunity, Human Rights and *Jus Cogens*: A Critique of the Normative Hierarchy Theory', *The American Journal of International Law*, Vol. 97 pp. 741–77; M. Potestá (2010): 'State Immunity and Jus Cogens Violations: The Alien Tort Statute against the Backdrop of the Latest Developments in the "Law of Nations"', *Berkeley Journal of International Law*, Vol. 28, 2, pp. 571–86. See also N. Saputo (2012): 'The Ferrini Doctrine: Abrogating State Immunity for Civil Suit for Jus Cogens Violations', *University of Miami National Security & Armed Conflict Law Review*, Vol. 2, pp. 1–37.

64. It should be noted that this notion of combatant 'immunity' according to which soldiers cannot be prosecuted for killing enemy combatants is not part of the doctrine of state immunity.

65. Furthermore, in recent years bilateral Status of Force Agreements (SOFAs), as we have seen them not least in Iraq and Afghanistan, have sought to provide combatants with further immunity from foreign prosecution. See C. Mason (2012): 'Status of Forces Agreement (SOFA): What Is It, and How Has It Been Utilized?' Washington, DC: Congressional Research Service. Available at http://www.fas.org/sgp/crs/natsec/RL34531.pdf. [Last visited 14 July 2015].

66. International Law Commission (1950): 'Principles of International Law Recognized in the Charter of the Nürnberg Tribunal and in the Judgement of the Tribunal, with Commentaries, 1950', *Yearbook of the International Law Commission*, Vol. II. The ILC reported, 'the general rule underlying Principle I [of the Charter of the Nürnberg Tribunal] is that international law may impose duties on individuals directly without any interposition of internal law. The findings of the Tribunal were very definite on the question of whether rules of international law may apply to individuals. "That international law imposes duties and liabilities upon individuals as well as upon States", said the judgement of the Tribunal, "has long been recognized." It added: "crimes against international law are committed by men, not by abstract entities, and only by punishing individuals who commit such crimes can the provision of international law be enforced."'

67. T. Graditzky (1998): 'Individual Criminal Responsibility for Violations of International Humanitarian Law Committed in Non-international Armed Conflicts', *International Review of the Red Cross*, 322, 29–56.

68. The Rome Statute of the International Criminal Court, Art. 28; Statue of the ICTY, Art. 7; Statue of the The International Criminal Tribunal for Rwanda, Art. 6.

69. Arrest Warrant, ICJ Reports [2002] 000 (14 February), pr. 45.

70. This has also recently been reaffirmed *inter alia* in the preamble to the United Nations Convention on Jurisdictional Immunities of States and Their Property, adopted by the General Assembly of the United Nations on 2 December 2004 (not yet in force). See H. Fox (2008): *The Law of State Immunity*, 2nd edition. Oxford: Oxford University Press, pp. 1ff; J. Bröhmer (1997): *State Immunity and the Violation of Human Rights*. Martinus Nijhoff Publishers: The Hague, p. 9

71. D. Akande and S. Shah (2011): 'Immunities of State Officials, International Crimes, and Foreign Domestic Courts', *European Journal of International Law*, Vol. 21, 815–52, p. 817

72. Fox, *Law of State Immunity*, p. 1.

73. United Nations Convention on Jurisdictional Immunities of States and Their Property. Adopted by the General Assembly of the United Nations on 2 December 2004. Not yet in force.

74. General Assembly Resolution 32/151 of 19 December 1977; Report of the International Law Commission on the work of its forty-third session, 29 April–19 July 1991, Doc. A/46/10 at pp. 8–151. As of 14 June 2010, there are 28 signatories to the Convention and 10 instruments of ratification have been deposited. According to its Article 30, the Convention requires 30 state parties in order to enter into force.

75. M. Akehurst and P. Malanczuk (1997): *Akerhurst's Modern Introduction to International Law*. London: Routledge, pp. 120–1.

76. Fox, *Law of State Immunity*, p. 737ff.

77. Ibid., p. 5; for a discussion of global public–private partnerships and immunity problems, see D. Aziz (2009): 'Privileges and Immunities of Global Public–Private Partnerships: A Case Study of the Global Fund to Fight AIDS, Tuberculosis and Malaria', *International Organizations Law Review*, Vol. 6, 2, pp. 383–419.

78. See Bröhmer, *State Immunity*; Akande and Shah, 'Immunities of State Officials', pp. 815–82; A. Bird (2010): 'Third State Responsibility for Human Rights Violations', *The European Journal of International Law* Vol. 21, 4, pp. 883–900.

79. Caplan, 'State Immunity'; Potestá, 'State immunity and Jus Cogens Violations; See also Saputo, 'The Ferrini Doctrine'.

80. The 1969 Vienna Convention on the Law of Treaties contains several rules pertaining to the category of *jus cogens*: Articles 53, 64, 66 (a) and 71.

81. M. Cherif Bassiouni (1997): 'International Crimes: *Jus Cogens* and Obligations *Erga Omnes*', *Law and Contemporary Problems*, Vol. 59, 4, pp. 68–74.

82. ICJ, *Barcelona Traction, Light and Power Company, Limited ICJ Reports 1970*, p. 32, paras 33–4.

83. Bassiouni, International Crimes, p. 65. Also relevant to consider here is the term 'intransgressible principles of international customary law'. The ICJ has stated that: '[the] fundamental rules [of humanitarian law] are to be observed by all States whether or not they have ratified the conventions that contain them, because they constitute intransgressible principles of international customary law' (ICJ, *Nuclear Weapons*, para 79). The term 'intransgressible principles of international customary law' had not previously been used but can be linked to the 1949 ICJ decision in *Corfu Channel*, where the Court held that certain international obligations could be based on 'elemental considerations of humanity applicable in wartime as well as in peacetime' (*Corfu Channel* (United Kingdom of Great Britain and Northern Ireland v. Albania) ICJ. 30 September 1947–15 December 1949), page 22.

84. See *Jones v. Ministry of Interior of the Kingdom of Saudi Arabia*, House of Lords, Judgement of 14 June [2006] UKHL 26.

85. See *Jones v. Ministry of Interior*, paras 43–5. In para. 44 the Court quotes Fox, *Law of State Immunity*, p. 525: 'State immunity is a procedural rule going to the jurisdiction of a national court. It does not go to substantive law; it does not contradict a prohibition contained in a *jus cogens* norm but merely diverts any breach of it to a different method of settlement. Arguably, then, there is no substantive content in the procedural plea of state immunity upon which a *jus cogens* mandate can bite.'

86. *Ferrini v. Federal Republic of Germany*, 128 ILR (2004) 658.

87. *Ferrini v. Federal Republic of Germany*, para. 11.

88. C. Tomuschat (2011): 'The International Law of State Immunity and Its Development by National Institutions', *Vanderbilt Journal of International Law*, 45, pp. 1105–40, p. 1127.

89. ICJ, Press Release, No. 2008/44, 23 December 2008.

90. ICJ, Application Instituting Proceedings, filed in the Registry of the Court on 23 December 2008, Jurisdictional Immunities of the State, (*Germany v. Italy*), p. 4.

91. ICJ, Jurisdictional Immunities of the State (*Germany v. Italy*: Greece intervening)—Judgement of 3 February 2012, para. 54.

92. In its decision of 3 February 2012, the ICJ found that 'the Italian Republic must, by enacting appropriate legislation, or by resorting to other methods of its choosing, ensure that the decisions of its courts and those of other judicial authorities infringing the immunity which the Federal Republic of Germany enjoys under international law cease to have effect'. It found that 'the Italian Republic has violated its obligation to respect the immunity which the Federal Republic of Germany enjoys under international law by declaring enforceable in Italy decisions of Greek courts based on violations of international humanitarian law committed in Greece by the German Reich.' Furthermore, 'that the Italian Republic has violated its obligation to respect the immunity which the Federal Republic of Germany enjoys under international law by taking measures of constraint against Villa Vigoni.' And finally, that 'the Italian Republic has violated its obligation to respect the immunity which the Federal Republic of Germany enjoys under international law by allowing civil claims to be brought against it based on violations of international humanitarian law committed by the German Reich between 1943 and 1945.' (para. 139 (1–4)).

93. Larry May (2011): *Global Justice and Due Process*. Cambridge: Cambridge University Press, p. 47.

3. COLLATERAL DAMAGE AND COMPENSATION

1. Christine Evans (2012): *The Right to Reparation in International Law for Victims of Armed Conflict*. Cambridge: Cambridge University Press, p. 1ff; Emanuela-Chiara Gilard (2003): 'Reparation for Violations of International Humanitarian Law', *International Review of the Red Cross*, Vol. 85, 851, pp. 529–53; Richard M. Buxbaum (2005): 'A Legal History of International Reparations', *Berkeley Journal of International Law*, Vol. 23, 2, pp. 314–46.

2. Kenneth Bullock (1995): 'United States Tort Liability for War Crimes Abroad: An Assesment and Recommendation', *Law and Contemporary Problems*, Vol. 58, 1, pp. 139–59, p. 141.

3. For an analysis of the global divide between the insured and uninsured see Mark Duffield (2007): *Development, Security and Unending War: Governing the World of Peoples*. London: Polity Press.

4. Frederic Borch (2003): *Army Lawyers in Military Operations from Vietnam to Haiti*. Washington DC: Office of the Judge General and Center of Military History, p. 28.

5. Liesbeth Zegveld (2003): 'Remedies for Victims of Violations of International

Humanitarian Law', *International Review of the Red Cross*, Vol. 85, 851, pp. 497–526.

6. The Canadian cases are *Bouzari v. Islamic Republic of Iran*, [2002] O.J. No. 1624 (QL) (O.S.C.J.) [Bouzari], *aff'd* (2004), 71 O.R. (3d) 675 (C.A.) [Bouzari (2004)], *leave to appeal to S.C.C. refused* [2004] S.C.C.A. No. 410; *Saleh v. United Arab Emirates* (2003), 15 C.C.L.T. (3d) 231 (O.S.C.J.) [Saleh]; and *Arar v. Syrian Arab Republic and Jordan*, [2005] 137 A.C.W.S. (3d) 823 (O.S.C.J.) [Arar]. The UK cases are *Mitchell et al. v. Al-Dali et al.*, Case No. A2 2004/0489 [Mitchell]; *Jones v. Saudi Arabia*, Case No. A2 2003/2155 [Jones]. Both appeals were decided together: [2005] 2 W.L.R. 808 (H.C.J.), rev'd [2006] 2 W.L.R. 1424 (H.L.).

7. *Filártiga v. Peña-Irala*, 630 F.2d 876 (2d Cir. 1980).

8. US Alien Tort Statute, 28 U.S.C. s 1350; *Filártiga v. Peña-Irala*, 630 F.2d 876 (2d Cir. 1980), p. 4

9. Michael Swan (2001): 'International Human Rights Tort Claims and the Experience of United States Courts: An Introduction to the US Case Law, Key Statutes and Doctrines', in Craig Scott (ed.): *Torture as Tort. Comparative Perspectives on the Development of Transnational Human Rights Litigation*. Oxford: Hart Publishing; Francois Larocque (2008): 'Recent Developments in Transnational Human Rights Litigation: A Postscript to Torture as Tort', *Osgoode Hall Law Review*, Vol. 46, pp. 605–56.

10. Larocque 'Recent Developments in Transnational Human Rights Litigation', p. 607;

11. *In re Iraq and Afghanistan Detainees Litigation*, 479 F. Supp. 2d 85 (D.D.C. 2007)

12. *Arar v. Ashcroft*, 414 F. Supp. 2d 250 (E.D.N.Y. 2006), *aff'd*, 532 F.3d 157 (2d Cir. 2008), *vacated and superseded on reh'g en banc*, 585 F.3d 559 (2d Cir. 2009); *El-Masri v. Tenet*, 437 F. Supp. 2d 530 (E.D. Va. 2006), *aff'd sub nom. El-Masri v. United States*, 479 F.3d 296 (4th Cir. 2007).

13. *Al Maqaleh v. Gates*, 604 F. Supp. 2d 205 (D.D.C. 2009), *rev'd*, 605 F.3d 84 (D.C. Cir. 2010); *Wazir v. Gates*, 629 F. Supp. 2d 63 (D.D.C. 2009).

14. Curtis A. Bradley and Laurence R. Helfer (2011): 'International Law and the U.S. Common Law of Foreign Official Immunity', *2010 Supreme Court Review*, pp. 213–72.

15. *Yousuf v. Samantar*, 552 F.3d 371 (4th Cir. 2009).

16. *Samantar v. Yousuf*, 130 S.Ct. 2278 (2010).

17. Beth Stephens (2011): 'The Modern Common Law of Foreign Officials', *Fordham Law Review*, Vol. 76, 5, pp. 2669–719, p. 2671; Bradley and Helfer, 'International Law'.

18. *Samantar*, 130 S Ct at 2292–93.

19. Timothy E. Donahue (2011): '*Samantar v. Yousuf*: A False Summit in American Human Rights Civil Litigation', *Boston College International and Comparative Law Review*, Vol. 34, 3, pp. 29–40, p. 40.

20. Ibid.
21. Stephens 'Modern Common Law'; Bradley and Helfer 'International Law'.
22. Charles F. Hollis (2011): 'Perpetual Mistrial: The Impropriety of Transnational Human Rights Litigation in United States Courts', *Santa Clara Journal of International Law*, Vol. 1, pp. 1–73, p. 33.
23. Ibid.
24. Ibid.
25. *Filártiga*, at 890; Hollis 'Perpetual Mistrial', p. 2.
26. ICTY, Appeals Chamber, *Prosecutor v. Tadić*, Judgement of 15 July 1999, IT-94-1-A.
27. Bruno Simma (2009): 'Universality of International Law from the Perspective of a Practitioner, *The European Journal of International Law*, Vol. 20, 2, pp. 265–97, p. 280.
28. Ibid.
29. Ibid.
30. 'An Act to Give Indemnity for Damages Caused by American Forces Abroad'. Act of 18 April 1918, chapter 57, 40 Stat (1918). See William R. Mullins (1966): 'The International Responsibility for Torts of International Forces', *Military Law Review*, Vol. 34, 59, pp. 59–101, p. 63 fn21.
31. Mullins, ibid.
32. John Fabian Witt (2008): 'Form and Substance in the Law of Counterinsurgency Damages', *Los Angeles Law Review*, Vol. 41, pp. 1455–82; Walerstein, Jordan (2009): 'Coping With Combat Claims', *Cardozo Journal of Conflict Resolution*, Vol. 11, pp. 319–51.
33. 10 USC § 2734 (b)(3)—Property loss; personal injury or death: incident to non-combat activities of the armed forces; foreign countries.
34. Paul von Zilbauer (2007): 'Civilian Claims on U.S. Suggest the Toll of War', *New York Times*, 12 April.
35. Documents received from the Department of the Army in response to ACLU Freedom of Information Act Request: Claims Filed Under the Foreign Claims Act by Civilians in Afghanistan and Iraq, Army Bates 18–22, 23–29, 30–34, 35–39, 40–43, 44–48, 49–51, 52–56 (released by the ACLU on 4 December 2007), available at http://www.aclu.org/natsec/foia/log.html. [last visited 15 July 2015]
36. Walerstein, 'Coping With Combat Claims', p. 319.
37. John Fabian Witt (2008): 'Form and Substance in the Law of Counterinsurgency Damages', *Los Angeles Law Review*, Vol. 41, pp. 1455–82, p. 1472ff; see also Jonathan Tracy (2005): 'Compensating Civilian Casualties: "I am Sorry for your Loss, and I Wish You Well in a Free Iraq"', A Research Report Prepared for the Carr Center for Human Rights Policy and Campaign for Innocent Victims in Conflict, available at http://civiliansinconflict.org/resources/pub/compensating-civil-

ian-casualties-i-am-sorry-for-your-loss-and-i-wish-you-we [last visited 15 July 2015]

38. Frederic Borch (2003): *Army Lawyers in Military Operations from Vietnam to Haiti*. Washington DC: Office of the Judge General and Center of Military History, pp. 24–5, 28, 41–2, 76, 85, 147, 111–13, 210, 211.
39. Walerstein 'Coping With Combat Claims', p. 347ff.
40. Ibid., p. 350.
41. For discussion of the possibility of expanding FCA to environmental damage, see Mark D. Sameit (2008): 'Killing and Cleaning in Combat: A Proposal to Extend the Foreign Claims Act to Compensate for Long-Term Environmental Damage', *William and Mary Environmental Law and Policy Review*, Vol. 32, 2, pp. 547–80.
42. Yaël Ronen (2009): 'Avoid or Compensate? Liability for Incidental Injury to Civilians Inflicted During Armed Conflict', *Vanderbilt Journal of Transnational Law*, Vol. 42, pp. 180–225.
43. Ibid.
44. Shunzo Majima (2009): 'Forgotten Victims of Military Humanitarian Intervention: A Case for the Principle of Reparation?', *Philosophia*, Vol. 37, 2, pp. 203–9.
45. Ronen, 'Avoid or Compensate?'
46. Documents received from the Department of the Army in response to ACLU Freedom of Information Act Request: Claims Filed Under the Foreign Claims Act by Civilians in Afghanistan and Iraq, Army Bates 18–22, 23–29, 30–34, 35–39, 40–43, 44–48, 49–51, 52–56 (released by the ACLU on 4 December 2007), available at http://www.aclu.org/natsec/foia/log.html. [last visited 15 July 2015]
47. Sarah Holewinski (2012): 'Making Amends', in Daniel Rothbart et al., *Civilians in Modern War*. Abingdon: Routledge, pp. 317–33, p. 329.
48. ICJ Statute, Art 38(1)(c) See Brian D. Lepard (2010): *Customary International Law. A New Theory with New Applications*. Cambridge: Cambridge University Press.
49. ICJ Statute Art. 38(1)(b).
50. Ian Brownlie (1998): *Principles of Public International Law*. Oxford: Oxford University Press, pp. 4–11; Michael Akerhurst (1977): 'Custom as a Source of International Law', *British Yearbook of International Law*, Vol. 47, pp. 1–53; Anthony D'Amarto (1971): *The Concept of Custom in International Law*. Ithaca: Cornell University Press.
51. ICJ Asylum Case (*Colombia v Peru*) [1950] ICJ Rep 266.
52. Michael Byers (2001): 'Power, Obligation and Customary International Law', *Duke Journal of Comparative and International Law*, Vol. 11, pp. 81–8.
53. Jean-Marie Henckaerts (2005): 'Study on Customary International Humanitarian Law: A Contribution to the Understanding and Respect for the Rule of Law

in Armed Conflict', *International Review of the Red Cross*, Vol. 87, 857, pp. 175–212, p. 178.

54. Ibid.; See also Jean-Marie Henckaerts (2007): 'Customary International Humanitarian Law: a response to US comments', *International Review of the Red Cross*, Vol. 89, 866, pp. 473–88, pp. 481–2.

55. For a great discussion of the legal science difficulty of coming to terms with the nature and role of international customary law, see Lepard: *Customary International Law. A New Theory with New Applications*. Chapter 1.

56. See Amanda Carrol and Marcus Schulke (2013): 'Compensating Civilians During War: A Place for Individuals in International Law', *Democracy and Security*, Vol. 9, 4, pp. 398–421; Sarah Holewinski (2012): 'Making Amends', in Daniel Rothbart et al.: *Civilians in Modern War*. Abingdon: Routledge, pp. 317–33, p. 325; U.S. Military Joint and Coalition Operational Analysis (JCOA) (2013): 'Reducing and Mitigating Civilian Casualties: Enduring Lessons', http://www. cna.org/sites/default/files/research/CIVCAS_Enduring_Lessons.pdf [last visited 15 July 2015]; Campaign for Innocent Victims of Conflict (2010): *Addressing Civilian Harm in Afghanistan: Policies & Practices of International Forces*, http://civiliansinconflict.org/resources/pub/addressing-civilian-harm-in-afghanistan [last visited 15 July 2015]; Center for Civilians in Conflict (2010): *United States Military Compensation to Civilians in Armed Conflict*, http://civiliansinconflict.org/uploads/files/publications/CENTER_Condolence_White_ Paper_2010.pdf [last visited 15 July 2015]; U.S. Government Accountability Office (2007): *The Department of Defense's Use of Solatia and Condolence Payments in Iraq and Afghanistan*, http://www.gao.gov/new.items/d07699.pdf [last visited 15 July 2015]; Jonathan Tracy 'Compensating Civilian Casualties: "I am Sorry for your Loss, and I Wish You Well in a Free Iraq"', A Research Report Prepared for the Carr Center for Human Rights Policy and Campaign for Innocent Victims in Conflict, http://civiliansinconflict.org/resources/pub/compensating-civilian-casualties-i-am-sorry-for-your-loss-and-i-wish-you-we [last visited 15 July 2015]

57. For a description of CERP, see Rebecca Patterson and Jonathan Robinson (2010): 'The Commander as Investor Changing CERP Practices', *PRISM*, 2, pp. 101–15.

58. Greg Mitchell (2010): 'WikiLeaks Confirms Shocking Civilian Death Toll—But US Has Been Paying Off Victims' Families for Years', *The Nation*, 23 October.

59. Holewinski, 'Making Amends', p. 325.

60. 'MoD pays £500,000 compensation to Afghan victims', *The Telegraph*, 1 January 2013, http://www.telegraph.co.uk/news/9774534/MoD-pays-500000-compensation-to-Afghan-victims.html [Last visited 2 March 2015]

61. 'Canada paid $1M compensation to Afghan civilians', *CBCNews* 9 June 2013 http://www.cbc.ca/news/world/canada-paid-1m-compensation-to-afghan-civilians-1.1124223 [Last visited 2 March 2015]

62. Crawford, *Accountability for Killing. Moral Responsibility for Collateral Damage in America's post-9/11 Wars*, p. 99.

63. UNAMA (2009): *Afghanistan Annual Report on Protection of Civilians in Armed Conflict, 2009*. Kabul: UNAMA Human Rights, p. 23

64. NATO (2010): NATO Nations Approve Civilian Casualty Guidelines, http://www.nato.int/cps/en/natohq/official_texts_65114.htm?selectedLocale=en [last visited 15 July 2015] Non-Binding Guidelines for Payments in Combat-Related Cases of Civilian Casualties or Damage to Civilian Property—ANNEX to SG(2010)0377 (approved on 11 Jun 2010).

65. United Nations (2010): 'Annual Report of the Special Rapporteur on Extrajudicial, Summary or Arbitrary Executions', United Nations General Assembly, A/HRC/14/24/Add.6, 28 May 2010, p. 22.

66. United Nations (2010): 'Report of the Secretary-General on the Protection of Civilians in Armed Conflict', United Nations Security Council, S/2010/579, 11 November 2010, p. 19.

67. Sarah Holewinski (2013): 'Do Less Harm. Protecting and Compensating Civilians in War', *Foreign Affairs*, Vol. 92, 1, pp. 14–20.

68. U.S. Military Joint and Coalition Operational Analysis (2013): *Reducing and Mitigating Civilian Casualties: Enduring Lessons*.

69. Ibid.

70. NATO (2010): Letter dated 11 October 2010 from the Deputy Secretary General of the North Atlantic Treaty Organization addressed to the Secretary-General/Quarterly report to the Security Council on the operations of the International Security Assistance Force, United Nations Security Council S/2010/548.

71. Michael Byers (1999): *Custom, Power and the Power of Rules. International Relations and Customary International Law*. Cambridge: Cambridge University Press, pp. 130–133.

4. LIFTING THE FOG OF WAR AND COLLATERAL DAMAGE

1. A. Madrigal (2013): 'DARPA's 1.8 Gigapixel Drone Camera Could See You Waving At It From 15,000 Feet', *The Atlantic*, 1 February 2013; See also B. Leininger et al. (2008): 'Autonomous Real-time Ground Ubiquitous Surveillance—Imaging System (ARGUS-IS)', *Proc. SPIE*, Vol. 6981.

2. T. Shanker (2013): 'Simple, Low-Cost Surveillance Drones Provide Advantage for U.S. Military', *New York Times*, 24 January 2014.

3. United Kingdom Ministry of Defence (2013): 'Miniature Surveillance Helicopters Help Protect Front Line Troops', 4 February, https://www.gov.uk/government/news/miniature-surveillance-helicopters-help-protect-front-line-troops [last visited 24. February 2013]

4. P.W. Singer cited in T. Shanker, 'Simple, Low-Cost Surveillance Drones'.

5. J.D. Herbach (2012): 'Into the Caves of Steel: Precaution, Cognition and Robotic Weapon Systems Under the International Law of Armed Conflict', *Amsterdam Law*

Forum, Vol. 4, 3, pp. 3–20; M. Coeckelbergh (2011): 'From Killer Machines to Doctrines and Swarms, or Why Ethics of Military Robotics Is Not (Necessarily) about Robots', *Philosophy & Technology*, Vol. 24, 3, pp. 269–78; M. Schulzke (2011): 'Robots as Weapons in Just Wars', *Philosophy & Technology*, Vo. 24, 3, pp. 293–306.

6. The wording of Article 57 is as follows:

   1. In the conduct of military operations, constant care shall be taken to spare the civilian population, civilians and civilian objects.

   2. With respect to attacks, the following precautions shall be taken:

      (a) those who plan or decide upon an attack shall:

         (i) do everything feasible to verify that the objectives to be attacked are neither civilians nor civilian objects and are not subject to special protection but are military objectives within the meaning of paragraph 2 of Article 52 and that it is not prohibited by the provisions of this Protocol to attack them;

         (ii) take all feasible precautions in the choice of means and methods of attack with a view to avoiding, and in any event to minimizing, incidental loss of civilian life, injury to civilians and damage to civilian objects;

         (iii) refrain from deciding to launch any attack which may be expected to cause incidental loss of civilian life, injury to civilians, damage to civilian objects, or a combination thereof, which would be excessive in relation to the concrete and direct military advantage anticipated;

      (b) an attack shall be cancelled or suspended if it becomes apparent that the objective is not a military one or is subject to special protection or that the attack may be expected to cause incidental loss of civilian life, injury to civilians, damage to civilian objects, or a combination thereof, which would be excessive in relation to the concrete and direct military advantage anticipated;

      (c) effective advance warning shall be given of attacks which may affect the civilian population, unless circumstances do not permit.

   3. When a choice is possible between several military objectives for obtaining a similar military advantage, the objective to be selected shall be that the attack on which may be expected to cause the least danger to civilian lives and to civilian objects.

   4. In the conduct of military operations at sea or in the air, each Party to the conflict shall, in conformity with its rights and duties under the rules of international law applicable in armed conflict, take all reasonable precautions to avoid losses of civilian lives and damage to civilian objects.

   5. No provision of this Article may be construed as authorizing any attacks against the civilian population, civilians or civilian objects.

7. Jean-Marie Henckaerts and Louise Doswald-Beck (2009): *Customary International Humanitarian Law*, Vol. 1. Geneva and Cambridge: ICRC and Cambridge University Press, p. 51.

8. Ibid.

9. For instance, the principle of precaution in environmental law applies to situations of armed conflict (depleted uranium, destruction of oil wells, use of poison) and is to be considered a strategy to guide policy in the face of scientific uncertainty about the environmental and health consequences of human action. Lesley Wexler (2006): 'Limiting the Precautionary Principle: Weapons Regulation in the Face of Scientific Uncertainty', *University of California Davis Law Review* Vol. 39, p. 459–527.

10. See for example Jean-François Quéguiner (2006): 'Precaution under the Law Governing the Conduct of Hostilities', *International Review of the Red Cross*, Vol. 88, 794–821.

11. Ibid., 798.

12. Michael N. Schmitt (2005): 'Precision Attack and International Law' *International Review of the Red Cross* Vol. 87, pp. 445–66, p. 461.

13. Bradley J. Strawser (2010): 'Moral Predators: The Duty to Employ Uninhabited Aerial Vehicles', *Journal of Military Ethics*, Vol. 9, pp. 342–68, p. 352.

14. See James Cavallaro et al. (2012): *Living Under Drones: Death, Injury and Trauma to Civilians from U.S. Drone Practices in Pakistan*. New York and Stanford: New York University Center for Human Rights and Global Justice and Stanford International Human Rights and Conflict Resolution Clinic, p. 29.

15. Thomas W. Smith (2008): 'Protecting Civilians ... or Soldiers? Humanitarian Law and the Economy of Risk in Iraq', *International Studies Perspectives*, Vol. 9, pp. 144–64, p. 146; the quote within the quote is from Eyal Benvenisti (2006): 'Human Dignity in Combat: The Duty to Spare Enemy Civilians', *Israel Law Review*, Vol. 39, 81–109, p. 93.

16. For a discussion of the dilemma, see Gabriella Blum (2011): 'The Laws of War and the "Lesser Evil"', *The Yale Journal of International Law* Vol. 35, 2, pp. 1–69, p. 59ff; David J. Luban (2011): 'Risk Taking and Force Protection', Georgetown Public Law and Legal Theory Research Paper, No. 11–72; Smith 'Protecting Civilians', p. 144.

17. Shanker, 'Simple, Low-Cost Surveillance Drones Provide Advantage for U.S. Military'.

18. Peter W. Singer (2010): 'The Ethics of Killer Applications: Why Is It So Hard To Talk About Morality When It Comes to New Military Technology?', *Journal of Military Ethics*, Vol. 9, 4, pp. 299–312.

19. This question is analogous to the question addressed by Gabriella Blum (2011): 'On a Differential Law of War', Harvard International Law Journal, Vol. 52, 1, 163–218. The question she poses is whether the United States, as the strongest military power

in the world, should be bound by stricter humanitarian constraints than its weaker adversaries. In other words, do different capabilities cause differentiated responsibilities?

20. Here we may look to the growing use of drone-based surveillance by the civil police. Apprehension towards the use of drones in this context springs from the risk that drone technology likely implies an intrusion into the private affairs of citizens. Unless we assume that completely different ethical standards apply at home and abroad, ethical dilemmas related to privacy and surveillance should be considered when drones are used in the non-Western world, where they are an equally intrusive form of control. In this way, uneasiness with regard to the control capability of civilian drones flows into the argument of this chapter: control is a material feature of drone technology no matter what the political or geographical context. See for example J. Stanley and C. Crump (2011): 'Protecting Privacy from Aerial Surveillance: Recommendations for Government Use of Drone Aircraft', Report by American Civil Liberties Union. New York: ACLU. The report argues that 'we need a system of rules to ensure that we can enjoy the benefits of this technology without bringing us a large step closer to a "surveillance society" in which our every move is monitored, tracked, recorded, and scrutinized by the authorities' (p. 1).

5. HOW BAD CAN BE GOOD

1. Voltaire (1755), 'Poem on the Lisbon Disaster: Or an Examination of the Axiom "All is Well!"', in Voltaire (1912): *Toleration and Other Essays*, trans. Joseph McCabe. New York and London: G.P. Putnam's Sons.

2. For two authoritative accounts of the role of pain and suffering in our intellectual life, see Joseph A. Amato (1990): *Victims and Values. A History and a Theory of Suffering*. New York: Greenwood Press, and Iain Wilkinson (2005): *Suffering. A Sociological Introduction*. London: Polity Press. A philosopher known for assuming that pain and suffering are the essential truth of human existence is Arthur Schopenhauer, who stated that 'you cannot do better than accustom yourself to regard the world as a penitentiary, a sort of penal colony, or ergasterion, as the earliest philosophers called it'. (Arthur Schopenhauer (2004): *On the Suffering of the World*. London: Penguin Classics, p. 14). Another famous philosopher who constantly turns to pain and its meaning is Nietzsche, who held that 'all belief is based on the feeling of pleasure or pain in the relation to the feeling subject' (Friedrich Nietzsche (1996): *Human, All Too Human: A Book for Free Spirits*. Winnipeg: Bison Books, para. 18, p. 25.). Post-war existentialists such as Gabriel Marcel, Albert Camus, Jean-Paul Sartre and Karl Jaspers also viewed pain and suffering as monopolisers of human thought. For some general accounts of the philosophical and sociological meaning of pain and suffering, see Arne Johan Vetlesen (2004): *A Philosophy of Pain*. London: Reaction Books; P.D. Wall (2000): *Pain: The Science of Suffering*.

New York: Columbia University Press; N. Grahek (2001): *Feeling Pain and Being in Pain*. Oldenburg, Denmark: BIS-Verlag, University of Oldenburg.

3. Vetlesen, *Philosophy of Pain*, p. 7.

4. Amato, *Victims and Values*, p. 15ff.

5. The commonly agreed definition of a state in international law was provided by the Montevideo Convention of 1933. It defined the state as a person of international law possessing a permanent population, a defined territory, a government, and the capacity to enter into relations with other states. During the last 20 years, it has increasingly been questioned whether state capacity should also be counted; that is, the state's capacity to deliver basic public goods such as school, health, food security and justice. Furthermore, it has been asked whether 'predatory' dictatorships and corrupt regimes that are unwilling to promote just basic good governance should be acknowledged as legitimate governments. These discussions started in the aftermath of the Cold War, as a number of African states in particular lost their superpower support and were revealed to be more or less without any governance capacity. For overviews of the discussions see, for instance, Edward Quashigah (1999): *Legitimate Governance in Africa: International and Domestic Legal Perspectives*. Hague: Kluver Law; Obiora Chinedu Okafor (2000): *Re-Defining Legitimate Statehood: International Law and State Fragmentation in Africa*. Hague: Martinus Nijhoff Publishers; Pierre Englebert (2000): *State Legitimacy and Development in Africa*, Boulder and London: Lynne Rienner Publishers.

6. The question of the limits to constitutional rights in the face of security governance has been treated extensively after the War on Terror raised the question of whether or not terrorists should enjoy the right to a fair trial, and if not, what this means for the self-identity of liberalism. The discussions in political theory about a possible 'permanent state of emergency' quickly reached back to the heated debate in the Weimar Republic about 'law or politics first', where the main positions were represented by the Catholic Nazi lawyer Carl Schmitt and the perhaps most important figure in European liberal constitution thought, Hans Kelsen. For a brilliant introduction to the Weimar debates on law and politics, see David Dyzenhaus (1999): *Legality and Legitimacy: Carl Schmitt, Hans Kelsen and Hermann Heller in Weimar*. Oxford: Oxford University Press.

7. Nicholas Rengger (2002): 'On the Just War Tradition in the Twenty-First Century', *International Affairs*, Vol. 78, 2, pp. 353–63.

8. Kateri Carmola (2005): 'The Concept of Proportionality: Old Questions and New Ambiguities', in Mark Evans: *Just War Theory*. Edinburgh: Edinburgh University Press, pp. 93–113, p. 94.

9. Judith Gardam (2004): *Necessity, Proportionality and the Use of Force by States*. Cambridge: Cambridge University Press, p. 86.

10. For a historical examination of the principle of distinction and how it relates to the concept of combatants and civilians in international law, see Helen Kinsella

(2011): *The Image Before The Weapon: A Critical History of the Distinction Between Combatant and Civilian*. Ithaca: Cornell University Press.

11. Augustine seems to have presented no clear-cut argument for the protection of the innocent, especially for the civilian, or non-combatants in times of war. See Richard Shelly Hartigan (1966): 'Saint Augustine on War and Killing: The Problem of the Innocent', *Journal of the History of Ideas*, Vol. 27, 2, pp. 195–204, p. 203; Louis J. Swift (1973): 'Augustine on War and Killing: Another View', *The Harvard Theological Review*, Vol. 66, 3, pp. 369–83. See also Colm McKeogh (2002): *Innocent Civilians: The Morality of Killing in War*. London: Palgrave, p. 29ff.

12. Hugo Slim (2008): *Killing Civilians*. New York: Columbia University Press, p. 29.

13. See Thomas Franck, 'On Proportionality of Countermeasures in International Law', *American Journal of International Law*, p. 715.

14. Nolen Gertz (2008): 'Just and Unjust Killing', *Journal of Military Ethics*, Vol. 7, 4, pp. 247–61.

15. Michael Walzer (2000): *Just and Unjust Wars* 2nd ed. New York: Basic Books, p. 137.

16. Robert L. Holmes (1989): *On War and Morality*. Princeton: Princeton University Press, p. 183; see also James Turner Johnson (1999): *Morality in Contemporary Warfare*. New York: Vail-Ballou Press, p. 129; Stanley Hauerwas and Paul Ramsey (2002): *The Just War: Force and Political Responsibility*. London: Rowman & Littlefield Publishers.

17. The killing of Osama bin Laden and targeted killings of confirmed terrorists may be said to be exceptions. The same thing applies to the Nürnberg Trials, where the US insisted on no death sentence without a trial. The generalisation may thus be said to have found its limits in the constitutional state.

18. Waltzer *Just and Unjust Wars*, p. 152.

19. Alison McIntyre (2001): 'Doing Away with Double Effect', *Ethics* Vol. 111, 2, 219–55, p. 255.

20. McIntyre, 'Doing Away with Double Effect', p. 221.

21. Here is a recent example of a philosopher applying the doctrine, one which focuses on the difference between terror bombing and strategic bombing: 'Terrence [the terror bomber] is a bomber pilot serving his country in what we will assume is a just war. Terrence realizes that his enemy's ability to continue to prosecute the war depends upon, among other things, the willingness of the enemy civilian population to continue to make sacrifices necessary to prosecute the war. Terrence also believes that that willingness is fragile and can be shattered if enough civilians are killed. Terrence, therefore, sets out on a bombing mission not only with intent to destroy a munitions factory that is supplying his enemy with weapons necessary to fight the war, but also the intent to kill a large number of civilians. We may be generous and assume that it is reasonable to believe, as he does, that his successful mission will shorten the war to the degree that fewer lives will be lost should he

fly the mission than should he refuse. Samuel [the strategic bomber] is a bomber pilot fighting in the same just war. Samuel also believes that civilian deaths will undermine his enemy's ability to continue the war. Samuel, however, in setting out on the same mission as Terrence, does not set out to kill civilians. Samuel realizes that a large number of civilians will be killed should his mission be successful; but those civilian deaths are not his aim. Similarly, we may assume that Samuel's success will, in the long run, save more lives than it will cost'. P.A. Woodward (2001): *The Doctrine of Double Effect: Philosophers Debate a Controversial Moral Principle*. Notre Dame: University of Notre Dame Press, p. 1

22. Joseph Shaw (2006): 'Intention in Ethics', *Canadian Journal of Philosophy*, Vol. 36, 2, pp. 187–224, p. 187.

23. James A. Aho (2006): *Confession and Bookkeeping*. New York: State University of New York Press; George Radford (2009): *The Philosophy of Bookkeeping*. La Vergne: Lightning Source UK Ltd.

24. Ibid.

25. Robert F. Berkhofer (2004): *Day of Reckoning: Power and Accountability in Medieval France*. Philadelphia: University of Pennsylvania Press, p. 5.

26. Berkhofer, *Day of Reckoning*, p. 123.

27. Ibid.

28. Daniel Bricker (2000): 'Innocent Suffering in Mesopotamia', *Tyndale Bulletin*, Vol. 51, 2, pp. 193–214.

29. For a brilliant account of the many historical receptions of the legend of Job, see Mark Larrimore (2013): *The Book of Job. A Biography*. Princeton: Princeton University Press.

30. From Michael Martin (1990): *Atheism: A Philosophical Justification*. Philadelphia: Temple University Press, p. 334.

31. Augustine, *The City of God*, 1.8–9.

32. Another version of providential thinking is represented by Kant. He also located evil as internal to order. But rather than explaining evil as an element of divine providence he describes it as a '*radical* innate *evil* in human nature' (1793/1996, p. 80) that, however, was impossible to put on final formula. The reason why the greatest philosophical rationalist resigned himself to further fleshing out the nature of evil was that he did not want to interfere with God's wisdom. To Kant, solving the problem of evil was not only beyond our reach but morally wrong insofar as a settled concept of evil would leave us without the possibility of morality. Furthermore, in his later work, he even proposed that any attempt to nail the problem of evil once and for all would amount to blasphemy in that it would be similar to trying to represent God in an act of idolatry that placed man above God. His position on natural or radical evil did not prevent him from developing a moral philosophy and proposing that working towards higher rationality could reduce the suffering of man, including ending all wars. In other words, he refused to speculate on the source of evilness but saw moral philosophy as a way of mak-

ing judgements about wrongdoing that may or may not have their source in the radical innate evil in human nature. For Kant, reasoning was a means to contain this dark side of man so as to prevent it from entering the world in the form of moral wrongdoing or even war. For an account of Kant's approach to the problem of evil, the possibility of morality, and idolatry, see Susan Neiman (2004): *Evil in Modern Thought: An Alternative History of Philosophy*. Princeton: Princeton University Press, pp. 57ff.

33. Acknowledging that a constituting paradox of the Christian God is that God can be both one and many (the Trinity), I will leave this debate aside. From the perspective of authority in governance, even the Trinity may be viewed as an integrated divine force.

34. Genevieve Lloyd (2008): *Providence Lost*. Harvard University Press.

35. Jean Hampton (1997): *Political Philosophy*. Oxford: Westview Press, p. 128.

36. Hampton, *Political Philosophy*, p. 130.

37. Laurie Calhoun (2002): 'How Violence Breeds Violence: Some Utilitarian Considerations', *Politics*, Vol. 22, 2, pp. 95–108, p. 96.

38. John Rawls (1971): *A Theory of Justice*. Harvard: Harvard University Press, p. 27, 29.

39. Joseph Raz (1988): *The Morality of Freedom*. Oxford: Clarendon Press, p. 271.

40. Rawls considers which principles of justice persons would choose if they were to make that choice from an imagined place beyond class, race, income and other forms of capital. Rawls' famous concept of the 'veil of ignorance' stands for an 'impartial' condition, where a person cannot see his or her own position in society, and therefore would need to choose principles of justice that were fair to all. Rawls' argument in *A Theory of Justice* with regard to utilitarianism is that it would probably not be preferred by rational and free-minded people because not all benefit from its principle: to accept utilitarianism from the bottom of society would mean to accept an unequal distribution of common good, something Rawls believes would not happen.

41. John Rawls (1993): *Political Liberalism*. New York: Columbia University Press, p. 22.

42. Paul Ricoeur (1995): *The Just*. Chicago: University of Chicago Press, p. 38ff.

43. Ibid., p. 39.

44. René Girard (1989) *The Scapegoat*. Baltimore: Johns Hopkins University Press; see also René Girard (1979): *Violence and the Sacred*. Baltimore: Johns Hopkins University Press.

45. Ricoeur, *The Just*, p. 43.

46. John Stuart Mill (1863): *Utilitarianism*. London: Parker & Son, and Bourn, p. 24.

47. Discussions of utilitarianism constantly revolve around the notion of sacrifice yet generally fail to consider the theories and functions of sacrifice. See, for instance, James Wood Bailey (1998): *Utilitarianism, Institutions, and Justice*. Oxford: Oxford University Press.

6. A DEATH WITHOUT SACRIFICE

1. Chris Hedges (2002): *War Is a Force that Gives Us Meaning*. Sioux City: Anchor Publishing, p. 3.

2. Stanley Hauerwas (2011): *War and the American Difference: Theological Reflections on Violence and National Identity*. Ada: Baker Publishing, p. 4.

3. John Tirman (2011): *The Deaths of Others. The Fate of Civilians in America's War*. Oxford: Oxford University Press.

4. Gregor Noll (2011): 'The Miracle of Generative Violence? René Girard and the Use of Force in International Law', unpublished working paper, Lund University Faculty of Law; Gregor Noll (2008): 'Sacrificial Violence and Targeting in International Humanitarian Law', in Ola Engdahl and Pål Wrange (eds): *Law at War: The Law as It Was and the Law as It Should Be. Liber Amicorum Ove Bring*. Martinus Nijhoff Publishers, pp. 101–12.

5. Caroline Cox (2004): *A Proper Sense of Honor: Service and Sacrifice in George Washington's Army*. Chapel Hill: University of North Carolina Press; Jesse Goldhammer (2005): *The Headless Republic: Sacrificial Violence in Modern French Thought*. Ithaca and London: Cornell University Press; Kelly Denton-Borhaug (2011): *US War-culture, Sacrifice and Salvation*, New York: Equinox Publishing Limited; Jon Pahl (2012): *Empire of Sacrifice: The Religious Origins of American Violence*. New York: NYU Press; Hauerwas, *War and the American Difference*; Mateo Taussig-Rubbo (2011): 'Sacred Property: Searching for Value in the Rubble of 9/11', in Winnifred Fallers Sullivan, Robert Yelle, and Mateo Taussig-Rubbo (eds), *After Secular Law*. Stanford: Stanford University Press, 322–40.

6. Carolyn Marvin and David Ingle (1996): 'Blood Sacrifice and the Nation: Revisiting Civil Religion', *Journal of the American Academy of Religion*, Vol. 64, 4, pp. 767–80; Carolyn Marvin and David Ingle (1999): *Blood Sacrifice and the Nation: Totem Rituals and the American Flag*. Cambridge: Cambridge University Press.

7. Ibid., *p. 135*.

8. Paul Kahn (2005): *Out of Eden. Adam and Eve and the Problem of Evil*. Princeton: Princeton University Press.

9. Mateo Taussig-Rubbo (2009): 'Outsourcing Sacrifice: the Labor of Private Military Contractors', *Yale Journal of Law and Humanities*, Vol. 21, 1, pp. 103–66; see also Mateo Taussig-Rubbo (2009): 'Sacrifice and Sovereignty', in Jennifer L. Culbert and Austin Sarat (eds): *State of Violence: War, Capital Punishment, and Letting Die*. New York: Cambridge Press, pp. 83–127.

10. By proposing that love is the primary nation-building relation rather the social contract or the threatening other in the form of a radical enemy, Paul Kahn offers an important critique of our times' obsession with otherness in the form of religion, radicalisation, terrorists; the racial or cultural other as the key to understanding the fundamental building blocks of political community. It might inspire

followers of Carl Schmitt's theory of the friend–enemy relationship as constitutive of political life to reconsider their adoption of a clearly harmful idea.

11. For a good overview of these debates, see Jeffrey Carter (2003): *Understanding Religious Sacrifice: a Reader*. London: Continuum.

12. Robertson Smith, cited from Susan L. Mizruchi (1998): *The Science of Sacrifice: American Literature and Modern Social Theory*. Princeton: Princeton University Press, p. 72.

13. Ibid., p. 72.

14. Jonathan Z. Smith (1987): 'The domestication of sacrifice', in R.G. Hamerton-Kelly: *Violent origins: Walter Burkert, René Girard, and Jonathan Z. Smith on ritual killing and cultural formation*. Stanford: Stanford University Press, pp. 191–205.

15. Kathryn McClymond (2008): *Beyond Sacred Violence*. Baltimore: Johns Hopkins University Press, p. 3ff; Hent de Vries (2001): *Religion and Violence: Philosophical Perspectives from Kant to Derrida*. Baltimore: Johns Hopkins University Press, p. 201.

16. Mizruchi, *The Science of Sacrifice: American Literature and Modern Social Theory*, p. 26.

17. Henri Hubert and Marcel Mauss (1893, 1981): *Sacrifice: Its Nature and Functions*. Chicago: University Of Chicago Press.

18. Claude Levi-Strauss (1962): *Totemism*. Chicago: University of Chicago Press.

19. Émile Durkheim (1915, 2009): *The Elementary Forms of the Religious Life*. London: Forgotten Books; Rene Girard (1982, 1986): *The Scapegoat*. Baltimore: The Johns Hopkins University Press.

20. Moshe Halbertal (2012): *On Sacrifice*. Princeton: Princeton University Press.

21. Douglas Hedley (2011): *Sacrifice Imagined. Violence, Atonement, and the Sacred*. New York: Continuum, p 2.

22. Ibid., pp. 161ff.

23. Ibid., p 7.

24. Marcel Deienne and Jean-Pierre Vernant (1989): *The Cuisine of Sacrifice among the Greeks*. Chicago: University of Chicago Press.

25. McClymond, *Beyond Sacred Violence*, p. 46.

26. I am referring here to E. Evans-Pritchard's classical study of the Nuer tribe's tradition of substituting a cow or an ox in their sacrificial practices. E. Evans-Pritchard (1956): *Nuer Religion*. Oxford: Oxford University Press, pp. 128–32.

27. Compare, Frits Staal (1993): *Rules Without Meaning: Ritual, Mantras and the Human Sciences*. New York: Peter Lang Publishers.

28. Marshall McLuhan (1964): *Understanding Media*. London: Routledge.

29. Claire King (2011): *Washed in Blood: Male Sacrifice, Trauma, and the Cinema*. Rutgers: Rutgers University Press. King argues that '[v]iewers of Hollywood action films are no doubt familiar with the sacrificial victim-hero, the male protagonist who nobly gives up his life so that others may be saved. *Washed in Blood* argues

that such sacrificial films are especially prominent in eras when the nation—and American manhood—is thought to be in crisis' (back cover description).

30. Mark Pizzato (2004): *Theatres of Human Sacrifice: from Ancient Ritual to Screen Violence.* Albany: SUNY Press.

31. For an account of the US government's neglect of soldiers returning from Iraq and Afghanistan, see Aron Glantz (2010): *The War Comes Home: Washington's Battle against America's Veterans.* Ewing: University of California Press; For an account of the US veteran experience from the 'forgotten war' in Korea, see Melinda L. Pash (2012): *In the Shadow of the Greatest Generation: The Americans Who Fought the Korean War.* New York: NYU Press; For an account of US veteran experiences from the 'dirty' war in Vietnam, see Wilbur J. Scott (2004): *Vietnam Veterans Since the War: The Politics of PTSD, Agent Orange, and the National Memorial.* Norman: University of Oklahoma Press; For a historical account of how America has related to veterans throughout its many wars, see James Wright (2012): *Those Who Have Borne the Battle: A History of America's Wars and Those Who Fought Them.* New York: PublicAffairs.

32. For a good account of the confused politics of the Afghanistan war and the impact on public opinion, see Tim Bird and Alex Marshall (2011): *Afghanistan: How the West Lost Its Way.* New Haven: Yale University Press.

33. For a discussion of the crucial distinction between sacrificing *for* and sacrificing *of* and the biblical and semantic legacy of this crucial distinction in the history of the idea of sacrifice, see Halbertal, *On Sacrifice.* Halbertal explains how a fundamental difference can be observed in the history of sacrificial practice between sacrificing *for* and sacrificing *of.* Sacrificing *of* is a structure that contains strong aspects of gift giving and involves a clear hierarchy and contains strong rituals. Sacrificing *for* involves a movement of self-transcendence, which means that the, according to Halbertal's analysis, biologically inherent drives for self-survival and self-preservation must be overcome. The 'ultimate' sacrifice is, in this sense, the ultimate overcoming of primordial inclinations to follow own interest and instead give it all up in the name of political and moral spheres or individuals or collectives. The art of sacrificing *of* is to balance the appropriate sacrifice and to accommodate the fear that the sacrifice might be rejected; the art of sacrificing *for* is self-transcendence and communicating self-transcendence.

7. COLLATERAL DAMAGE OR ACCIDENT?

1. Paul Virilio (1993): 'The Primal Accident', in Brian Massumi: *The Politics of Everyday Fear.* Minneapolis: University of Minnesota Press, pp. 211–21, p. 212.

2. Brendan Wallace and Alastair Ross (2006): *Beyond Human Error. Taxonomies and Safety Science.* New York: Taylor Francis; John Davies et al. (2003): *Safety Management. A Qualitative System Approach.* New York: Taylor Francis.

3. Aristotle's philosophy and, not least, his concept of the accident, has had massive

influence and constitutes a major scholarly field in itself. A good place to start is the recent book by John Dudley (2012): *Aristotle's Concept of Chance: Accidents, Cause, Necessity, and Determinism*. New York: State University of New York Press.

4. Aristotle (1872): *Aristotle in Two Volumes, Vol. II* (edited by George Grote et al.). London: John Murray, available online scanned through Google books, p. 321. For a brilliant treatment of the history of the accident in the history of ideas see Ross Hamilton (2008): *Accident: A Philosophical and Literary History*. Chicago: University Of Chicago Press.

5. Ibid., p. 43.

6. John C. Burnham (2009): *Accident Prone: A History of Technology, Psychology, and Misfits of the Machine Age*. Chicago: University Of Chicago Press; Michael Witmore (2001): *Culture of Accidents: Unexpected Knowledges in Early Modern England*. Stanford: Stanford University Press; Peter D. Norton (2008): *Fighting Traffic: The Dawn of the Motor Age in the American City*. Michigan: The MIT Press.

7. John G. Burke (1966): 'Bursting Boilers and the Federal Power', *Technology and Culture*, Vol. 7, 1, pp. 1–23; John Kennedy Brown (1988): *Limbs on the Levee: Steamboat Explosions and the Origins of Federal Public Welfare Regulation, 1817–1852*. Middlebourne, WV: International Steamboat Society.

8. Roger Cooter and Bill Luckin (ed.) (1997): *Accidents in History: Injuries, Fatalities, and Social Relations*. Atlanta: Editions Rodopi, p. 4.

9. Cooter and Luckin, *Accidents in History*, p. 38.

10. Patricia Owens (2003): 'Accidents Don't Just Happen: The Liberal Politics of High-technology "Humanitarian" War', *Millennium: Journal of International Studies*, Vol. 32, 3, pp. 595–616, p. 605; Morton J. Horwitz (1992): *The Transformation of American Law, 1870–1960: The Crisis of Legal Orthodoxy*. Oxford: Oxford University Press.

11. William Lucy (2006): *Philosophy of Private Law*. Oxford: Oxford University Press, p. 53. See also the authoritative history of attitudes towards tort law in the US, Edgard White (2003): *Tort Law in America: An Intellectual History*. Oxford: Oxford University Press.

12. This cost-and-who-shall-pay perspective on tort, or the *liability-rule view* on tort as it is called in legal circles, sets the general approach to tort in the US. It is inherently sceptical of the notion of duty by rejecting the idea that the payment of damages in a tort case is an instance of an injurer being held to account for having breached an obligation to conduct themself in certain ways towards the victim. For a discussion of this, see John C.P. Goldberg and Benjamin C. Zipursky (2006): 'Seeing Tort Law From the International Point of View: Holmes and Hart on Legal Duties', *Fordham Law Review*, Vol. 75, pp. 1563–91.

13. For a discussion hereof, see Alan Dershowitz (1997): *Reasonable Doubts: The Criminal Justice System and the O.J. Simpson Case*. New York: Touchstone.

14. Benjamin C. Zipursky (2005): 'Philosophy of Tort Law: Between the Esoteric and the Banal', in Martin Golding and William Edmundson (ed.) *Blackwell Guide to Philosophy of Law and Legal Theory*. Hoboken: Wiley-Blackwell, pp. 122–38, p. 128. The mainly practical approach to tort law does not mean that a philosophy of tort is irrelevant to consider. For an overview of the debates on the theory of tort law, see Gerald J. Postema (ed.) (2001): *Philosophy and the Law of Torts*. Cambridge: Cambridge University Press; David G. Owen (1996): *Philosophical Foundations of Tort Law*. Oxford: Oxford University Press; and Joel Levin (2008): *Tort Wars*. Cambridge: Cambridge University Press. For a feminist perspective on tort law, see Janice Richardson and Erika Racklec (2012): *Feminist Perspectives on Tort Law*. London: Routledge.

15. Zipursky, 'Philosophy of Tort Law', p. 122.

16. See Jeremy Waldron (1995): 'Moments of Carelessness and Massive Loss', in Owen: *Philosophical Foundations of Tort Law*, pp. 387–408, p. 387ff.

17. Edward Hall Alderson, *Blyth v Birmingham Waterworks Co.* (1856).

18. For a discussion of the concept of negligence in the context of international humanitarian law, see Yael Ronen (2009): 'Avoid or Compensate? Liability for Incidental Injury to Civilians Inflicted During Armed Conflict', *Vanderbilt Journal of Transnational Law*, Vol. 42, pp. 181–225.

19. Insurance today institutes something akin to a global North–South divide: those who have effective insurance may recover relatively easily from losses and accidents, while those who don't may simply lose everything. For an intriguing analysis of how insurance divides the entire human population, see Mark Duffield (2007): *Development, Security and Unending War: Governing the World of Peoples*. London: Polity.

20. Guido Calabresi (1970): *The Cost of Accidents. A Legal and Economic Analysis*. New Haven: Yale University Press.

21. Nan Goodman (1998): *Shifting the Blame. Literature, Law, and The Theory of Accidents in Nineteenth-Century America*. Princeton: Princeton University Press, p. 37.

22. Goldberg and Zipursky, 'Seeing Tort Law'.

23. Goodman, *Shifting the Blame*, p. 66.

24. Owens, 'Accidents Don't Just Happen'.

8. A PRIVATE CALL FOR COLLATERAL DAMAGE?

1. Paul, Romans 13:1.

2. Gary T. Schwartz (1991): 'The Myth of the Ford Pinto Case', *Rutgers Law Review*, Vol. 43, 1, pp. 1013–68, p. 1021.

3. It can be noted that the debates of the "Value of Statistical Life" and cost-benefit analysis in public policy gained enormous traction in the early 1970. Hence I see how the Ford Pinto and the GM Chevrolet memos also grew out of a historical

context. For an of over the literature on "The Value of Statistical Life" that has developed since the 1970s, see S. Madheswaran (2004): A Brief Bibliographical Survey, Bangalore Institute of Social and Economic Change, SANDEE Bibliography No. 8—04.

4. See Schwartz, *The Myth of the Ford Pinto Case.*
5. Ibid., p. 1021.
6. Andrew Pollack (1999): $4.9 Billion Jury Verdict In G.M. Fuel Tank Case, New York Times, July 10, 1999.
7. Schwartz, *The Myth of the Ford Pinto Case*, p. 1014.
8. Andrew Pollack (1999): $4.9 Billion Jury Verdict In G.M. Fuel Tank Case, New York Times, July 10, 1999.
9. "Value Analysis of Auto Fuel Fed Fire Related Fatalities," prepared by Edward Ivey, GM Advance Design Unit, 29 June 1973.
10. Marianne M. Jennings (2012): *Business Ethics. Case Studies and Selected readings.* Mason: South-West Cengage Learning, p. 457.
11. Andrew Pollack (1999): '$4.9 Billion Jury Verdict In G.M. Fuel Tank Case', New York Times, July 10, 1999.
12. Kip Viscusi (2000): 'Corporate Risk Analysis: A Reckless Act?', *Stanford Law Review*, 52, pp. 547—597.
13. John G. Burke (1966): 'Bursting Boilers and the Federal Power', *Technology and Culture*, Vol. 7, 1, pp. 1–23.
14. Non-state armed force has been treated extensively since the mid-1990s when the topic of private military and security companies started to rise to the level of something like an academic field of its own. Today there is a huge academic and popular literature on this topic, which, however, is mainly preoccupied with institutional challenges, including the tension between private force and the state's monopoly on force, and historical explorations of the place and role of private force. A good place to start is Janice Thomson (1994): *Mercenaries, Pirates, and Sovereigns: State-Building and Extraterritorial Violence in Early Modern Europe.* Princeton: Princeton University Press.
15. See the webpage of the international trade organisation for private military and security companies, the International Stability Operations Associations, at http://www.stability-operations.org/ [last visited 15 July 2015]
16. Many political scientists and other scholars have studied the Bible to gain insights about power, sovereignty, law, authority, leadership and similar topics of general relevance to contemporary politics. See for instance Paula R. Abrahamson (2012): *Politics in the Bible.* London: Transaction Publishers; Michael Walzer (1985): *Exodus and Revolution.* New York: Basic Books; Ira Sharkansky (1996): *Israel and Its Bible. A Political Analysis.* New York: Garland Publishing; Joshua A. Berman (2008): *Created Equal: How the Bible Broke with Ancient Political Thought.* Oxford: Oxford University Press; Paul Kahn (2005): *Out of Eden. Adam and Eve and the Problem of Evil.* Princeton: Princeton University Press.

17. Sarah Percy (2007): *Mercenaries: The History of a Norm in International Relations.* Oxford: Oxford University Press.

18. Ibid., pp. 97–105.

19. Ibid., pp. 161–2.

20. Moshe Halbertal and Avishai Margalit (1992): *Idolatry.* Cambridge: Harvard University Press, p. 22, 108ff.

21. Hence, interpretation is used as guessing to fill the textual gaps, rather than to reveal a world behind the text. For a discussion of ways to read the Bible, see J.G. McConville (2006): *God and Earthly Power. An Old Testament Political Theology: Genesis–Kings.* New York: T & T Clark, pp. 1–11.

22. Halbertal and Margalit (1992): *Idolatry*, p. 214; Steven Weitzman (1997). *Song and Story in Biblical Narrative: The History of a Literary Convention in Ancient Israel.* Bloomington: Indiana University Press, p. 10.

23. II Samuel 16:6, in Robert Alter (2000): *The David Story: A Translation with Commentary of 1 and 2 Samuel.* New York: W.W. Norton & Company.

24. Other passages mentioning mercenaries are II Samuel 15:19–22 (David on mercenary loyalty), II Samuel 27:1–12 (David as Philistine mercenary), Jeremiah 46:20–21 (on Egypt's mercenaries), II Samuel 25:6, II Samuel 5:6,7 (David and his men marched to Jerusalem to attack the Jebusites). See also: Israel Finkelstein (2006): *David and Solomon.* New York: Free Press, p. 16, 289–92; John H. Walton, Victor Harold Matthews, Mark W. Chavalas (2000): *The IVP Bible Background Commentary: Old Testament.* Downers Grove, IL: InterVarsity Press. Another theme in the Bible regarding loyalty and warrior commitment is the issue of vassals who are kings that shift loyalty towards stronger kings due to the benefits of fighting under the flag of the strongest.

25. II Samuel 23:8–39, in Alter, *The David Story.*

26. Finkelstein, *David and Solomon*, p. 46.

27. II Samuel 15:19–22. Other translations are: 'Why will you also go with us? Return and remain with the king, for you are a foreigner and also an exile; return to your own place' (The New American Standard Bible, 1995), and 'Then the king said to Ittai the Gittite, "Why do you also go with us? Return, and stay with the king; for you are a foreigner, and also an exile. Return to your own place"' (World English Bible).

28. II Samuel 15:21, in Alter, *The David Story.*

29. II Samuel 18:4, in Alter, *The David Story.*

30. Halbertal and Margalit, *Idolatry*, p. 219ff.

31. D.M. Gunn (1980): 'From Jerusalem to the Jordan and Back: Symmetry in 2 Samuel XV–XX', *Vetus Testamentum*, Vol. 30, 1, pp. 109–13.

32. I Samuel, 22:18, 17–18.

33. Alter, *The David Story*, p. 132, fn 8.

34. Joseph Lozovyy (2006): 'Saul, Doeg, Nabal and the "Son of Jesse": Readings in 1 Samuel 16–25'. unpublished Ph.D thesis, University of Edinburgh, pp. 103–48.

35. Matthew 6:24, Luke 16:13.
36. William L. Moran (1992): *The Amarna Letters*. Baltimore: Johns Hopkins University Press; W. Murnane (2000): 'Imperial Egypt and the Limits of Power', in R. Cohen and R. Westbrook (eds), Amarna *Diplomacy*. Baltimore: The Johns Hopkins University Press, pp. 101–11
37. Rémi Brague (2008): *The Law of God. The Philosophical History of an Idea*. Chicago: University of Chicago Press, p. 5.
38. Brian S. Rosner (1999): 'The Concept of Idolatry', *Themelios*, Vol. 24, 3, pp. 21–30.
39. Brian S. Rosner (2007): *Greed as Idolatry: The Origin and Meaning of a Pauline Metaphor*. Grand Rapids: Eerdmans, p. 148.
40. Halbertal and Margalit, *Idolatry*, p. 108.
41. Ibid., p. 236–42.
42. Rosner, *Greed as Idolatry*.
43. Halbertal and Margalit, *Idolatry*, p. 113f.
44. Nicolo Machiavelli (2003): *The Prince*. Harlow: Longman Publisher, p. 46.
45. Matthew Trundle (2004): *From the Late Archaic Period to Alexander*. New York: Routledge, p. 30ff.
46. Ibid.
47. I imply here a critique of contemporary debates on the relationship between religion and politics, which have recently been organised around names such as Leo Strauss and Carl Schmitt. I suggest an alternative way of enquiring into political–theological problems across the disciplinary divides. I suggest using a particular figure, in this case that of the mercenary, to organise a cross-disciplinary perspective that does not need to consider whether there is a difference between religious and political concepts. In that way this book may be said to be an enquiry into the political theology of collateral damage, which cuts across established disciplinary boundaries.

9. WITH OR WITHOUT A CENTRE

1. Claire Cutler Virginia Haufler, and Tony Porter (ed.) (1999): *Private Authority and International Affairs*. Albany: State University of New York Press; Hans Krause Hansen and Dorthe Salskov-Iversen (2008): *Critical Perspectives on Private Authority in Global Politics*. Basingstoke: Palgrave MacMillan; Richard A. Higgott, Geoffrey R.D. Underhill and Andreas Bieler (ed.) (2000): *Non-State Actors and Authority in the Global System*. London: Routledge.
2. See Michel Foucault (2008): *The Birth of Biopolitics*. London: Palgrave; Trent H. Hamann (2009): 'Neoliberalism, Governmentality, and Ethics', *Foucault Studies*, Vol. 6, pp. 25–36
3. Wendy Larner and William Walters (ed.) (2004): *Global Governmentality: Governing International Spaces*. London: Routledge, pp. 8–9.

4. Jason Read (2009): 'A Genealogy of Homo–Economicus: Neoliberalism and the Production of Subjectivity', *Foucault Studies*, Vol. 6, pp. 25–36.

5. In addition to global security governance, such governance practice is observable today on all levels: in health care, as a move from patient (passive) to client (active) (Sue McGregor (2001): 'Neoliberalism and health care', *International Journal of Consumer Studies*, Vol. 25, 2, pp. 82–9), or from patient to consumer (Christine Hogg (1999): *Patients, Power and Politics: From Patients to Citizens*. London: Sage); in state building and international development aid (Mark Duffield (2008): *Development, Security and Unending War*. Cambridge: Polity); and in education (Gavin Patrick Kendall (2005): 'The Neo-liberal Turn in Education', *International Journal of Learning*, Vol. 12, 2, pp. 137–44; M.A. Peters (2002): 'Foucault and Governmentality: Understanding the Neoliberal Paradigm of Education Policy', *The School Field*, Vol. 7, 5/6, pp. 59–80).

6. In the words of Ronald Reagan, 'government is not the solution to our problem; government is the problem'. Ronald Reagan (1981): Inaugural Address, January 20.

7. James N. Rosenau (2006): *The Study of World Politics: Volume 1: Theoretical and Methodological Challenges*. London: Routledge, p. 14.

8. Michael Hardt & Antonio Negri (2000): Empire. Harvard University Press.

9. Claire Cutler, Virginia Haufler and Tony Porter (eds) (1999): *Private Authority and International Affairs*. Albany: State University of New York Press, p. 13.

10. Cutler, Haufler and Porter *Private Authority*, p. 15.

11. Ibid.; Robert Keohane (2002): *Power and Governance in a Partially Globalized World*. New York: Routledge, 284.

12. Rita Abrahamsen and Michael C. Williams (2009): 'Security beyond the State: Global Security Assemblages in International Politics', *International Political Sociology*, Vol. 3, pp. 1–17, p. 3.

13. John Rapley (2006): 'The New Middle Ages', *Foreign Affairs*, Vol. 85, 3, pp. 95–103.

14. Robert O. Keohane (2003): 'Governance in a Partially Globalized World', in David Held and Anthony McGrew: *Governing Globalization*. London: Polity. pp. 326–47, p. 326.

15. C. Barry and T. Pogge (2005): *Global Institutions and Responsibilities: Achieving Global Justice*. Oxford: Blackwell.

16. Inge Kaul, Isabelle Grunberg and Marc A. Stern (1999): *International Cooperation in the 21ˢᵗ Century*. Oxford: Oxford University Press.

17. The UN Global Compact is a strategic policy initiative for businesses that are committed to aligning their operations and strategies with ten universally accepted principles in the areas of human rights, labour, environment and anti-corruption. By doing so, business, as a primary driver of globalisation, can help ensure that markets, commerce, technology and finance advance in ways that benefit economies and societies everywhere. See http://www.unglobalcompact.org/ [last visited 15 July 2015]

18. Garret Hardin (1968): 'The Tragedy of the Commons', *Science*, Vol. 162, 3859, pp. 1243–8.

19. Thomas Weiss (2000): 'Governance, Good Governance and Global Governance', *Third World Quarterly*, Vol. 21, 5, pp. 795–814; Craig Murphy (2000): 'Global Governance: Poorly Done and Poorly Understood', *International Affairs*, Vol. 76, 2, pp. 789–804.

20. Kaul, Grunber and Stern *Global Public Goods*; I. Kaul, P. Conceicao, K. Le Goulven and R. Mendoza, (2002): *Providing Global Public Goods: Managing Globalization.* Oxford: Oxford University Press; Joseph Stiglitz (2006): Global Public Good and Global Finance. Does Global Governance Ensure that the Global Public Interest is Served?' in Jean–Philippe Touffut (ed.) *Advancing Public Goods.* Chamberley: Edward Elgar Publishing; O. Morrissey, D. te Velde and A. Hewitt (2002). 'Defining International Public Goods: Conceptual Issues', in M. Ferroni and A. Mody (eds): *International Public Goods: Incentives, Measurements and Financing.* Dordrecht: Kluwer Academic Publishers.

21. Mateo Taussig-Rubbo (2009): 'Sacrifice and Sovereignty', in J. Culbert and A. Sarat (eds.): *State of Violence: War, Capital Punishment, and Letting Die.* New York: Cambridge Press; Mateo Taussig-Rubbo (2009): 'Outsourcing Sacrifice: the Labor of Private Military Contractors', *Yale Journal of Law and Humanities*, Vol. 21, 1, pp. 103–66

22. Steven L. Schooner & Collin D. Swan (2010): 'Contractors and the Ultimate Sacrifice', GWU Legal Studies Research Paper No. 512, GWU Law School Public Law Research Paper No. 512. See also Steven L. Schooner (2008): 'Why Contractor Fatalities Matter', Parameters, Vol. 38, 3, pp. 78–91.

23. Ibid.

24. Ibid.

25. Moshe Schwartz and Joyprada Swain, *Department of Defense Contractors in Iraq and Afghanistan: Background and Analysis*, available at http://www.fas.org/sgp/crs/natsec/R40764.pdf

26. Taussig-Rubbo, 'Outsourcing Sacrifice'.

27. For an account of Hugo Grotius, see Anthony F. Lang (2010): 'Authority and the Problem of Non-state Actors', in Eric A. Heinze and Brent J. Steele (ed.): *Non-State Actors and the Just War Tradition*, London: Palgrave Macmillan, pp. 47–53.

28. James N. Rosenau (1995): 'Governance in the Twenty–First Century', *Global Governance*, Vol. 1, pp. 13–43.

29. For an account of Weber in international relations studies, see Tarak Barkawi (1998): 'Strategy as a Vocation: Weber, Morgenthau and Modern Strategic Studies', *Review of International Studies*, 24, pp. 159–84; for an account of the public–private distinction in organisation theory, see James L. Perry and G. Hal (1998): 'The Public–Private Distinction in Organization Theory: A Critique and Research Strategy', *The Academy of Management Review*, Vol. 13, 2, pp. 182–201; for an

account of the project of modernity in international relations theory, see Richard Devetak (1995): 'The Project of Modernity and International Theory', *Millennium*, Vol. 24, 1, pp. 27–51. See also R.B.J. Walker (1993): *Inside/Outside: International Relations as Political Theory*. Cambridge: Cambridge University Press. Walker claims that theories of modernity and theories about international relations have been systematically obscured by claims about socio-scientific epistemology and that it is necessary to be suspicious about the modernist categories, which have been treated as 'the main highway to a better life' (p. 50ff).

30. See Heinrich Meier (2006): *Leo Strauss and the Theological–Political Problem*. Cambridge: Cambridge University Press.

31. See http://www.etymonline.com/index.php?term=subject/ [last visited]

32. See Niels Åkerstrøm Andersen (2004): 'The Contractualisation of the Citizen— on the Transformation of Obligation into Freedom, *Social Systems*, Vol. 10, 2, pp. 273–91; (2006): *Partnerskabelse*. København: Hans Reitzels Forlag; (2007): 'Creating the Client Who Can Create Himself and His Own Fate—the Tragedy of the Citizens' Contract', *Qualitative Sociology Review*, Vol. 3, 2, pp. 119–43; (2008): 'The World as Will and Adaptation: The Inter–discursive Coupling of Citizens' Contracts', *Critical Discourse Studies*, Vol. 5, 1, pp. 75–89.

33. Genevieve Lloyd (2008): *Providence Lost*. Harvard University Press.

ACKNOWLEDGEMENTS

This book has benefited from discussions with and comments from many people. I owe a particular debt of gratitude to Davinia Abdul Azziz, Stefano Guzzini, Henrik Bjelke Hansen, Jessica Lerche, Lars Nørgaard, Sine Molbæk-Steensig, Luke Patey, and my much appreciated colleagues at the Danish Institute for International Studies. Thanks also to the Bikuben Foundation, the Klitgården Foundation, the San Cataldo Foundation, and especially the Danish Research Council for financial support. I am grateful to Michael Dwyer at Hurst Publishing for taking on this book. My deepest thanks go to my partner and love of my life, Anne Østrup.

INDEX

Absalom, 142f
accidents, 119—131
  accident law, 84, 125ff, 168
  Aristotle on, 119ff, 128, 163, 197f
  and collateral damage, 61f, 84
  Ford Pinto, 135ff
  Foreign Claims Act, 61
  and military operations, 61
  and miracles, 121f
  and Oedipus Rex, 122
  and private corporations, 135
  and religion, 128
  and technology, 124f
  tort law, 61, 126ff, 198f
  US Indemnity Act, 61
  Virilio on, 120f
accountability
  and accidents, 94, 125
  and bookkeeping/record keeping, 92
  command structures, 139, 149
  and decentralization, 28
  history of, 92f
  for human rights violations, 50f
  legal concept, 20, 92f, 139
  and network-centric warfare, 28
  and 'new world order', 151
  private corporations, 137
  and public sphere, 156
  and sin, concept of, 92

  and utilitarianism, 101
Adam and Eve, 6, 79f, 93, 127, 167
Additional Protocols to the Geneva
  Conventions (1977), 17, 19, 21, 35,
  73, 78, 188
Afghanistan
  checkpoints, 25
  Bagram brake-failure accident
    (2006), 62
  civilian casualties, 9, 10, 13, 29, 97,
    117; see also compensation
  and Cold War, 18
  and Collateral Damage Estimation
    (CDE), 13, 22
  collateral damage rule, knowledge
    of, 29
  compensation in, 10, 33, 59, 62, 64,
    66ff
  contractors, 158f
  counterinsurgency, 18
  drones, 75
  'forgotten victims', 9
  and habeas corpus, 59
  immunity, 59, 179
  International Security Assistance
    Force (ISAF), 33, 67, 69, 75
  and International Human Rights
    Law (IHRL), 53, 59

INDEX

INDEX